SPECIAL TREATMENT

SPECIAL TREATMENT

Student Doctors at the
All India Institute of Medical Sciences

ANNA RUDDOCK

STANFORD UNIVERSITY PRESS
STANFORD, CALIFORNIA

STANFORD UNIVERSITY PRESS
Stanford, California

© 2021 by the Board of Trustees of the Leland Stanford Junior University. All rights reserved.

Printed in the United States of America on acid-free, archival-quality paper

Library of Congress Cataloging-in-Publication Data
Names: Ruddock, Anna, author.
Title: Special treatment : student doctors at the All India Institute of Medical Sciences / Anna Ruddock.
Other titles: South Asia in motion.
Description: Stanford, California : Stanford University Press, 2021. | Series: South Asia in motion | Includes bibliographical references and index.
Identifiers: LCCN 2021018466 (print) | LCCN 2021018467 (ebook) | ISBN 9781503614925 (cloth) | ISBN 9781503628250 (paperback) | ISBN 9781503628267 (epub)
Subjects: LCSH: All-India Institute of Medical Sciences. | Medical education--India. | Teaching hospitals--India. | Occupational prestige--India. | Social medicine--India.
Classification: LCC R814.A84 R83 2021 (print) | LCC R814.A84 (ebook) | DDC 610.71/154--dc23
LC record available at https://lccn.loc.gov/2021018466
LC ebook record available at https://lccn.loc.gov/2021018467

Cover photo: Anna Ruddock

Cover design: Christian Fuenfhausen

Typeset by Kevin Barrett Kane in 11/15 Adobe Caslon Pro

For my parents

CONTENTS

SPECIAL TREATMENT

CHAPTER 1

"AIIMS IS AIIMS"

THE MAIN GATES to the All India Institute of Medical Sciences (AIIMS) in Delhi are next to the metro station on Aurobindo Marg, a busy artery that runs through the south of the city. When I arrive on this occasion, it is a late March morning; the air is warm but not yet vibrating with the full heat of summer. The young man who sells flower-patterned plastic wallets to protect medical histories is standing in his usual place just outside the gates. I pass him and turn left at the tree that provides shade for a few of the thousands of people who spend hours at AIIMS waiting—for consultations, for tests, for results, for information about where to go next. A road skirts the edge of the campus, a cordon separating pedestrians from a huddle of stationary green and yellow auto-rickshaws and the passing traffic. When a gap appears between vehicles, I step over the fraying red rope and cross to the concourse that extends out from the main outpatient building. Small clusters of people sit on the floor, many on sheets made from recycled plastic packaging, bright with primary colors. As the sun gets stronger, people squeeze more tightly into the segments of shade cast by roof and walls. Sometimes patients are obvious—identifiable by dressings on a wound or a drainage bag on the floor beside a frail body—but not always. The inability to distinguish patients at first sight makes visible the fact of shared affliction—how illness and treatment seeking extend beyond the skin of an individual to encompass a network of surrounding people.

Opposite, outside a waiting hall under construction, some women have laid rinsed-out clothes over a railing to dry. I watch as a security guard shouts at them and gestures aggressively with his *lathi*, a wooden baton, toward the clothes. The women reluctantly pull the garments from the railing. (When I walked back through a few hours later, different clothes hung in their place.) The queue outside the pediatric outpatient department on my left has already subsided—those who didn't reach the front before the appointments ran out will try again tomorrow. Outside the generic drugs pharmacy the queue will disperse only when the shutters are lowered in the late afternoon.

Medical students are rarely noticeable around this area of AIIMS, but it is with and through these throngs of patients, an average of 10,000 passing through each day, that India's most esteemed young doctors are formed.

Turning right, I enter the institution's administrative and educational nerve center. This is the boundary between the clinical and the academic worlds of AIIMS—between the hospital and the college. The sudden absence of patients and families is striking; they are not permitted to congregate here. If they drift off course during the effort to navigate the hospital labyrinth, they will be policed away from this haven—a large quadrangle laid with a well-irrigated jade-green lawn, edged with palm trees and rose beds, and stone curbs painted in warning stripes to discourage sitting. The huddle of buildings seems to cushion sound, which adds to the qualitative difference between the two environments. It is calm here, amid students and faculty milling among the hostels, library, offices, and consultation rooms. This is a different place, where precarity is hidden.

I skirt the quadrangle and cross the road, passing into the heart of student life. The men's hostels stand on one side of the tree-lined road (the women's hostels are pointedly situated on the opposite side of the campus). On the other side are the photocopying and stationery shop, general store, and outdoor café. Students are suddenly everywhere, chatting in groups or walking purposively toward the hospital in their white, or graying, coats with stethoscopes slung around their necks. These, we are informed by the media and the medical establishment, are examples of India's "best"—its most gifted, dedicated, promising medical students. And there are moments, even when I am in the thick of uncovering the many caveats and complications that this description disguises, that I find myself looking at these young people as though they really are different—special—somehow.

It was 2016 and I had returned to AIIMS to visit two students, Purush and Sushil. I first met them during the final year of their MBBS degree; their experiences, among others, inform this book. Now they were studying for the fiercely competitive postgraduate entrance exams that would determine the type of medicine they would specialize in. We discussed their preferred courses and colleges. Sushil acknowledged that studying somewhere else might lend him a broader perspective. Then he paused and looked at me. "But AIIMS is AIIMS," he said with a grin. Simply put, what follows is an attempt to understand what this exceptionalism means: for students at AIIMS, for the doctors they might become and the patients they might treat, and for the deeply inequitable landscape beyond the institution's gates.

INTRODUCING AIIMS

The All India Institute of Medical Sciences opened its gates in 1956, but as I describe in chapter 2, the seeds for the institution were planted while India was still a British colony. Modeled on the prestigious Johns Hopkins University in the United States, AIIMS embodied the primacy of science and technology in independent India's developmental project. It was intended to set a new standard in Indian biomedical research and practice while also training new generations to remedy the ills of a vast and impoverished emergent nation.[1] Today, AIIMS is an enormous and ever-expanding government-funded teaching hospital. It is anomalous in India's public healthcare landscape for employing many of the country's most respected doctors, who provide a high standard of care at nominal cost to predominantly poor and marginalized patients who often travel long distances in search of help.

Faculty members	701
Non-faculty staff	9,625
Teaching departments and centers	55
Undergraduate	
MBBS, nursing, paramedical	818
MBBS graduates since 1961	3,059
Postgraduates	1,844
Total outpatients (excluding outreach sites)	3.5 million (~10,000/day)
Admissions	234,000
Surgical procedures	177,000
Beds	2,300 (265 private)
Annual budget (2017–2018)	INR 2,400 crores (~£270 million)

FIGURE 1 AIIMS Snapshot 2016–2017. Data from AIIMS Annual Report 2016-2017. https://www.aiims.edu/images/pdf/annual_reports/Annual%20Report_Web_16_17.pdf

The AIIMS Act of 1956 declares AIIMS an institution of national importance. Its three founding objectives are to set national standards in undergraduate and postgraduate education, to establish the highest standard of facilities for training in "all important branches of health activity," and to achieve self-sufficiency in postgraduate education[2]—while providing care to some of the country's most underprivileged patients. This complex mandate makes for a formidable and unrelenting challenge. Figure 1 captures the scale for which the institution is famous and hints at the pressure under which it operates.[3]

People acquainted with healthcare in India often have an opinion about AIIMS, especially in northern India, and even more so if they have lived in Delhi. It is a phenomenon as much as a concrete landmark. It is not uncommon to know someone who has been treated at AIIMS or, within a particular milieu, to know someone who knows someone whose relative is or was an AIIMS doctor. But impressions also form during years of passing within sight of the modernist complex, whose neon sign alerts the city to its presence. Or while stuck in traffic outside the hospital gates, where patients and families sleep on the pavement for want of anywhere else. Or through the media, which fuels public perceptions of the institution, for better and worse,[4] and which these days brings news of the next generation of All India Institutes being established around the country.[5] Even if AIIMS means little to an individual, from many locations in Delhi it is possible to reorient oneself via the ubiquitous road signs pointing the way to the institute. AIIMS is *there*: embedded in the landscape of Delhi, and in imaginations both within and beyond the city.

Ethnographic studies of medical institutions in the Global South, while still relatively few, often share a concern with the ways in which resource scarcity reveals the instabilities and contingencies of biomedicine in different terrains, demanding improvisation on the part of both medical professionals and patients in order to achieve some form of therapeutic outcome in straitened circumstances.[6] Patients and doctors at AIIMS, meanwhile, suffer more from limited time and space than from an explicit lack of institutional resources, pressured though these are. If anything, the pressure on resources at AIIMS illuminates how profoundly they are lacking beyond its gates, as patients crowd into the OPD to seek the care they cannot access elsewhere.[7] AIIMS is not, however, an aesthetically therapeutic environment for either patients or doctors. It is crowded, confusing, uncomfortable, not always clean. It sometimes suggests less an effort to impart health than a perpetual scramble to stave off decay.[8]

A dedicated government budget does ensure that AIIMS is equipped, staffed, and maintained to an unusually high standard for an Indian public healthcare facility. In principle, the 1956 AIIMS Act also guarantees the independence and autonomy of the institute. In practice, however, AIIMS has always been a political institution that has periodically suffered from and sometimes colluded with direct interference in its functioning. The central government minister of health and family welfare is also president and chairman of AIIMS, and members of Parliament and civil servants account for half of the 18-member institute body and just under half of the governing body.[9] The directorship of AIIMS is known to be a political appointment, and several senior faculty members wryly informed me that they would never be considered for the position because they were not on sufficiently good terms with the powers that be. A retired faculty member told me that political interference became routine only in the 1980s, when AIIMS became the hospital of choice for politicians, following the fatal shooting of Indira Gandhi in 1984.[10] However, T. N. Madan cites an informant telling him in the 1970s that "the long arm of the government is very visible in the manner in which the institute is run."[11] In the last few years, wrangling over the locations of new branches of AIIMS has reemphasized their political nature.

"Corruption talk" is ubiquitous at, and in relation to, AIIMS. It ranges from the *jaan-pechaan*, or personal connection, that some patients utilize to access treatment, to allegations of kickbacks from off-campus pathology laboratories, caste-based discrimination toward students and faculty, and allegations of systemic malpractice. In the chapters that follow, I don't attempt to analyze corruption as a distinct entity, or to interrogate the truth or falsity of allegations—rather, where corruption talk arises, I approach it as an illustration of how AIIMS reflects the values and practices of the broader society in which it is embedded.[12]

Officially AIIMS is a tertiary institution, and the lack of a tiered public healthcare system in India means that AIIMS actually exists as an independent entity, as illustrated by the vast number of self-referrals to the hospital. For the majority of patients without privileged access to individual doctors who are directed to the hospital, to be "referred" to AIIMS does not involve internal communication within a healthcare system as the term might imply. Rather, it is to be "sent"—the Hindi *bhej dena* more accurately reflects the experience of being told to seek further treatment at AIIMS by a doctor who has reached the limit of ability or inclination to treat a complex and/or chronic condition.[13] Some patients are directed to seek an appointment at a particular department, with no guidance about how to navigate the appointment system or the overwhelming hospital campus itself. Others are simply instructed to "go to AIIMS," feeding an impression of the institution as an almost mythical site of last resort. On arrival, the pursuit of treatment often reverts to square one.

This fragmented system has complex consequences for both patients and doctors at AIIMS, as I illustrate in chapters 5 and 6. It also influences the impressions made upon students at an institution that, as well as being a famous public hospital, occupies a seemingly unassailable position atop the hierarchy of Indian medical education.

In recent years, the position of AIIMS as the country's most prestigious medical college has been formalized by the promotion of an annual ranking of colleges by the news magazine *India Today*. During my research, a framed cover of the magazine declared this continued domination from a wall in the office of the institute's academic dean. AIIMS is also the only Indian medical college in the Centre for World University Rankings' top 1,000 degree-granting institutions. In 2018, India's Ministry of Human Resource Development added a new medical college category to its own National Institutional Ranking Framework (NIRF). In a group of 25 colleges, AIIMS New Delhi occupied the top spot by a significant margin, set apart even from its fellow institutions in the top five: Post Graduate Institute of Medical Education and Research in Chandigarh, Christian Medical College in Vellore, Kasturba Medical College in Manipal, and King George's Medical University in Lucknow. As with all exercises, the metrics used by the NIRF invite scrutiny and are open to interpretation.[14] What is most interesting for the purposes of this book, however, is the inclusion in the NIRF of a "perception" score, which combines survey data from employers and research funders, academic peers, and the general public about their perceptions of the colleges, together with the number of postgraduate students admitted from "top institutions" each year. AIIMS is unique in the medical college category for having a perception score of 100. What does it mean for a single medical college to be considered so unequivocally "the best"—for the doctors it trains and for the society in which they will practice?

STUDYING AIIMS

Writing about the challenges and rewards of conducting "public ethnography," Didier Fassin notes that while ethnography must pay attention to understudied social locales, it also retains salience in "spaces saturated by consensual meanings."[15] In the first circumstance, he writes, ethnography "illuminates the unknown; in the second, it interrogates the obvious." Studying AIIMS fulfills both criteria. It is notably understudied and thus constitutes a "black hole of ethnography" in Fassin's terminology,[16] and yet as a nationally renowned institution uniquely embedded in the imaginations of diverse Indian publics, it is also a repository of unchallenged assumptions. Few of these assumptions have been addressed by social scientists.[17] In work on treatment seeking, AIIMS arises periodically as a feature in the healthcare landscape, often to emphasize the uneven scale and quality of provision.[18] In these contexts, AIIMS is a remote and exceptional site, usually mentioned only as an outlier among public hospitals. Through this book, I seek to add nuance to this portrayal by suggesting that AIIMS influences the broader landscape in both imagination and practice and therefore, by extension, the experiences of patients and trainee doctors who may never personally attend the institute. In considering this wider influence, I aim to make an implicit case for the validity and import of studying institutions that appear at first glance to be disconnected from the broader context in which they exist.[19]

This book is an anthropological study of AIIMS New Delhi as a provider of undergraduate medical education, informed by ethnographic research I conducted between January 2014 and May 2015.[20] At the heart of the book is an argument that while AIIMS fulfills an invaluable public function by providing high-quality treatment to poor patients, its approach to medical education renders it complicit in the reproduction of inequalities that define the society and the healthcare landscape in which it operates. Social inequalities—expressed through caste, class, and gender hierarchies, for example—coupled with the neglect of public healthcare fuel enormous demand for treatment at an institution that exacerbates power asymmetries and does very little to acquaint its students with medicine's potential to be a transformative social endeavor. The "excellence," for which an AIIMS education is renowned, is narrowly defined by the careers its graduates go on to pursue. On the whole, as I make clear in the chapters that follow, AIIMS is about middle-class students learning from poor and marginalized patients in order to eventually treat rich and privileged patients, upholding the institute's reputation for excellence in the process.

The social hierarchy necessary to maintain this order of things is reproduced during the undergraduate medical program, or MBBS, as I show in a series of chapters. These take us from the entrance exam that reproduces the prestige attached to AIIMS by virtue of unmanageable demand, through exclusionary upper-caste narratives of "merit" that inform the experiences of trainee doctors from marginalized caste and tribal groups, into the AIIMS hospital to demonstrate how the power differential between doctors and patients goes unaddressed during the MBBS, and finally to the point of graduation as students make decisions about their futures based on a hierarchy of medical practice entrenched during their education.

Given the status of AIIMS in the public imagination and its mandate to set standards for Indian medical education, I contend that its promotion of such a narrow conception of excellence among trainee doctors has implications for medicine in India more broadly. As such, this book can be read as a larger argument for paying greater attention to the relationship between medical education and the reproduction of health and social inequalities.

INDIA'S HEALTH SYSTEM:
"WORKING AT CROSS PURPOSES"

Understanding the landscape beyond its gates is crucial for understanding the function and the symbolism of AIIMS—as a provider of both medical care and education.[21] India is riven by health inequalities that are produced by myriad influences, including caste, class, gender, religion, and geography, and their intersection with social determinants such as access to clean water, food, and education.[22] For example, the mortality rate for children under 5 years old born into Adivasi or Scheduled Tribe communities is 15% higher than the national average, and overall infant mortality rates between rural and urban areas differ by 17 percentage points.[23] When it comes to gender, a 2011 study found that the risk of dying between 1 and 5 years old was 75% higher for girls than for boys. Illustrating regional disparities, a girl born in the states of Chhattisgarh or Madhya Pradesh is five times more likely to die in the first year of life than a girl born in Kerala. These disparities are all compounded by the weaknesses of India's public healthcare system.[24]

In the years since the inception of India's National Rural Health Mission in 2005, public healthcare infrastructure has improved, although it remains profoundly inadequate.[25] Again, the distribution is uneven, exacerbating health inequalities. While 68% of India's population lives in rural areas, 73% of public hospital beds are located in urban centers. In Goa, one hospital bed exists for every 614 persons; in Bihar one bed exists for every 8,789 persons. Nationally, there remains a general rural shortfall of 22% of required primary health centers.[26] Bihar and Uttar Pradesh are persistently cited as two of the states whose population suffers from the most significant shortfall in facilities—both states are heavily represented among patients at AIIMS. Where facilities do exist, absent staff and/or poor-quality care may lead patients to bypass the local health center and seek care elsewhere.[27] One consequence of this inadequate and unreliable provision is that public tertiary care institutions are forced to compensate by providing primary care.[28] This, as I show in the chapters that follow, is precisely the situation at AIIMS.

Despite the concern professed through eloquent policy documents and commitments,[29] government spending on public healthcare remains persistently low, at 1.2% of gross domestic product in 2018, compared to China's 3.1% and the United Kingdom's 7.6%.[30] Unsurprisingly, then, both the pursuit and the provision of healthcare in India is a largely private enterprise—and actually it always has been.[31] Public healthcare was neglected by the British regime in colonial India, and it did not receive concerted government attention following the nation's independence in 1947.[32] That the colonial legacy of weak infrastructure impeded the enactment of postindependence health policy is clear. What it doesn't explain is why the idea of public healthcare has never been a political priority, or why it has been consistently underresourced even in times of high economic growth.[33]

Serious discussions of healthcare were virtually absent from the Constituent Assembly debates that took place between 1946 and 1950 among the architects of newly independent India.[34] Where "health" is mentioned in the records of the debates, it is most frequently in association with "the health of the body politic" or healthy versus unhealthy national sentiment. In the final draft of the Constitution, health is subordinated to the Directive Principles, where it forms part of "the programme of social transformation . . . to be realized in the fullness of time," rather than being articulated alongside Article 21, which dictates the right to life.[35] The conundrum persists about why the newly independent government did not prioritize equitable public healthcare, resource constraints notwithstanding.

The lack of public deliberation of policy issues around essential human services such as health and education both reflects and feeds the perception that they are largely inconsequential for electoral politics. This cannot be attributed to an idea that those most in need of these public services do not vote, because India's poor *do* vote, and in famously large numbers.[36] It does appear true, however, that voters do not generally mobilize around education or healthcare, nor do politicians see sufficient short-term gain in campaigning around health.[37] Mehta suggests that a partial explanation for this scenario lies in the fact that the Indian state has rarely "been governed by a public philosophy; it is rather a high stakes or competitive game in which individuals or groups seek advantages on particularistic lines." He claims that "the two sustaining associations of the state"—the "public" or the "common"—have worn very thin in India.[38] From the perspective of health, however, we have to ask how substantial these associations ever were and—from the perspective of this book—what the consequences of this disassociation have been for medical education.

What has changed in terms of private provision of healthcare is the scale. Lucrative opportunities for corporate chains of large, urban, "superspecialty" hospitals have expanded since the liberalized restructuring of the Indian economy in the early 1990s,[39] through tax exemptions, subsidized land allocation, and lower import tariffs on medical equipment.[40] Between 2002 and 2010, the private sector contributed to 70% of the increase in total hospital beds across the country.[41] Private treatment does not ensure a superior standard—the unregulated and vastly differentiated nature of the private sector makes for uneven and unpredictable standards of care.[42] In urban India, medical care may be visibly available, but it is often of poor quality and can be financially devastating.[43]

Increased incomes allow some people to end their dependence on unreliable public services, and in the process their choice of healthcare becomes an act of conspicuous consumption that speaks to their relative wealth and social status.[44] But in many cases in India, seeking private treatment is not a lifestyle choice; it is the only option. People compensate for inadequate public healthcare with personal "out-of-pocket" spending on private treatment. Often described as "catastrophic spending," healthcare costs entrench poverty: in 2011–2012, 55 million Indians were estimated to have fallen below the poverty line as a result of medical expenditure.[45] Relating people's experiences of this fragmented, unreliable, and financially punitive semblance of a health system in poor Delhi neighborhoods, Das concludes that illness in these circumstances lends a destabilizing sense of "incoherence" to the lives of the poor.[46] Whether the recent establishment of *mohalla*, or community, clinics by Delhi's local government will offer remedy to people living amidst such precarity remains to be seen.[47]

MEDICAL EDUCATION IS PART OF A HEALTH SYSTEM

In their work on medical education in South Africa, Pentecost and Cousins write that "understanding the doctor as a social figure is staked on the possibility of being attuned to the historical and political contexts that shape medical training and practice."[48] I have included the brief sketch of India's troubled healthcare system in the previous section in order to illuminate the need for greater attention to the norms that are established through medical training at an elite government-funded institution and their influence on the wider healthcare landscape via understandings of what it means to be "the best" kind of doctor. The aspirational horizons of young Indians who hope to become doctors are set and maintained by a preeminent institution that was designed to do exactly that. The road to socially sanctioned excellence in medicine begins with winning a place at AIIMS.

The striking figure of ten thousand outpatients a day is regularly used to illustrate the overwhelming demand for treatment at AIIMS. Arguably, however, the numbers for which the institution is most famous are those associated with the notoriously fierce competition for admission to the five-and-a-half-year-long MBBS. Differentiated from their peers at the moment of admission, AIIMS students are catapulted into an exclusive club, one whose membership is aspired to by many but achieved by only a tiny minority of applicants. As I discuss in chapter 3, at the time of my research this was 72 people from around 80,000 hopefuls who took the annual entrance exam, with its success rate of less than .001%.[49] Those ranked highest—the "toppers"—are profiled with their families in the national news, and future applicants seek their advice. Most of the students who feature in this book graduated in 2016 and 2017, joining a network of MBBS "AIIMSonians" that had yet to exceed 3,000 members since the first cohort graduated in 1961. While AIIMS New Delhi has recently increased its annual MBBS intake to 100 in line with the new All India Institutes, it retains its reputation in part due to an insistence on keeping student numbers small and exacerbating the competition for entry in the process.

The impact of AIIMS on the national imagination far outweighs the number of doctors it has contributed to the country's health workforce (especially in the public sector), particularly when emigration is taken into account, as I discuss in chapter 6. India's ostensible shortage of qualified practicing doctors is well known. According to the World Health Organization (WHO), which recommends a doctor-patient ratio of 1:1000, India stands at 0.7:1000.[50] The absence of reliable and consistent data makes agreement about the exact number of healthcare professionals elusive, however, with even the WHO's 2016 *Health Workforce in India* report relying on information from the 2001 census.[51] The Indian Government has declared a desirable density of 85 doctors to every 100,000 people. Even going by the highest estimate of current doctors, the country would still require approximately 49% again of its existing workforce to achieve this ratio.

The ratio measure admits little insight into the uneven density of doctors, and of their qualifications, across regions and sectors.[52] For example, the 68% of India's population living in rural areas is served by only 33% of the country's doctors. In 2014, only 11.3% of all biomedical doctors were working in the public sector, and of them barely 3.3% were employed in rural areas.[53] Consequently, not everyone agrees that training more doctors is the right priority for improving India's health outcomes and inequities. Others disagree about the specific type of doctor the country most needs. Community health centers in rural parts of many northern and northeastern states face shortfalls of specialists exceeding 80%.[54] For some, this is the greatest priority, while for others, the most urgent need is for well-trained generalists.[55] Nor does the policy conversation about the doctor-patient ratio address the structures of medical education that produce this outcome. As I discuss in chapter 6, AIIMS plays an implicit role in the debate about priorities through its singular focus on superspecialization as the career path befitting its graduates. At the same time, however, the 80% shortfall of specialists in northern states cannot be understood independently of the fact that Maharashtra and the four southern states of Andhra Pradesh, Karnataka, Kerala, and Tamil Nadu account for more than 50% of India's total seats in medical colleges.

As I write, there are 542 medical colleges in India recognized by the Medical Council of India, which together provide almost 77,000 MBBS seats, making India officially the largest producer of doctors in the world. This figure continues to increase. Around 279 colleges are government owned and funded, reflecting a recent commitment to increasing the public provision of medical education. The rest are private institutions, many of which are located in wealthier southern states.

Different medical colleges have traditionally had different routes of entry; until 2016 there were around 35 separate entrance exams for the country's 412 medical colleges. The All India Pre-Medical Test allocated 15% of seats at state government colleges on a pan-India basis—in 2015, more than 600,000 students competed for 3,700 MBBS seats. Private colleges often conducted separate entrance exams. In April 2016, however, a Supreme Court ruling mandated that all medical college admissions be subject to passing the single National Eligibility cum Entrance Test.[56] AIIMS, along with the Post Graduate Institute of Medical Education and Research in Chandigarh and the Jawaharlal Institute of Postgraduate Medical Education and Research in Pondicherry, is exempt and continues to hold its own entrance exam, which maintains a reputation as the country's most challenging.

As I discuss in chapter 6, the MBBS degree has been devalued in India to the extent that few graduates go into practice without at least one post-graduate qualification. Seats for postgraduate training are scarce. While the government has announced an expansion of medical colleges intended to provide 40,000 seats, at the time of my research there were 18,000 annual places at institutions around the country. One consequence of this situation, which some consider a key impediment to the provision of adequate public healthcare, is a loss of doctors.[57] Dr. Raman Kumar, president of the Indian Academy of Family Physicians, estimates that there are approximately 300,000 MBBS graduates not in full-time practice due to their relentless pursuit of a postgraduate seat.[58] This competition also has a direct impact on MBBS education, as most students prioritize studying for postgraduate entrance exams over gaining clinical experience during their intern year, exacerbating the devaluation of general practice.

Rent seeking and corrupt practices have long been synonymous with the Medical Council of India and medical education,[59] most publicly through monetized exam cheating such as that exposed in the notorious Vyapam scheme in Madhya Pradesh.[60] A 2015 Reuters investigation found that since 2010, one out of every six medical colleges, or around 69 institutions, had been accused of fraudulent practices, whether bribing Medical Council officials to pass inspections, bussing in healthy locals to pose as patients in order to persuade inspectors that students were gaining sufficient clinical experience, demanding capitation fees, or rigging exams.[61] Another report showed that almost 60% of India's medical institutions had failed to produce any research papers during the previous decade. Of those that did, 40% of the output came from the country's top 25 institutions, with AIIMS faculty among the most published.[62]

Patel and colleagues note that "the medical curriculum focuses on clinical applications of medicine, which, along with lucrative career options in the specialist private sector and limitations of infrastructure and opportunity in the public health-care sector, leads many medical graduates to specialise and work in the private sector."[63] While this is no doubt true, in this book I also explore some of the less immediately visible influences on student aspirations and the obstacles that preclude the alternative futures that some students envisage in defiance of the conventional wisdom that confirms a (super)specialized career as the most appropriate achievement for an AIIMS graduate. Bearing in mind that this aspiration is also common to the majority of medical students beyond AIIMS, I question the role of India's most prestigious medical college in setting standards and expectations for trainee doctors, arguing that from this angle the institution is complicit in the inequitable landscape beyond its gates.

YOUTH, ASPIRATION, AND THE REPRODUCTION OF INEQUALITY

In this book I focus on a specific institution that trains students for a specific profession. That said, my interest is not so much in how particular clinical knowledge and skills are imparted and adopted, and the implications of this transmission for medical practice, as exemplified by other studies.[64] Rather, this project was motivated by an interest in a particular prestigious institution and how it influences students in the process of becoming doctors. In that light, this book also reflects a burgeoning interest among social scientists in the many meanings of being a young person in contemporary India.[65] It is in many ways about youth and the heady, often disorientating, combination of aspiration and fear, confidence and self-doubt, idealism and hard-learned pragmatism that youth entails. This might be said about young people anywhere in the world, but the need for richer and more nuanced understanding feels particularly urgent in a country where 56% of the population is younger than 25 years old—this translates as upward of 700 million people.[66]

The stories of India's young people are overwhelmingly stories of a vast and growing middle class—whether they reflect the tenuous social mobility of new generations, or the anxieties of those who feel that their historical privilege is under threat from these new entrants, particularly when caste enters the equation. In 2008, following a government policy to increase the number of seats reserved for students from socially disadvantaged groups, the number of annual MBBS seats at AIIMS was increased from 50 to 72. As I mentioned earlier, in September 2016, AIIMS New Delhi announced that from 2017 it would increase its annual MBBS intake to

100 students in line with the new branches being established. At the time of my research, the 72 seats were divided into four categories. Three of these categories reflect India's affirmative-action policy for higher education, known colloquially as "reservation"; there were 5 seats for Scheduled Tribes, 11 for Scheduled Castes, and 19 for Other Backward Classes. The remaining 37 seats made up the so-called general category. Students from upper castes, whose socioeconomic dominance in the country obscures the fact that they are not a numerical majority, dominate the general category which, as I show in chapter 4, works both to obscure and to affirm the role of caste on campus.[67]

In 2006, AIIMS was at the heart of an agitation by upper-caste members of the medical fraternity against the extension of affirmative action to include students from communities collectively termed Other Backward Classes, or OBCs.[68] In contrast with the overt violence of that period, caste-based discrimination appears to operate more subtly at AIIMS these days than at some other medical colleges, but it remains insidious, and the suicides of marginalized students are a shameful reality. In chapter 4 I show how the social dynamics of reservation-based difference have a clear influence both on student experiences and on perceptions of who has the right, and the ability, to practice medicine with the credentials of an AIIMSonian.

The AIIMS entrance exam ranking system obscures miniscule differences in marks behind whole integers, as is the case at all of India's most competitive colleges. Empirically, this renders the concept of the topper rather meaningless, but being ranked first bestows a powerful and enduring identity on those individuals nonetheless. Conversely, rank also serves as a weapon in ideological narratives about the exclusion of "meritorious" students as a result of affirmative-action policies that reserve seats for candidates from marginalized caste and tribal groups.[69] However, as I show in chapter 3 through an analysis of the 2018 MBBS entrance exam results, what is revealed when the top 3,000 of 374,000 candidates all score in the 99th percentile is not the admission of less capable students, but the overwhelming demand for higher education that India lacks the institutional capacity to absorb and convert into better life chances for its enormous population of young people. Individuals possess their own narratives while also being one of hundreds of millions of people collectively coming of age at a moment when the state is simply not equipped to fulfill its promise of a bright future for young people who apply themselves.[70] Before questions about quality—both of education and of life—are even approached, estimates suggest that 1,000 new universities and 50,000 colleges would need to be built by 2022 to accommodate the increasing number of eligible students.[71]

For those young people who do find their way into higher education, the privilege often proves dubious. Infrastructure, administration, curricula, and teaching vary enormously, fueling a conveyor-belt approach to education in which students accumulate poor-quality degrees and graduate into a market that offers little chance of sustainable employment.[72] For those fortunate to gain access to reputable universities, the current political moment has its own implications, as the ruling Bharatiya Janata Party imposes a Hindu nationalist agenda on state institutions and rewards private donors in confirmation of the capital-political nexus at the heart of Indian governance.[73]

To apply the sociologist Pierre Bourdieu's well-known concept, AIIMS is the greatest repository of social and cultural capital in Indian medical education and this capital is directly convertible into economic security.[74] As a consequence, most (but not all) AIIMS students are insulated from the fear that their graduating credentials will not bolster their career prospects and broader life chances. That said, for the majority of students in a predominantly middle-class institution, the capital bestowed at admission and confirmed at graduation is an augmentation of the existing advantages that enabled their route to AIIMS and that are consolidated during their time at the college. Thus, while confidence in the future is one of the more tangible legacies of an AIIMS MBBS, the privileges necessary to access the institution in the first place also set it apart. The immediate status of becoming an AIIMS student, however, also entails the pressures of the expectations of subsequent achievements befitting an AIIMSonian, which students must confront and negotiate as they approach graduation.

Researching elite institutions and the experiences of a group of comparatively privileged young people (though some far more so than others) is still relatively new territory for the anthropology of India. It means foregrounding the experiences of upwardly mobile young doctors—a demographic that troubles traditional categories of "suffering subjects" in both anthropological and development discourse more broadly, as Jocelyn Chua notes in her work on middle-class young people in Kerala.[75] In this book I pay more attention to the experiences of elite doctors-in-formation than to those of the many marginalized patients through whom they learn their profession. But without this attention we forgo opportunities for insight into how student doctors come to understand not just clinical medicine but also their roles and responsibilities as social actors imbued with status and power in the eyes of both the patients they will go on to treat and the wider society in which they live.

This book catches a group of young people at a liminal stage in their lives. They reach AIIMS already in possession of social knowledge that will inform their approach to medicine but that is also open to suspension and reinterpretation.[76] The "freedom" that many students described as integral to their AIIMS experience is encountered in different ways and has particularly troubling implications for those who need support that the institution is ill-equipped and sometimes unwilling to provide. It was partly the delicate nature of this life stage that led me to focus on MBBS students. There are of course many other students at AIIMS in different departments, including nursing and paramedical students, PhD candidates in biomedical research, and the many postgraduates pursuing specialist qualifications.

Officially, AIIMS is a tertiary institution providing specialized treatment, but, as we will see, patient demand, which is driven by a lack of supporting primary and secondary infrastructure, has always compromised this focus. Equally, although AIIMS was established to train specialists, it also has a founding mandate to set standards in undergraduate medical education. It is the MBBS entrants who embody the mythical aura of AIIMS—whose names reach the newspapers, having survived a staggeringly competitive admissions process. These students are the institute's most impressionable: the MBBS is their first experience of higher education, and for many it is their first time living away from home. They are the students with the most decisions still to make about their futures, decisions that will be heavily influenced by their formal and informal learning during their five and a half years at AIIMS.

It is during the MBBS that perceptions of excellence in medicine are established and expectations of the ideal AIIMSonian—and by implication the ideal doctor—are confirmed. Although a certain default understanding might already be in place among postgraduate students, the liminal position of undergraduates allows for the critical interrogation (as well as the confirmation) of an apparently conventional wisdom. Therefore, while this book is about experiences at an elite medical college—an environment explicitly designed to train doctors—it is also about the possibilities of higher education more broadly. Many of the themes and observations in this book are undoubtedly applicable to any Indian medical college, and in some cases to any institution of higher education. What distinguishes AIIMS, however, is its status and consequently the way in which it operates as both a structure and an idea. Or, to borrow from Sarah Pinto's work on health and medicine in rural North India, how it is a site of both imagination and practice.[77] For patients and aspiring doctors alike, for passersby outside the hospital gates or people consuming media coverage of its latest scandal, AIIMS represents both what medical practice and education are in India and what they *could be*.

I show that many AIIMS doctors deserve admiration for the excellent treatment they provide to disadvantaged patients under the pressures of insufficient time and space. I contend, however, that as an educational institution, AIIMS relies on a reputation that interprets excellence through a narrow lens of exam results and career prospects; thrives on a spectacular asymmetry between the demand for higher education and the ability to absorb it; and as a result, has little incentive to consider its original mandate and teach medicine as a social endeavor. In the process, AIIMS abdicates institutional responsibility for confronting the complex power hierarchies and social structures that determine health inequalities, patient experiences, and the experiences of AIIMS students themselves.

STRUCTURE

The book follows a broadly chronological structure. In chapter 2, I tell the story of the creation of AIIMS, drawing on historical sources and interviews with some of the institute's first students and faculty. I show how the institute was a product of and a response to the politics of medical education in colonial India, and I discuss the tensions inherent in its mandate to embody global standards of biomedical prowess while also addressing the needs of the predominantly poor and rural population of a newly independent nation. In chapter 3, I trace the long process of gaining admission to AIIMS as an MBBS student and argue that possession of social and economic capital is necessary not only for winning a place but even for realistically aspiring to sit the entrance exam. Drawing on the history and anthropology of Indian education, I outline the legacy of a reliance on memorization, or "mugging up," to understand how these pedagogical orientations inform the admissions process. Reflecting on the minute differences between the percentile scores of thousands of candidates, I introduce the concept of a "biographical number" as a means to explore the social function and subjective content of exam rankings, and suggest that what the admissions data reveals above all else is the inability of Indian institutions to absorb the overwhelming demand for higher education, with profound implications for young people and their futures.

Chapter 4 takes us through the gates of AIIMS and into the lives of its students. Reflecting on the discourse of "freedom" that I often heard from students, I interpret the MBBS as a liminal period in the lives of students, which offers transformative possibilities that nevertheless contain their own limits. This thread becomes a discussion of affirmative action at AIIMS, and the ways in which a discourse of caste and meritorious achievement slips in and out of view at the institution, reflecting how students think about themselves and each other as citizens and future doctors.

In chapter five, I discuss "patient labor," a phenomenon whereby students appreciate the number and diversity of AIIMS patients as an educational asset, at an institution that conditions those students to become (super)specialized clinicians unlikely to provide the frontline care that many patients come to the hospital for lack of. I also draw on ethnographic material from wards and outpatient clinics to show how a hidden curriculum naturalizes structural inequalities that play out in the clinical encounter, imparting impressions to students of what it means to be a good doctor and a responsible patient.[78] Integrating other ways of learning about medicine, such as through the humanities, would, I argue, create space for reflection on the social role of the doctor and open up possibilities for addressing rather than reproducing inequalities.

"AIIMS killed the GP," a former director told me, and I explore the implications of this statement for student aspirations and Indian healthcare in chapter six. I consider how medical practices are differently valued and legitimized, and how this informs students' ambitions. I discuss the process of graduating from AIIMS as an achievement with a social life in the present and implications for the future, for both individual students and the networks in which they are embedded.[79] I discuss the complex discourse that steers AIIMSonians toward superspecialized urban practice as the career path most befitting the country's "best" new doctors, ending with two short stories of female students who challenged this conventional wisdom by envisaging alternative futures, only to find them precluded by social—gendered—expectations of appropriate trajectories for AIIMS graduates.

I conclude the book by reflecting on the existence and experience of AIIMS in imagination and practice, and the implications of how the institution understands and promotes ideas of attainment and excellence.[80] Writing in a time of pandemic, I argue that this particular moment demands a political reckoning with the real nature of public health in India, and a reassessment of what the country needs from medical education—particularly at an institution mandated to set national standards. Integrating the humanities into the MBBS curriculum, I suggest, would create space for interrogating rather than naturalizing social inequalities and for self-reflection among students about the role of the doctor in society. By reimagining medical education, AIIMS could promote the potential of higher education to inspire and foster social change, earning in the process its reputation for excellence. Unless this happens, I conclude, the inhumanity of India's social and health inequalities is unlikely to be remedied.

CHAPTER 2

THE BEGINNING
Establishing AIIMS

IT IS UNWISE, if not impossible, to approach the contemporary life of an institution without considering its history. This is even more critical in the case of a postcolonial institution like AIIMS: conceived upon the threshold of Indian independence from British rule and created in the image of prestigious Western institutions to be preeminent in the field of Indian medical education and research while remaining mindful of the needs of a largely impoverished population. In the following pages, I trace the story of the All India Institute in Delhi from conception to inauguration, drawing out the tensions and the complexity that continues to influence the life of AIIMS today.

Each year, students at AIIMS organize an enormous weeklong cultural festival called Pulse that attracts medical students from colleges around the country. When I attended, I took the opportunity to ask some of the visitors what they thought of AIIMS. Their responses made clear that AIIMS New Delhi is understood to be in a class of its own:

> Obviously it's our dream college. We want to join it.
> —Second-year MBBS student, Government
> Medical College Kota, Rajasthan

They are best in everything . . . the best doctors are over here. Many things.
—Second-year MBBS student, CM Medical College, Chhattisgarh

Best in India. Best in Asia . . . Quality of education, lifestyle, thinking, everything.
—Third-year MBBS student, Assam Medical College

AIIMS, we call it medical heaven of east . . . when we take coaching for medical test, we dream to study in AIIMS, but can't reach.
—Second-year MBBS student, Government
Medical College Haldwani, Uttarakhand

When I asked these visiting students what made AIIMS the best, they spoke about the quality of doctors and their medical practice; resources and technology; the diversity of patients and diseases; and the self-perpetuating fact that it attracted the nation's highest-ranked students. Some also mentioned the institute's historical pedigree. An MBBS student from the Government Medical College in Jammu told me that AIIMS was India's first medical college, which was one reason it was better-equipped than others.

AIIMS was conceived as part of a colonial survey, informed by global expertise, and ultimately realized with the support of international donors as a unique embodiment of independent India's scientific and developmental ambition. But it was far from being the country's first medical college. At the moment of independence in 1947, India had 22 medical colleges, and by the time the first cohort of MBBS students at AIIMS graduated in 1961 that number had increased to 57.[1] But the student's misperception illustrates several things: the absence of history from medical curricula, the stature of AIIMS in the contemporary imagination, and the association of value with longevity. For this student, it was logical to assume that AIIMS was India's first medical college, which all subsequent institutions strived to emulate.

THE POLITICS OF MEDICAL
EDUCATION IN COLONIAL INDIA

By the mid-nineteenth century, India had been subject to different forms of British rule for more than 200 years. At this point, various medical colleges in India were teaching Western medicine, including Madras Medical College and Calcutta Medical College (both inaugurated in 1835), Grant Medical College in Bombay (1845), and Lahore Medical College (1860).[2] These were followed in the early twentieth century by Lady Hardinge Medical College for Women in Delhi and others in Patna, Lucknow, Bombay, and Visakhapatnam.[3]

Some preexisting institutions provided hybrid instruction in Western and indigenous medicine. At the Native Medical Institution in Calcutta, for example, students were taught European medical texts translated into Indian languages and they took classes in the indigenous medical systems of Unani and Ayurveda. This arrangement reflected a political moment in which the parallel existence and occasional syncretism of Western and Indian knowledge systems was tolerated by the colonial administration, and also expressly promoted by the era's "Orientalists." An attitudinal shift came with both the report on medical education requested by the governor of Bengal William Bentinck in 1833 and Thomas Macaulay's infamous Minute on Indian Education in 1835, which argued for the promotion of Western science and literature through exclusively English-medium curricula.[4]

The Calcutta Medical College was established in 1835 in place of the preexisting Native Medical Institution. The first institution in India to teach Western medicine solely in English, its mission was to teach "the principles and practice of the medical science in strict accordance with the mode adopted in Europe."[5] This bureaucratic consolidation of Western medicine's supremacy over indigenous practice extended into the twentieth century: by the 1920s, in Roger Jeffery's words, medical education "was caught between conflicting pressures of nationalism and a swiftly changing, increasingly scientized European medicine."[6] The Medical Registration Acts and Medical Degrees Act passed between 1912 and 1919 had excluded indigenous practitioners from claiming the title of "doctor." However, the 1919 Montagu-Chelmsford Reforms allowed Indian nationalist politicians to implement policies despite the opposition of British medical advisers, and the Indian National Congress began to pass resolutions in support of indigenous medicine. The two positions were never fully reconciled within the party: self-proclaimed modernizers such as Jawaharlal Nehru, who would become India's first prime minister, supported the expansion of Western medicine, while the new regional legislative councils supported indigenous medicine on nationalist and economic grounds.[7]

Before 1860, other than at the colleges I have mentioned, medical education in India generally took the form of apprenticeships, as it did in Britain. Between 1860 and 1914, however, the Indian Medical Service (IMS), a colonial institution with an entrance exam, determined and controlled the hierarchy of medical education.[8] Medical schools, which offered short courses for employment in auxiliary medical services, were subordinated to medical colleges, whose courses led to university qualifications that allowed a student to take the IMS exam and whose degrees, from 1892, were recognized by the British General Medical Council (GMC) in London. In an effort to stress the parity between Indian and British institutions, Indian colleges periodically raised their entrance requirements, creating a new market for the medical schools among candidates who did not qualify for college entrance.[9]

The numbers of medical colleges, schools, and students grew hesitantly during the nineteenth and early twentieth century, although figures for those who passed the final exams belie the broader impact of medical education. For example, of 2,511 students enrolled at medical colleges in 1916–1917, only 512 sat the final exams, and of those, 329 passed.[10] However, there were plentiful opportunities for students who left the colleges without a formal qualification to enter private practice, or to take up appointments in one of India's many princely states not directly governed by the British, given the absence of a regulated medical market.[11] This was a somewhat paradoxical outcome for the colonial government from a functional perspective. But there appears to have been less concern among those who considered colonialism an opportunity to disseminate Enlightenment science among subject populations alongside the service of British domination, as this 1885 report from the Bengal Administration suggests: "The object [of medical education] was not merely to secure a constant supply of subordinate medical officers for the Government service but also to raise the standard of medical knowledge and encourage the practice of medicine and surgery on established scientific principles. That private practitioners possessing the necessary qualifications should be able to compete successfully with public medical charities is a satisfactory result."[12]

Unsurprisingly, greater objection was raised when Indian doctors threatened the private practice of British IMS members. In response, the IMS determinedly prevented Indians from attaining prestigious positions as attending doctors and teachers at major hospitals. The grip of the IMS tightened in the early twentieth century as the GMC began to scrutinize Indian medical education more closely. In 1930, the GMC withdrew recognition of Indian degrees until an Indian medical council was established. As Jeffery puts it, "The rhetoric was that Indian graduates who wished to practice in Britain should meet British standards, but the implications were to affect the patterns of medical education in and for India thereafter."[13]

The Medical Council of India was established in 1933, and the medical schools were excluded from its terms in an effort to dismantle India's "two-tier" system of medical education. Where possible, schools were to be upgraded to colleges; otherwise, they were to close. The policy received wide support in India: school-educated doctors hoped to receive the benefits of college graduates, and for the nationalists, it resolved the notion that medical schools were second-class institutions that prompted international mistrust of Indian qualifications. In 1938, the colonial administration decided to close the medical schools altogether.[14]

"A GRAVE MORAL QUESTION"

The politics of medical education in early twentieth-century India was dominated by the tussle between Indian and British doctors and medical students to gain access to IMS recruitment and, by extension, to coveted positions at the most well-regarded medical colleges. Until the 1850s, employment as a doctor did not demand any official qualification. Before 1800, only 6% of doctors had attended a medical school, and at least half had no qualification of any kind. By 1860, however, a growing number of IMS recruits had gained a diploma from the Royal College of Surgeons in London or from the Scottish Royal College of Physicians.[15] Competitive examinations for entry to the IMS were first held in 1855 and were theoretically open to Indians, but the location of the examination centers in London ensured that, in practice, by 1913 only 55 Indians had joined, forming 5% of the service. By 1921, this had risen to only 6%.[16] Some of these early recruits resigned from the service soon after joining, citing discrimination by British officers; such testimonies would become more audible during the 1920s and 1930s.[17]

In response to the monopoly of the IMS, Indian doctors formed their own organizations such as the Bombay Medical Union (BMU) in 1883 and the Calcutta Medical Club in 1906. At a time of rising nationalism, the BMU in partnership with nationalist politicians demanded greater inclusion of Indian doctors in the IMS and more opportunities for Indian medical graduates outside the IMS in government medical colleges.[18] In 1913, the BMU wrote to the Royal Commission on the Public Services in India, demanding that the IMS examinations be held simultaneously in Britain and India, arguing that the supposedly "open" biennial IMS examinations in London were to all intents and purposes "shut" to the majority of Indians.[19] Indicating just how naturalized the sense of British ownership of its colony had become, the British Medical Association sent its own memorandum to the same commission warning against the "Indianization" of the Indian Medical Service, spluttering that Indians trained in "our colleges" posed a "grave moral question" for the future welfare of India in general and the standard of medical education in particular":

> The Government of India and the millions it rules will obviously be the first losers, and in this loss its European and Indian subjects will share alike. More gradually, but with equal certainty, the standard of education will fall, thereby inflicting lasting injury on the health of the people. Last, but not the least, comes a grave moral question; India wants our best, in all departments of service. Those who know the Indian most intimately, and who admire most intelligently his many excellent qualities as a professional man, cannot blind themselves to the fact that his standards are still far from being those of his British brother.[20]

This tactic, in which a dominant social group sought to protect its privilege by professing a concern for scientific standards, would be deployed almost a hundred years later by upper castes in protesting the expansion of affirmative action to include more reserved seats in medical colleges for students from underprivileged communities, as I discuss in chapter 4. Back in 1913, the Royal Commission on Public Services made some concessions in response to the BMU's petition and recommended that recruitment to senior posts be made both in England and in India. But it rejected the main demand to hold competitive exams simultaneously in England and India.[21] The Indian Students Association, which represented Indian students studying in England, sent a statement to the same commission asking that teaching standards at Indian medical colleges be improved. It held that despite the curriculum being equal to its British equivalent, poor teaching placed Indian students at a disadvantage when competing with British students in the IMS exams.[22]

Between 1909 and 1915, the president of the Indian Students Association was Dr. Jivraj N. Mehta, a medical student who would go on to be active in the movement for Indian independence and to hold roles as chief minister of the newly formed Gujarat state, as well as Indian high commissioner to the United Kingdom.[23] Mehta returned to India in 1915 and soon became involved in setting the agenda for nationalist medical education. In a post–World War I context of strained human and financial resources, the British administration actively supported the establishment of private medical institutions in India. In 1926, the King Edward Memorial hospital and Seth Gordhandas Sunderdas Medical College opened in Bombay, funded by entrepreneur Seth Gordhandas. Mehta became the first dean of the joint institution and defined its principles of medical education in accordance with the Indian nationalist agenda. It was one of the first Indian medical colleges to be almost exclusively staffed by Indian doctors outside government service (and implicitly outside the IMS)—a policy that incurred inevitable accusation from British doctors and IMS officers that the institution was "an anti-government and political movement" in the wake of the non-cooperation movement of 1919–1920 led by the Indian National Congress against imperial rule. These two institutions in

Bombay represented the ambitions of an emergent nation and its struggle for autonomy. In doing so, they presaged the establishment of the All India Institute of Medical Sciences thirty years later in the context of a newly independent state.[24]

"AN INDIAN INSTITUTE ESTABLISHED
IN INDIA, FOR THE TRAINING OF
INDIAN WORKERS BY INDIANS"

The Health Survey and Development Committee was appointed in October 1943 and was subsequently known as the Bhore Committee after its chair, Sir Joseph Bhore, a senior civil servant. It was partly an effort to assuage the Indian elite through a demonstration of concern for national welfare in the wake of the recently launched Quit India movement, but it also presaged a broader postwar shift in the West from laissez-faire to greater state interventionism.[25] Its task was twofold: to conduct a "broad survey of the present position in regard to health conditions and health organisation in British India" and to provide "recommendations for future developments."[26]

The four-volume Bhore Report presented in 1946 was implicitly critical of the colonial neglect of Indian public health and of the defeatist attitude of the civil service in the face of a task of such magnitude. The report promoted the dovetailing of preventive and curative care, with recommendations encompassing medical care, education, and administration. Although it was not without dispute, the report endorsed the policy that saw the closure or upgrade of medical schools.[27] A minority of members argued for the rapid expansion of all levels of medical education, but the report ultimately recommended that India focus its limited resources on "the highly trained type of physician whom we have termed the 'basic doctor.'"[28]

In 1943, the year of the Bhore Committee's appointment, the colonial government invited Professor A. V. Hill, secretary of the Royal Society in London, and a deputation, to visit India and "advise it on the future of scientific research in the context of development."[29] Their report focused on education:

For the most effective way of producing a change in all this would be to set out deliberately to create teachers and research workers of a new kind, people who would devote their lives to the single object of advancing in India the art, science and practice of medicine. For this purpose a great All-India Medical Centre should be established, an "Indian Johns Hopkins" staffed in all departments by the ablest people available anywhere, employed full-time and adequately paid. The students of the All-India Medical Centre should be highly selected ones, preferably with good degrees in arts or science as a start: and since a large proportion of the most desirable students cannot meet the financial cost of a long training in medicine, all who require help should be given it in the form of scholarships or bursaries. . . . The intention of the All-India Medical Centre would be to produce the future leaders of Indian medicine and public health, the teachers and research workers.[30]

During the visit, Hill had detailed discussions with members of the Bhore Committee about an institute that would reflect this need for greater integration, the plan for which was briefly known as "Prof. Hill's scheme."[31] Following the submission of Hill's report in 1945, C. G. Pandit, a London-trained virologist who was director of the King Institute of Preventive Medicine and Research in Madras, was deputed to accompany J. B. Hance, the director general of the IMS, on a research trip to the United Kingdom, United States, and Canada "to study and report on the modern trends in medical education and research." The trip placed particular emphasis on Johns Hopkins University, which was Hill's suggested model for an "All-India Medical Centre."[32] The terms of reference included the following: "Enquiries should be directed primarily towards securing information which would be of value in the preparations of plans for the organization of a medical training and research center, the purpose of which will be to train men, who will eventually be leaders of the medical profession, especially teachers and research workers. *It should be borne in mind that the primary object of such an institution will not be advancement of scientific knowledge, but the training of students.*"[33] In Britain, the Goodenough Committee, which was established to inquire into the changes required in medical education in Britain, released its report in 1944, recommending "the reorganization of medical education and research," particularly for a comprehensive National

Health Service.[34] The wartime deputation under Hance and Pandit stated in its own report that, "throughout the English speaking world a great renaissance in health provision and education is in formulation and the end of hostilities will see a burst of progress in matter [*sic*] of health unprecedented in history."[35] This reformist enthusiasm permeated discussions during the consultation period, particularly at the University of Oxford, which was developing its own plans for an undergraduate medical school that would adopt innovative teaching arrangements.[36]

Following consultations with the medical faculty of Liverpool University, Professor R. A. Morlan sent a letter to the committee urging that the specificities of India be given as much consideration as international models in establishing the new institute. India, he said, promised new scope for preventive medicine and research, all of which could be part of its new medical training:

> In both teaching and research, it could be held that relevance to India should decide priorities. I do not mean simply utility but relevance in [a] wider sense. . . . The whole problem of geography in relation to disease affords an instance of a long term programme of research to which individuals could contribute and the institute could act as the unifying agency and building up its own peculiar prestige, team spirit and continuity. . . . One would think that medical anthropology could be cultivated in India as nowhere else. Similarly, the problem of "putting over" preventive medicine affects all the world but India affords a unique laboratory for research in the borderland between education and medicine. I hope this makes clear what I mean by relevance as a strategic aim. The Institute should be *itself*, an Indian [*sic*], not a transplanted Johns Hopkins or Mount Vernon.[37]

Two years later, the Bhore Report included the recommendation that an "All-India Medical Institute" be established:

> The objects of the Institute should be 1) to bring together in one place educational facilities of the very highest order for the training of all the more important types of health personnel and to emphasize the close interrelation which exists between the different branches of professional education in the field of health; 2) to promote research of the highest type . . . ; 3) to co-ordinate training

and research; 4) to provide postgraduate training of an advanced character in an atmosphere which will foster the true scientific outlook and a spirit of initiative; 5) to inspire all persons who undergo training, undergraduate or postgraduate, with the high ideals of the profession to which they belong and 6) to promote in them a community outlook and a high degree of culture, in order that they may become active apostles of the progressive spirit in whatever field they may be called upon to serve.[38]

According to Pandit, the plan was shelved for some time because of financial constraints; the upgrading of certain departments in existing medical colleges was agreed to as an interim measure, "where suitable leadership was available."[39] Nevertheless, the newly independent Indian government recorded its intention to establish the recommended institution in its first five-year plan (1951–1956), and the project was revived by the allocation of a $1.25 million grant by the Government of New Zealand under the auspices of the Colombo Plan.[40] The foundation stone of the All India Institute of Medical Sciences (AIIMS) was laid by New Zealand's minister of industries and commerce in 1952, and the institute opened in 1956.

JAWAHARLAL NEHRU AND THE SCIENCE OF DEVELOPMENT

> The emergence and existence of India is inseparable from
> the authority of science and its functioning as the name
> for freedom and enlightenment, power and progress.
> —G. Prakash, *Another Reason*

The AIIMS foundation stone embodies the intention to place science and technology at the heart of postcolonial national development.[41] Warren Anderson reminds us that the concept of the postcolonial denotes more than a simple "celebration of the end of colonialism." Rather, "it signals a critical engagement with the present effects—intellectual and social—of centuries of 'European expansion' on former colonies and on their colonizers."[42] David Arnold expands with specific reference to India: "Postcolonial science might be presented as literally that: as sited temporally after colonialism. But India's independence was long anticipated and its science had by the 1930s reached a point of maturity—in institution building, individual achievement, and international recognition—that encouraged high expectations of what would happen once colonial constraints were removed. [Nehruvian science] began its 'postcolonial' career more than a decade before independence in 1947, just as it continued long after that date to grapple with the legacies of colonial rule and its continuing manifestations."[43] AIIMS was initially conceived in a report commissioned by the British colonial administration. That it was finally built and inaugurated under the auspices of an independent Indian government, with international funding, suggested less an epistemic break in scientific discourse than an opportunity to build on the legacy of Jivraj Mehta and others through a potent narrative that blended the challenges facing the new nation with the promise of scientific remedy. Referring to India's first prime minister, Jawaharlal Nehru, Jahnavi Phalkey describes this developmental discourse as "Nehruvian optimism."[44]

David Arnold suggests that Nehru's understanding of science was not only technical but also "philosophical and literary," which informed his determination to confirm "the centrality of science in the autobiography of the Indian nation."[45] Science was to serve national interests and inform the redress of social ills including disease and poverty. AIIMS represented this intention and also stood as a symbol of the new government's determined march toward a transnational standard of modernity as represented by science.[46] Despite Pandit's stated ambition for AIIMS to be an "Indian institute established in India, for the training of Indian workers by Indians," the institute carried a wider mandate. When A. L. Mudaliar, chair of the AIIMS planning committee, spoke at the first meeting of the Central Council of Health in 1953, he argued that undergraduate education at AIIMS should be "along the most modern lines that are accepted in international circles": "It is very important for us to realise that we must look to international standards. . . . When it comes to a question of helping in the cure of the sick and the general welfare of the community you cannot afford to forget international standards or lower your standards below the international level. If you do that, you will be the worse for it."[47]

During my time in Delhi, I interviewed several of the first faculty and students to work at and attend AIIMS. Dr. S joined the department of anatomy in 1957. Her account illustrated the determination that AIIMS emulate the most prestigious Western medical colleges:

It was highlighted everywhere—it was going to be the best institute. I was told that a delegation went around the world, picking up and interviewing outstanding Indians in different medical colleges in England, in the USA. And Professor N. H. Keswani, the professor that they had selected for anatomy, was outstanding; he was awarded the Outstanding Achievement Award by Mayo Clinic. So, the name of Mayo Clinic in those days, and hearing these very westernized people, young people, without much of that old culture of "yes-sir no-sir" appealed to me very much. So I was offered the job and I took it. And before I knew, I was deep into research. . . . In my early days the atmosphere in the institute was very nice. It was like a family. And the students, you did not treat them as students, everybody knew everyone. . . . I mean the first batch of students, they must have attended my wedding, they were all there, you know! That's why I started liking it and continued to work there. The place certainly was very congenial; it was not like any other place.

[The administration asked for] feedback from the students about the teachers, and things, everything—these were very modern techniques. [They] introduced a very, very excellent course, a detailed course, on neuro-anatomy. In those days, hardly any neuroanatomy was taught anywhere. . . . There was hue and cry from everyone, that why—do you want to make everybody a neurosurgeon or what? . . . But now neuroanatomy is important everywhere. So the influence on medical education, of the institute, was great. There was a lot of resistance from other centers—that this fellow is teaching, he is American, he is loud, he doesn't know, and she from Oxford has her head in the clouds, and things like that. But finally the entire country picked up the methods of examination and teaching in basic sciences. And then the huge number of postgraduates that have gone from here to there, they are all over, and they are following the same methods of teaching and research.

As Dr. S recalled, it was not only teaching methods and curricula that were incorporated from the United States and United Kingdom, but several faculty members themselves were handpicked and encouraged to return to India to be part of the new institute. Meanwhile, the experiences of Drs. S and V both illustrate how the character of AIIMS reflected that of Delhi's political elite:

> I qualified from Lady Hardinge Medical College. In those days that was the only medical college in Delhi. And after that I went to what was called in those days Irwin Hospital, because I wanted to specialize in surgery. After doing my house job, I was planning to go to England like everyone else, to do FRCS [Fellowship of the Royal College of Surgeons]. Due to many reasons, I could not go immediately. Because this institute was coming up, and my mother was a politician . . . I knew the ruling elite in those days very intimately. The All India Institute of Medical Sciences had already been planned. And Rajkumari Amrit Kaur was the president of the institute. She told my mother (I shouldn't say I was a political victim, but at that time I felt so) that if our children go abroad to study, who will study here? So I was forced to explore the possibility of getting a job here. And they did not have any clinical departments; they had just started basic sciences. Since I wanted to be a surgeon, I applied for a job in anatomy. I was interviewed very informally on a Sunday, and I was selected for the post of what they called a tutor, the junior most teacher in the Department of Anatomy. And I think I joined the All India Institute of Medical Sciences on 2nd February 1957.
>
> —Dr. S

> I joined AIIMS in 1960. [In] 1959 the hospital was started, so amongst the clinical faculty I would be amongst the early ones who joined. You see at that point in time, it was Rajkumari [Amrit Kaur] and Pandit Nehru. She would pick up the phone and say, "I want this," and he would say, "All right, you will have it." There was no bureaucracy in between. I can give my own example. I was working at Lady Hardinge Medical College; when the AIIMS advertisement for faculty came, I was selected. Normal course of events. And when I had to leave Hardinge to join AIIMS, the principal said, "I can't relieve you, I have no one else." She said, "Whenever a substitute comes, I will relieve you."

So what could I do? I kept on getting letters from AIIMS asking, "When are you going to join? When are you going to join?" And I would write back saying, "I cannot leave till I get permission to leave." So I get another letter saying, "If you do not join by this date, it will be assumed that you are not interested." Now what could I do? I was in a dilemma. So I looked around; how could I go and meet Rajkumari Amrit Kaur and explain my dilemma to her? There was no other way I could handle this situation. So then I found a friend who rang her up and said I have a damsel in distress. . . . So Rajkumari said to me: "Look, I cannot let you go away from Hardinge till someone else comes. But I can tell the director at AIIMS that you will join as soon as possible, and not to send these letters to you." So this would normally bypass the rules. [Without her intervention], I would have never joined AIIMS.

—Dr. V

For Dr. C, one of the first MBBS students to attend AIIMS, a personal connection to Delhi politics was also key to his arrival at the new institute where he went on to spend his career:

In those days Delhi did not have its own state medical college. So they used to nominate five students from Delhi to attend different institutions in India. So I got admission in Gwalior. Agra was my domicile, so I appeared there also, and got through. Finally, AIIMS—the result came in the last. And I must say there was a health ministry official who was somewhat related to us, to my father. And he told me, "What are you doing, this is going to be the biggest institution in the country and you are thinking of Agra and Gwalior and all that. This is rubbish. You wait for the [AIIMS] result, and if you get through, fine." So that's how it was. So I got through to the All India Institute. I spent 47 years of my life there. It's more than half my life I suppose. And I saw AIIMS being built brick by brick.

The complexity of the mandate for the new institution was expressed most explicitly through the speech by Health Minister Rajkumari Amrit Kaur, when she presented the All India Institute of Medical Sciences Bill to Parliament on February 18, 1956. The speech highlights all that was intended to be unique about AIIMS, but it also contains insurmountable contradictions of purpose that have had consequences for medical practice within and without the institute. Toward the beginning of the speech, Kaur asserts:

> Medical education must, above all, take into account the special needs of the country from the point of view of affording health protection to the people. . . . [T]he continued prevalence of various forms of preventable causes of sickness and suffering necessitates special emphases, if I may so put it, on the preventive aspect of medical care. Further, the extent to which [a doctor] develops a community outlook and a desire to serve the people. Medical education, moreover, is receiving considerable attention in all the progressive countries of the world. I have had the privilege recently to see what is being done in the USA, in the USSR, in Scandinavia and even in the UK to bring it more and more into consonance with present day needs and to promote an increasing realization of the object of equipping the future doctor to give of his best to the community. India cannot afford to keep apart from this broad and steady program of development that is taking place in other parts of the world.[48]

In a converse arrangement to that at the Gordhandas Sunderdas Medical College in Bombay decades earlier, the speech goes on to note the special measure of prohibiting private practice by AIIMS doctors and compensating them with higher salaries to ensure their exclusive focus on the institute, and the importance of a residential campus to ensure a personal *guru-shishya*, or teacher-student, relationship, in the spirit of one Indian tradition of education.

Dr. V remembered this relationship as one of the strengths of the institution in the early days, although she noted the absence of a strategy or model to ensure that graduates did indeed replicate the new teaching methods of AIIMS in other states:

> The best thing that the founders of AIIMS did was to build houses on the campus. So everyone was available on the premises when the hospital came up . . . so that you had the full attention of the faculty to deliver services and to teach. And it was thought that if you have only 50 students then you can experiment with methods of teaching, whereas in the larger medical schools you have 100 students, 150 students, that's too big a number to be able experiment on teaching modules. That was the idea. But unfortunately that never

happened. Because one was not able to create models, because we never built an area where you could invite people who could stay there and teach. You see? We had to provide for people who would come in, we would train them and they could go back to the states and teach. That model was not prepared. Therefore, models of education were really not set by AIIMS. But they acted as role models to the 50 students that came in.

Students were to be given "ample opportunities to participate in both urban and rural health work," and the curriculum was to encourage "a community outlook and also promote powers of initiative and observation and of drawing conclusions from them." The institute would be "given the powers and functions of a University because it will probably make revolutionary changes, as I hope, in curriculum as well as in modes of teaching," and it would "enjoy a large measure of autonomy in order that it may fulfil the objectives." While the government would provide the primary funding for the maintenance of the institute, Kaur hoped that "philanthropy also will come to the aid, as it so often does, of such institutions because, after all, serving the cause of sick and suffering humanity is always something that appeals to those who would like to give."

In the conclusion of her speech, she stressed that the future of the institute lay in the hands of its members:

> I believe it will be their devotion to duty, their desire to promote their work and the spirit of altruism that will actuate [*sic*] them to subordinate personal considerations, as I believe the noble profession of medicine should do, to the fulfilment of the objectives to be achieved that will eventually create and maintain the atmosphere which is necessary for an Institute like this. I therefore do hope that in presenting this Bill for acceptance by Parliament today, the legal structure that is created may facilitate the medical education in the institute and that, through the influence it exerts, the standards of different forms of professional training in the field of health throughout the country will be raised.[49]

The ambition articulated for the new institution was formidable.[50] AIIMS was intended to transform the nature of medical education and practice in the nation while deliberately catering to a small number of students to ensure a unique pedagogical experience. Students were to develop a community outlook, a commitment to national service in both rural and urban settings, and a preventive orientation (an echo of the Bhore Report), and also to emulate Western "progress" while responding to Indian needs, while the greater purpose was to focus on postgraduate specialization and the training of teachers. In 1973's *Medicine and Society*, Henry Miller described this as the "Indian predicament," which is "characteristic and understandable. Unless the government trains a medical *corps d'élite* it will be unable to undertake the practical research into preventive medicine that is central to the Indian situation. Furthermore, it will demoralize the medical profession to whom involvement in high technology is a matter of national pride, even if it is not always so easy to justify on utilitarian grounds."[51]

FORESEEING THE CHALLENGE OF AIIMS

By 1956, the first year of AIIMS, "technology" was taking precedence over "science" as a key trope in Nehru's speeches. He spoke often about the need to think about the demands of the national planning process "in technological terms."[52] Great energy went into the establishment of the Indian Institutes of Technology (IIT) in the 1950s, a set of institutions that, more broadly than AIIMS, were expected to produce graduates who would shape the future of the country. Indeed, in his convocation address at IIT Kharagpur in 1951, Nehru stated that while administrators continued to be important in national governance and development, "the time has now come when the Engineer [*sic*] plays an infinitely greater role than anybody else."[53] Arnold suggests that "medicine and public health never stood quite so high in Nehru's esteem" as more explicitly technological pursuits.[54] In the speeches that Arnold cites, however, what is striking is less a lack of esteem for medicine and public health than Nehru's grappling with two separate but related challenges. First, that technology did not offer and could not be considered a magic bullet for public health; and second, how to reconcile a principle of quality over quantity in medical education with the glaring need for a huge number of trained healthcare professionals. These tensions have always been, and remain, intrinsic to AIIMS.

Despite Nehru's commitment to technology as a primary tool of national development, in the 1950s he was well aware of the pitfalls of adhering to high technology alone as a public health solution and he foresaw the detrimental consequences of a singular focus on individualized, curative, and largely urban medicine. Whether or not it was the lingering influence of the Bhore Report, a result of Nehru's own observations, or both, he maintained his conviction that social and preventive medicine should take priority, even as he watched the opposite trend become entrenched: "The actual day-to-day work of a doctor should become more and more preventive than actual treatment, although the latter is of importance. We put up big hospitals and that is inevitable. You must have some big hospitals where there is a concentration of work, but one cannot put up these big hospitals all over India, or even smaller hospitals but rather on a large scale. We should evolve some way of giving medical services to the villagers, because I am constantly thinking as to how to deal with them."[55] At the second convocation of AIIMS in 1964, Nehru articulated his ongoing preoccupations with quantity versus quality, technologized curative medicine versus preventive public healthcare, urban versus rural practice, and here he also dwelled on his concern that India's traditions of indigenous medicine and learning should not be forgotten. In comparison with the rousing call to arms Nehru delivered to the graduates of IIT Kharagpur in 1951, his 1964 address was notably sober, almost weary, as he confronted the divergent challenges that the country still faced in its effort to improve the health of its people.[56] He noted with approval the study of preventive and social medicine at AIIMS and stated that he considered it "particularly important in the modern age."[57] The subject should be, Nehru said, "the dominant function of the Institute and the people who go out of this Institute, because social medicine prevents those things happening which require treatment later on. I hope enough attention will be paid to the social aspects of medicine."[58]

This challenge echoes the parliamentary speech of Amrit Kaur in 1956, wherein the AIIMS mandate was to be at once an exclusive center of cutting-edge research and technology and also an incubator of doctors who would take social and preventive medicine to the rest of India. "It is comforting," Nehru went on, "to find that your Institute has not so much cared for quantity as for quality. It is essential that we should have higher standards at the top as these will determined the quality of work below to a large extent."[59] Having discussed the need for rural doctors, he then admitted the overwhelming scale of the challenge and his own uncertainty about the remedy:

> One thing that troubles me is that in spite of such fine institutes as this one, yet there are vast areas in this country . . . where the benefits of modern medicine do not reach and sometimes we are rather overwhelmed by the problem. So many people are wanted there—qualified physicians, surgeons and properly equipped institutions—and we have so few. It is obvious that, however good an institute like this may be, that is essential of course; one can only be satisfied if it reaches down to the villages and if thousands, hundreds of thousands of villages feel the impact of it. I do not know how we are going to train the people in such large numbers to go there; and I will suggest to you, those who are trained, have received the benefit of training at these special institutes, should always bear in mind the need of the people of India who live in the villages. Because they are in numbers as well as otherwise the real people of India and unless we know them, we do not function properly. And then how to deal with such vast numbers and how long it will take enough people to go there, is a difficult matter. Whether it is conceivable to have institutes at these villages, some kind of assistance to serve the community, bring up the real cases to experts or how to deal with it, I do not know. But something has to be done to bring modern medicine to the great majority of our people in the country.[60]

There is a retrospective poignancy to these words of an increasingly frail statesman who had once regularly noted the robustness of his health and the rarity with which he consulted doctors, but who could not offer answers to the questions of illness and death that afflicted so much of the population, beyond vaguely articulated hopes. Within two months of his address at AIIMS, Nehru died at the age of 74.

As was predictable given its complex mandate, opinions also differed between people directly involved with AIIMS about how the imagined institution should translate into practice. Dr. V. Ramalingaswami, director of AIIMS from 1969 to 1979, expressed concerns in his Jawaharlal Nehru memorial speech of 1975:

The distortions and incongruities that characterize the present system are many—the over-emphasis on doctors and specialists, on hospitalized individual medical care to the detriment of frontline primary health care of the masses of the people, curative services to the neglect of preventive services, urban orientation to the neglect of rural masses, the draining away of limited resources in the provision of advanced levels of health care to a relatively small segment of the population . . . the distorted health manpower structure that mismatches the needs and, in the end, the wide gap that exists between the capabilities of modern medicine and the unfulfilled expectations of people. . . . Physicians in developing countries become estranged from their own people in the course of their training. The ablest men and women are not tackling the most acute and difficult problems.[61]

During this same period, the sociologist T. N. Madan found a sense of identity crisis among doctors at AIIMS. Some faculty members felt that "a drastic redefinition" of institutional goals was required, to reflect its educational success and the attention being paid to its role in community medicine and, by extension, national development. Others disagreed and felt the priority should be to reemphasize its tertiary specialist orientation, and to replicate the institution around the country.[62]

This sense of unease persists among present AIIMS faculty who acknowledge the inherent challenge of an institution founded to reflect Indian parity in the global discourse of scientific progress while sensitizing skilled clinicians to the needs of their most disadvantaged fellow citizens. Dr. V explained to me how the lack of supporting infrastructure meant that AIIMS was unable to ever be an exclusively tertiary institution, given the large number of patients who sought primary and secondary care at the hospital, a challenge that has since multiplied and is definitive of the contemporary life of the institute (and many ostensibly tertiary hospitals across India).

There was an infectious energy in the national ambitions articulated through AIIMS, as well as an almost poignant recognition of the scale of the challenge expected to be met. AIIMS was tasked with becoming India's premiere medical institution, combining the finest research and medical facilities with high-quality training of new generations of Indian doctors. It was also intended to apply social medicine to the nation's widespread health challenges, many of which were, and continue to be, entangled with poverty and social exclusion. This complex mission ensured that AIIMS was immediately caught between the scientific and the technological emphases of development, the wider social determinants of health, and the inadequate medical infrastructure in most of the newly independent country. The absence of supporting infrastructure immediately threatened the institution's mandate as a center for tertiary care while also doing nothing to ensure that AIIMS graduates were willing and able to establish careers at home rather than leaving the country, as so many of them did. Many of these tensions endure today.[63]

In 1970, 25 years after his research expedition, C. G. Pandit was invited to speak at the AIIMS Annual Day. "Annual Day, to my mind, is a day of stock taking," he wrote in his memoir, where he records the conclusion of his address:

> When I look at this campus, with its beautiful and impressive lawns, note the sharing of the campus by the staff and students, admire the highly developed laboratories, and clinical departments, and inevitably reflect on all that you have done and achieved, I feel that you have created here an "island of excellence." But will it always remain a lonely island, or as some others would put it, an ivory tower? Or, on the other hand, will you be helping in making this country an archipelago with many islands of excellence in it? Excellence must not be isolated in islands but must flow into the main stream of national life. Was that not the dream of the original planners of the Institute?[64]

AIIMS is a product of and a response to the politics of medical power and knowledge in colonial India as well as an emblem of—and challenge facing—the ambition of a newly independent state. This book goes on to explore what it means for AIIMS to be "an island of excellence," in Pandit's words, and the degree to which it has influenced "the main stream of national life," connecting the demanding ideals of the institute's founders with the complex realities of education, health, and medicine in today's India.

CHAPTER 3

GETTING IN

Being the Best

GIVEN THE HERITAGE and prestige of AIIMS, is it not surprising that it is the top choice of college for so many aspiring doctors. In this chapter, I introduce the students who appear throughout the book and trace how they went from being schoolchildren considering a medical career to trainee doctors profiled in the media for winning a seat at India's most coveted medical college. In doing so, I pay particular attention to the social phenomenon that is the AIIMS MBBS entrance exam and the way that it illuminates and entrenches inequalities, while working to fuel narratives that firmly associate concepts of achievement and "merit" with upper casteness via the "general category." Looking particularly at the function of exam ranking, I present the concept of biographical numbers as a means of exploring the subjective impact of rank on students' sense of self and their potential futures.

WHY MEDICINE?

In their writing about medical students in South Africa, Pentecost and Cousins return to the work of Eisenberg and Kleinman on the "social decision" to become a patient.[1] This decision, Eisenberg and Kleinman note, is usually made in consultation with others, against "a background of values" that include class and culture. "The same can be said for the decision to become a doctor," Pentecost and Cousins argue. In this section I give examples of how this social decision took place for the student doctors I came to know at AIIMS.

In newly independent India the medical and engineering professions promised financial security and social status, and were promoted as integral to the vision of national development. Together with the civil services they formed a trifecta of prestige that has remained largely intact among India's middle classes.[2] For many school students, their families and teachers alike, medicine and engineering have historically been considered interchangeable career options. In Bourdieu's terms, they continue to bestow all three forms of capital: economic, social, and cultural.[3] Since the establishment and growth of India's information technology (IT) sector, however, and the increase in opportunities for careers in software engineering, rather than the more traditional civil engineering, the narratives attached to each option have begun to diverge. During her research among doctors in Kerala, Wilson found a growing disconnect between the perception and the reality of a doctor's lifestyle, which is often defined by low pay, challenging conditions (in both public and private settings), and, at least in the early years, unrelenting competition over seats for postgraduate training.[4] In many cases, it is medicine's *cultural* capital, reflected through social status and value in the matrimonial market that sustains its appeal. Even cultural capital can suffer these days, though, in comparison with that associated with careers in IT, finance, or entrepreneurship, all of which are celebrated in contemporary narratives of national development and India's place in the world, and all of which tempt young people with an unreliable promise of ever-greater material comfort and security.[5]

Nevertheless, ambitious middle-class students still regularly speak of medicine and engineering in the same breath. It remains the case in India's education system that academic aptitude is quantified through performance in maths and sciences—numeracy is everything. Most students are streamed following exams in class 10 at age 15–16, with maths and sciences commanding the most respect (in contrast with the vaguely termed "arts" or "commerce"). As we will see, among the AIIMS students I spoke to, everyone had made a choice between maths (implying an undergraduate course in engineering) and science (implying medicine), with occasional students such as Anjali continuing to study both. "Arts," which encompasses the humanities, has no place in the life of India's medical students. The implications of this absence for how students understand medicine, patients, and themselves as young doctors became apparent during my research, and I draw attention to them in the chapters that follow.

The majority of AIIMS patients are from northern India, with a minority traveling from further afield for specialist treatment. Almost all the patients and their companions I spoke with at the hospital were from in and around Delhi itself and the northern states of Bihar and Uttar Pradesh, both of which suffer from some of India's most inadequate public healthcare infrastructure. Students, however, present a more pan-Indian face of AIIMS. This regional diversity coupled with similarly middle-class backgrounds has consequences for social dynamics among students, as I describe in chapter 4.

Tashi was a fourth-year MBBS student when we first met at the AIIMS rural health project in Ballabhgarh, Haryana. He was one of a small number of students from Northeast India, and was from an Adivasi or Scheduled Tribe community, although he had attended a prestigious private boarding school from a young age. Of all the students I spoke with, Tashi most clearly articulated an equivalence between medicine and engineering, and, by extension, between India's most prestigious educational institutions. When I first asked why he had chosen to study medicine, he said: "I thought I could never do engineering!" It transpired that he had briefly studied engineering at an Indian Institute of Technology (IIT), the equivalent of AIIMS, with its own ferociously competitive entrance exam:

> During my 12th [year at school], when I was giving the entrance exam, I was thinking I will go to IIT. So I went there, I thought that I could never do it, I left it and I came here. That's why I am here in medicine. There was no motivation . . . that I was interested or something like that.

Being "interested or something like that" is not, then, a requirement for winning a seat at India's most prestigious medical college. Excelling at multiple-choice exams, however, very much is. While at AIIMS, given his lack of interest in medicine, Tashi decided to pursue a career in the civil services, and by the time we met, he had begun studying for another notoriously difficult examination process. A third success would complete his portfolio of prestige; whether it would bring him fulfillment was a different question.

Sushil was an intern in the final year of his MBBS when we met. He was from northern India and also had begun an engineering course after school, albeit at a college he dismissed as "not good." His mother, whom he described as illiterate, advised him to seek guidance from a teacher at his old school:

> I went to my teacher to see her. She told me, "You should go for medicine since you have scored so much." I was the topper in my school. So she told me, "You should go for the medicine line." I said, "OK, let's see." So I went there to Kota [for exam coaching] and got selected.

Other students had specifically chosen medicine, but often with reference to engineering as the only obvious alternative. Azam was a fourth-year student from Kerala. His father wanted him to be an engineer, but he chose medicine, he said, having been inspired by the doctors he encountered during his childhood. Those childhood experiences continued to influence his approach to medicine, and he aspired to be a pediatrician.

Dilip, from Rajasthan and also in his fourth year, felt that he had made an unconventional choice by pursuing medicine rather than engineering. "Most people choose engineering," he said, "because they don't want to study for more than four or five years of college." Dilip's reasons for studying medicine suggested a confidence in his ability to go far in his chosen profession, not only reflecting the advantages that made his admission more likely but also confirming the convertible social and cultural capital bestowed upon AIIMS students:

> [In medicine] you get maybe more opportunities to become famous, people know you for your work and then maybe you can go to . . . much more heights of your career than one would do in engineering.

Priya was an intern and also from Rajasthan. She echoed Dilip's assessment that medicine was a more demanding course of study than engineering, and she also noted the appeal of a doctor's social status, adding its potential to ensure a comfortable life. A career in engineering would have been harder work given its itinerant nature, she thought,[6] whereas

> in the medical field you tend to set-up nicely, make your own, have your private set-up, whatever, and that gives you a lot of respect. I really like that. I like communicating with people so . . . that's why I chose and later on I realized that, OK, I was satisfied with that.

It took Priya time to feel satisfied with her decision because her favorite subject at school had been maths, which inclined her toward engineering. However, she also enjoyed biology, and—crucially—she reasoned that a career as a doctor was "better; suitable for a girl."[7]

The role of gender in career decision making was also raised by a group of students from CM Medical College in Chhattisgarh, who I spoke with during their visit to AIIMS for the Pulse festival. One student told me that medicine was "the best profession for girls." Her friends agreed, explaining that medicine allowed for financial and professional independence, which made it particularly appealing to women. Anthropologists have written about the calculations that inform parents' educational strategies for their daughters, including the need for domestic labor and a child's marriage prospects.[8] Wilson found that a significant aspect of the capital attached to medicine in Kerala was its utility in the matrimonial market; while online matrimonial sites have specific sections for doctors, a dedicated service also exists at the website DoctorShaadi.com.[9] I found suggestions of similar calculations by the families of AIIMS students. I first met Neha, a fourth-year student from Punjab, in January 2015. Like Tashi, she was in the process of planning a strategy that would allow her to study for the civil services entrance exam alongside the demands of the MBBS curriculum. However, Neha's aspirations became so entangled with questions of marriage and kinship that by the time I left Delhi, she intended to apply for postgraduate medical training in the United States. As Anjali, another student from Rajasthan, struggled to forge a career path based on her own interests, she too was finding the shadow of marriage expectations increasingly difficult to compartmentalize. Such considerations were not confined to female students. Santosh, an intern, was filled with foreboding at the prospect of marriage. Like Neha and Tashi, he hoped to join the civil services after completing his MBBS, but he was anxious about the incompatibility of his envisioned career with the family life that would be expected of him. Any prospect of his family accepting his choice not to marry was out of the question: the stigma of being unmarried was akin to "being a criminal, or worse," he said. I return to these stories, and the ambition to join the civil services, in chapter 6.

Rahul, from Himachal Pradesh, told me that his pursuit of medicine was a response to his mother having been denied the opportunity when she was young. She had missed out on a seat at the medical college in her home state by just 11 marks and was offered a place at a dental college in a different state instead:

> [But] at that time people were very conservative, so nearby there was an agricultural university and my grandmother said you should go there only, it's nearby home, just a kilometer or so. So [my mother] said that when I have a son or daughter, he or she should become a doctor, so I decided to become a doctor.

Shankar, an intern from Delhi, described a similar influence, albeit less directly:

> My mother had a dream to become a doctor. But she could not become a doctor. So I decided to become a doctor. But it was not driven by . . . when I decided, when we had to choose, when we finish our 10th grade, at that time it is mainly driven by what are the outcomes of the career, I mean employment opportunities and all. So that was what it was mainly, but not . . . I did not have so much self-awareness about me, what I wanted to do at that time.

Of the students who noted the role of family in influencing their decision, Shyam and Balraj, both from Madhya Pradesh, and Raheem, a second-year surgical senior resident from Andhra Pradesh, were the most explicit about their parents having imposed a preference on them.[10] Shyam's father was a radiotherapist; when I asked if this had any influence on Shyam's motivation to study medicine, he said: "Yeah, most of it. He pursued me and I got pursued! I liked physics much more than biology, for that matter, so yeah." Shyam sounded unconvinced by the wisdom of his choice, but he took a pragmatic view: "It's OK; I mean, there are too many engineers. So I always knew there was not very much scope in the engineering part. I am in a good field, I am in a good place so I'm happy with it." When we spoke, he had begun studying for the US Medical Licensing Examination, a multiple-part exam that students must pass in order to pursue postgraduate training in the United States. He had plans to return to India afterward to open a chain of clinics providing affordable treatment in peri-urban and rural areas.

Neither Balraj nor Raheem came from medical families, but both attributed responsibility for their decision to their parents:

> Actually, initially my parents wanted that. See, nobody was a doctor in my family so I didn't have any idea regarding what doctors are or what medicine is, and they wanted me to study this. So that was the reason that I took it. But now I am enjoying.
>
> —Balraj

> Frankly speaking it was my parents' wishes. I never had any such [ideas about becoming a doctor]. Even later on once I was in this field, I never thought . . . I just thought that I have to do this, I have to do this, and things went on their way.
>
> —Raheem

By the time we met, Balraj aspired to be a neurosurgeon, and his enthusiasm for the field was palpable when he spoke. Raheem was about to graduate with an MCh in gastrointestinal surgery, one of only 33 people to do so in India each year.

The most vivid account of a lack of autonomy in the process of choosing a medical career came from Dr. D, who had studied at AIIMS in the mid-1970s: "Nobody asked me. In fact I didn't know about AIIMS until I appeared in the examination. So it was my father who filled up all the forms; I just signed those forms without knowing anything, what the options were that were available. My career path was chosen by my father."[11]

Not all parents supported their child's medical ambitions. These examples are at odds with Wilson's findings that parents in Kerala preferred their children to study medicine rather than engineering, to the dismay of some students who said their parents did not appreciate the years of intense study involved in becoming a doctor.[12] Neha was drawn to medicine having witnessed her uncle's treatment for a chronic illness over many years: "So I wanted to do something. My parents were not at all supportive of my decision. They said you will spend your whole life studying; you won't have anything else in your life. Then I said, no, I want to be a doctor."

Ashish's parents were both doctors, and their initial objection to their son's choice challenged any assumption of the automatic reproduction of capital in medical families. They were concerned about Ashish committing to so many years of study before he began earning a living. It is also possible that they had concerns about their son's affinity for sustained academic application. Following his first MBBS exams, he told me, he "lost direction" ("I was basically having fun," he said), and he had to retake two midsemester exams. "My parents gave me a big scolding," he said, adding that he was almost back on track. Ashish had convinced his parents of his commitment, and he explained to me that he was motivated more by medical science as an academic subject than as a route to clinical practice: "I wanted to know more about the human body. That is why I opted for this." This affinity for biological science, as opposed to a general aptitude for academic study that makes science a default gateway to a career, receives less attention as a motivator of medical careers than the pursuit of capital. But it was not unusual at AIIMS—several students visiting for Pulse also told me that it was an interest in biology and human anatomy that inspired their choice and ensured their ongoing commitment to a demanding course of study.

Purush, an intern from Rajasthan, was drawn to medicine by the same fascination: "the enigma, the human body, and how it works and all." But this attraction was coupled, he explained, with a desire to alleviate what he saw as "widespread gloom in society—there is so much pain and suffering." This social dimension was not an uncommon aspect of students' motivation, but it was rarely cited as a primary reason for their choice of a career in medicine.

In her work on medical education in Malawi, one of very few studies of medical education in a postcolonial state, Claire Wendland writes that for many of the students she spoke with, the combination of sociocultural capital and job security made medicine an appealing option. The same is true in India and, we might presume, the rest of the world. In Wendland's experience, however, most Malawians "understood medicine as a vocation, a duty, or an opportunity to 'uplift our nation.'" The desire to become "agents of development" through medicine was underpinned by a Christian ethos that fueled a motivation to "heal Malawi."[13] Among medical students in South Africa, Pentecost and Cousins found examples of the "antisocial and pragmatic" attitudes that Kasper and colleagues have written about with regard to Harvard Medical School students.[14] "Antisocial" attitudes included rejection of the idea that doctors should play roles akin to social workers, whereas "pragmatism" meant that any knowledge beyond the bounds of the technical-clinical was irrelevant.[15] And for the South African students, there was a concern to be equipped with expertise on par with that of their peers in the Global North, where many of them planned to emigrate.[16] We will see these themes arise for AIIMS students in the chapters that follow. The most notable contrast with the students in Wendland's work in particular was that most AIIMS students who spoke of "development" or the politics of healthcare intended to leave medicine following their MBBS, most commonly for a career in the civil services. Purush was unusual: unlike others he told me he intended to continue with medicine as a means to ameliorate the "pain and suffering" he saw around him.

For many of Wendland's student informants in Malawi, "medicine felt less like a choice than an inevitability," given their status as highly educated members of a tiny urban elite and the dearth of alternatives in the small, impoverished nation.[17] At AIIMS, for some students it was growing up in a medical family that made the career feel inevitable.[18] Vivek, from Haryana, spoke of a mixture of motivations: the intellectual challenge of complex diagnosis and medical innovation, combined with a varied work life and the capacity to help people in need. He acknowledged, however, that this conclusion was largely informed by having witnessed such opportunities as he grew up surrounded by doctors—although his parents were not enthusiastic about his choice, given the amount of work involved.

In contrast, the response of Mihir, an intern from Haryana, suggested that he felt his horizons had been limited by both of his parents and several other family members being doctors, to the extent that he overrode his preference for maths in order to pursue medicine:

> My favorite subject was always maths. I didn't want to go into biology, but I couldn't visualize myself as anything other than a doctor. I had to get into biology by force. I suppose it's because my parents are doctors and it's the only profession I was exposed to during my growing years.

Anjali was the latest of five generations of doctors, a lineage that had a clear impact on her perceptions of medicine and healthcare as she grew up:

> Every single person I know is a doctor! I mean I didn't know you had to take an appointment from a doctor, because all I needed to do was just call up and say, "Hey, Aunt, this is the problem." Seriously! Probably until sixth standard, I genuinely thought that if you study, if you work hard, you are going to be a doctor. Like, there is no other option out there. That's genuinely what I thought.

Despite this inculcation of medical habitus at home, as she progressed through school, Anjali became aware of other possible options that depended on her choice of subjects.[19] Her reflections confirm how future-determining educational choices at school are structured and valued, and why students at AIIMS only ever spoke of having to choose between maths and science:

> Yes, so, in 10th standard you are supposed to choose between biology and mathematics, and arts is . . . I was like 16 at that point and the conception was that humanities was for those who cannot make it to the sciences and you never really choose to go into humanities. And commerce was full of those who had a businessman kind of family. So science was the natural option and between biology and maths there was a choice, so I just took both of them, and I studied both of them, unlike anyone else in my school. And then

when the time came to decide, I had the option of going into engineering, which is another hot thing to do in India, and becoming a doctor. I wasn't sure of myself, I didn't know what I liked more. I was like, "OK, this is a safe choice, might as well do it."

For Nikhil, however, who came from rural Uttar Pradesh, having grown up around medicine was an unequivocal inspiration. His father was not a trained physician, but his educated status in their village meant that people approached him for medical advice, and he was later selected for some first-aid training through a government program. His premature death was also a factor in Nikhil's decision to study medicine:

> Actually from the beginning when I saw my father doing something to treat, giving some pain relief . . . Someone came with pain and my father gave something, the person would say, "Thank you, doctor," and that would give me pleasure. I feel better that I can treat, if someone calls me doctor, I feel very passionate. And I want to help people this way. And the other thing is my father was suffering from brain tumor and he expired when I was in class 7. So at that time I turned more towards medical science. . . . I felt I had to do something more in this field, so that I can make other children happy; some sentiments are related to this.

Growing up in a medical family had a different connotation for Nikhil than it did for Mihir or Anjali, and yet for all that Nikhil's father would not be considered "a proper doctor" by students at AIIMS—indeed, he would likely be dismissed as a "quack"—it was Nikhil whose early observation of the social life of medicine encouraged him to become a doctor. It was not a default option that he felt compelled to choose.

"NONCOMBUSTIBLE DATA": A BRIEF HISTORY OF MUGGING UP

> We in India are apt to pay more attention and more time to book-learning than to the practical side. In our country there is far too much of a habit of memorizing things in order to pass examinations. It is a very dangerous habit. Apart from a person not

learning anything, he becomes stultified and possibly is not capable
of growth later on. I think it is essential that the practical side is
stressed much more in all our scientific pursuits and education.
                                        –Jawaharlal Nehru, speech to the Medical
                                        Education Conference, New Delhi, 1955

Sabra, a Maldivian student in her intern year, laughed when she recalled
the pedagogical culture shock she experienced during her first year at
AIIMS.[20] She had struggled to learn all the examination material in the
limited time available: "For us it was a lot of cramming, so we were like,
how are the Indians doing this?! They are so smart! It was very difficult for
all the foreign nationals. We kept on failing." She remembered a conversation with a friend studying medicine at Imperial College in London. The
difference, she said, was that the books her friend used for reference, to
supplement lecture notes and seminar learning, were those that AIIMS
students tried to commit to memory in their entirety. The disadvantage
was not being able to retain the large volumes of information she read. But
on the upside, she said, the catchall approach to "mugging up" meant that
"without knowing, we kind of learn a lot of things, I guess."

As in so many things, education in contemporary India is notable for its
diversity of form. Schools vary in terms of provenance, language, religion,
exam board, and whether they are government, nongovernmental organization, or private initiatives. This variation notwithstanding, and despite periodic government efforts at educational reform, rote memorization and the
accumulation of facts through mugging up continues to dominate the school
experience of many students.[21] Students navigate regular cycles of highly
competitive examinations, following which they are assigned a numerical rank
in a matrix of achievement, with determinist consequences that often cement
preexisting social advantages and disadvantages.[22] What may appear to be
largely a question of the mechanics of learning contains its own histories—of
definitions of and control over knowledge, and the techniques and purposes
of its transmission. The currents that ripple through contemporary Indian
education reflect the influences of three intersecting eras: the precolonial, the
postcolonial, and, arguably most viscerally, the colonial era itself.[23]

The systematization of colonial influence over Indian education began with the 1835 English Education Act, forever associated with Thomas Babington Macaulay's Minute on Indian Education. The minute advocated for English as the main medium of instruction in place of Persian and for the civilizing influence of a curriculum based on Western science and literature. Informed by Victorian Britain's twin preoccupations with morality and scientific rationality, a system of education was deployed in parts of India that worked to reproduce British behavioral values, establishing and maintaining a loyal elite, and imparting "knowledge" to those hitherto denied it—while simultaneously providing a moral justification for empire.[24]

The colonial motivations fueling the expansion and systematization of education were various: the creation of a loyal elite, and the dissemination of what were considered the Enlightenment's rational, scientific fruits; education for girls; and teaching in vernacular languages—all intertwined with "moral uplift" through Christian ethics. With the imposition of the new education system, however, the British administration made an unequivocal statement about the definition of, and control over, valid forms of knowledge. This is not to say that the colonial system extinguished all other forms of learning, but with the opening of the civil services to Indians in 1833 the colonial curriculum became the established pathway to the salaried benefits of government employment.[25]

"Textbook culture," as Kumar has called it, grew out of and was institutionalized by formalized procedures for teacher recruitment, the subsequent devaluation of the profession, the colonial administration's "elaborate machinery for inspection," plus rapidly entrenched evaluation methods that led to the award of scholarships and qualification certificates.[26] Teachers were subordinated to a low rung of an institutional ladder, reduced to low-paid government servants responsible for shepherding students through exams.[27] Despite policy architects' ostensible concerns about comprehension and analysis, textbooks quickly became the de facto curriculum, cemented by the identification of specific portions that would be used in examinations: "what meaning the lessons in the textbooks could have had for the student was inextricably linked to the urgency to pass in the examination."[28]

With notoriously high failure rates, fear of examinations (among those in a position to take them) became a naturalized part of a materially comfortable Indian childhood. In his 1910 short story "Bade Bhai Sahab," the much-loved author Premchand captured the discombobulation of taking exams that held little relevance for students beyond a strategic need to pass:

> And you'll have to study English history. Remembering the names of kings isn't easy. There were eight Henrys—do you think it's easy to remember what happened during each one's reign? And if you write Henry VIII instead of Henry VII you lose all your marks. Gone. You won't even get a zero. . . . [B]ut why care about these exams?! Just write whatever is written in the book. All they want is that we keep putting words on paper. And they call this process education. But in the end, what's the use in studying these absurd things?[29]

The demands of the colonial administration for order and control likely took precedence over concerns about the substantive content of education and its capacity to foster critique and contemplation.[30] At the university level in particular, Kumar argues that exams became a method of establishing and maintaining an acceptable norm of achievement. A centralized educational bureaucracy set standards for scholarships, employment, and promotion, and in doing so, it projected an argument for colonial rule based on "principles and impartial procedures."[31] Considering Bourdieu's ideas about how academic credentials produce cultural capital enriches this analysis: "With the academic qualification, a certificate of cultural competence which confers on its holder a conventional, constant, legally guaranteed value with respect to culture, social alchemy produces a form of cultural capital which has a relative autonomy vis-à-vis its bearer and even vis-à-vis the cultural capital he effectively possesses at a given moment in time."[32] As a form of cultural capital in colonial India, a particular type of education became, and remains, a powerful means of distinguishing oneself; a differentiation made tangible and objective through mark sheets, certificates, and medals that proclaimed achievement from their proud positions on walls or in cabinets.[33] While these material expressions of achievement continue to be important signifiers of cultural capital in the present, their capacity for conversion, particularly for school leavers, cannot always be taken for granted: uncertainty about this capacity informs decisions in some families about whether to continue a child's education beyond a certain age.[34]

THE AMBIGUITIES OF EDUCATION; OR, THE OPPORTUNITY TO ASPIRE

Aspiration is a key trope in campaigns for improving access to education. Children who declare their intention to become a teacher or a doctor in order to improve the lives of those around them are presented as emotive proof of education as the engine of social mobility and development.[35] The support of socially minded donors, campaigns by nongovernmental organizations suggest, continues to ensure that aspiration plus determination will equal success for newly educated children. Although a rhetorical association between the education of the poor and the development of the Indian nation has been audible since the 1940s, the Right to Education Act was not passed until 2009. Subsequently, India has seen enrollment rates improve, particularly in primary education.[36] Enrollment does not guarantee attendance or completion, however, and the monitoring of this crucial dimension is still unreliable. Nor does it speak for quality.

Scholars have challenged the idea that education possesses an inherently positive value, independent of context. Patricia Jeffery argues that "education *as it is practised* is profoundly ambiguous in its effects."[37] Levinson and Holland describe education as a "contradictory resource," "conferring advantages and bringing about social mobility for some while reinforcing positions of inequality for others."[38] While the great expansion of India's middle class is a visible demonstration of social mobility that stems at least in part from increased access to education, Jeffery and colleagues suggest that there has been an analytical overemphasis on the creation of human capital through access to education and insufficient attention to "issues of power, social change, and the meanings attached to education."[39]

This speaks in particular to the machinations through which the cultural capital of academic achievement may or may not be converted into economic opportunity, and how this may change over time, as Bourdieu describes: "Because the material and symbolic profits which the academic qualification guarantees also depend on its scarcity, the investments made (in time and effort) may turn out to be less profitable than was anticipated when they were made (there having been a *de facto* change in the conversion rate between academic capital and economic capital)."[40] In colonial India, opportunities for education in English were exploited by comparatively wealthy upper-caste families in order to ensure that their children were equipped with the "skills, knowledge and certificates" necessary for employment in the colonial administration.[41] In the contemporary context, the perceived advantage conferred by English-medium education is more significant than ever, even as standards vary; as other forms of capital influence access to opportunities; and as quandaries arise about the denigration of regional languages as the mode of instruction.[42]

All the AIIMS students I spoke with had been to English-medium schools, and all were privately educated, other than Purush and Nikhil—both students from Scheduled Castes (SC) who had attended selective government schools for academically gifted children from disadvantaged backgrounds. Two students I met came from famously elite boarding schools, but "convent" education—at one of the many Catholic or Jesuit schools established by missionaries across colonial India—was much more common.

Sushil was from a Scheduled Tribe (ST) community and was convinced that without his English-medium schooling he would not have been at AIIMS. He explained that he wouldn't have had such an education if his father had not left his home village after completing class 8 and subsequently secured a government position with the Indian Railways. His father then pursued his secondary education through a correspondence course. As Sushil put it:

> I came to the city, and I got my early education in an English-medium school, that's why it became possible. A guy from a reserved caste, who has studied in a Hindi-medium school, can't get up to here. It's not possible.

Aspiration is complicated by factors including caste, class, religion, and gender.[43] Official statistics that reflect increasing school enrollment and attendance celebrate achievement while obscuring heterogeneous experience.

More children are attending school in India than ever before, but their experiences of education and the opportunities that await them are diverse and deserving of attention. The opportunity to translate aspiration into achievement is not available to everyone, and of those who make the attempt, not all are rewarded for their efforts. As Peggy Froerer puts it, "By disregarding the differentiated ways in which schooling is experienced and valued by people within a similar demographic, the 'intrinsic benefits' that are supposedly associated with education will remain restricted to a privileged few."[44]

I have noted the complex nature of education in part as groundwork for troubling the discourse of "meritocracy" that we will encounter later in the book—but also in an effort to suggest that while winning a place at AIIMS is exceedingly difficult, getting a toehold on the aspirational ladder that leads to taking the entrance exam constitutes a challenge of a different magnitude. As Deshpande notes in his discussion of the advent of the modern examination, exams are "downstream events" and access is regulated by social structures that ensure the reproduction of inequalities by, for example, denying equal access to education.[45] "In every country," write Bourdieu and Passaron, "the inequalities between the classes are incomparably greater when measured by the *probabilities of candidature* . . . than when measured by the *probabilities of passing*."[46] In this respect, AIIMS students have much in common with the Malawian medical students of whom Clare Wendland writes: "by the time they stepped between the painted metal gates and entered the medical school, and to an extent far greater than their North American or European counterparts, they were already exceptional."[47]

"*LAKHS* OF PEOPLE JUST MUGGING STUFF"

A dependence on rote learning and memorization is increasingly being called into question by aspirational parents as well as scholars of education.[48] It is seen to connote low-status government schooling and an outdated pedagogy that ill prepares upwardly mobile children for cosmopolitan working life and citizenship. Of course, a historical tradition of rote learning does not transpose directly onto contemporary competitive examinations, nor is the AIIMS entrance exam solely a test of memory. Memorization still dominates studying techniques, but the exam also demands that this content be appropriately managed and deployed in order to answer questions correctly. The function of rote learning here is therefore more complex than that required for a school exam or a historical university entrance test. The AIIMS admissions process contains echoes of the past rather than offering a direct equivalence. Nevertheless, it remains the case that without considerable training in these skills, a candidate is unlikely to win a place at AIIMS. Officially, any student who has completed class 12 exams in English, physics, chemistry, and biology with a pass of 60%—or 50% for SC/ST candidates—is eligible to sit the AIIMS entrance exam. This eligibility criterion is partly what sustains the idea of the mass entrance exam as a leveler—as an unmissable opportunity for young people from less privileged backgrounds to access a life of greater security through one of the country's most esteemed colleges. There is an enormous market for this promise; the prestige of the exam depends on huge numbers of candidates signing up to it and then failing to make the cut—they act, in Deshpande's stark description, as "cannon fodder."[49] But while it is technically possible to leave school with marks of 60% and then take the AIIMS entrance exam, doing so is unheard of. As Purush explained: "In school I did well and all, but that's not enough for this premedical thing."

Subramanian notes that coaching for college entrance exams in India is as old as the institutions themselves.[50] What is more recent is the explosion of coaching as an industry catering to an enormous market of aspiring IITians and AIIMSonians—the vast majority of whom will not get in. All of the MBBS students I spent time with had attended coaching classes to prepare them for the AIIMS entrance exam. Most had attended classes during their final two years of school, beginning as they entered class 11. Deepak, in his intern year, recalled the coaching regime: "From two to eight, classes. Everyday almost. And it was a long process with tests every few weeks. And in the end, after finishing school we have a test series that we prepare for." The National Council of Educational Research and Training science textbook became Deepak's constant companion: "We used to sleep with it, be with that book every time we can. . . . I would say I have read that book six or seven times. Whenever we get time, just read that book, that's it." He shook his head as he recalled the subordination of an adolescent social life to exam preparation: "I watched only three or four movies in two years, that's it. It was like that."

Balraj took coaching classes during class 12, noting that he attended for "just one year." The process was intense: "Actually we had to study a lot, 14–15 hours a day at a stretch. And during the three, four months just before the exam it was more intense, like 17–18 hours per day." For Nikhil, preparation involved leaving his hometown in Uttar Pradesh and moving to Delhi to attend a coaching institute for five hours a day, four days a week. His elder brother encouraged the move, advising him, "If you join coaching, then you will get a competitive environment, you can compare yourself, see where you stand." Life in Delhi revolved around the competitive ethos of the institute: "Coaching was the only thing, nothing else. And I was here alone as a paying guest, so no friends, only coaching."

Nikhil's experience of leaving home to attend a coaching institute was not unique. Purush was selected for secondary schooling at the Jawahar Navodaya Vidyalaya in Rajasthan—a network of government schools established to provide free secondary education to gifted students from rural areas—where he lived from class 6 to class 12. Having developed an interest in biology and anatomy, he moved to Kota, also in Rajasthan, to attend a coaching institute for a year. Sushil also spent a year in Kota for coaching, an experience he described as "*lakhs* [hundreds of thousands] of people just mugging stuff."

Historically famous as a railway hub, in recent years Kota has gained a reputation as India's premier coaching city, preparing students for engineering and medical entrance exams, and spawning an industry in the process worth, with its associated hostels, copy shops, and so on, an estimated Rs. 2000 crore (£200 million) a year.[51] A Google search returns a list of nearly 200 coaching institutes—from small home-based setups to franchises with branches across the country. Online fora such as Quora are filled with prospective students seeking advice about which institute to attend, with variables including financial resources, specialist subjects, and those best for "droppers" or "repeaters"—those who have already failed entrance exams for medicine or engineering colleges. Krish, a student from Kerala in his final year, decided to pursue medicine only when he reached class 11. His preparation suffered, he said, from a poor maths teacher, which prompted him to take a year out to study for the entrance exams after completing class 12. "I am a dropper," he told me.

A year's tuition in Kota costs between Rs. 50,000 and 1 lakh (£400–£1,000), with accommodation and additional expenses totaling at least Rs. 80,000 (£800).[52] In a dystopian twist to a tale of relentless examinations, given the high demand and the development of a hierarchy among institutes, some of the most popular coaching establishments hold their own admissions tests, for which separate coaching centers have been established.[53] Tie-ups between schools and coaching centers mean that some students attend full-time coaching classes, returning to school only to take class 12 exams. A growing number of "dummy schools" have been set up to facilitate this scenario, in which the substance of education from class 6, or 11 years old, can be geared toward college entrance exams. The student ranked third in the 2016 AIIMS entrance exam had been taking coaching classes since class 9. Family investment in such strategies produces what Susan Bayly describes in a Vietnamese context as "achiever collectivities," whereby the ostensible achievement of a single individual disguises the involvement of multiple actors.[54] Later in the book, I suggest that an awareness of this collective investment has consequences for the career choices of some AIIMSonians.

Kota's coaching environment is described in *Revolution Twenty20*, a book by India's highest-selling English-language novelist, and IIT Delhi alumnus, Chetan Bhagat, who writes for and about India's young and aspirational urban middle classes.[55] Gopal, the story's protagonist, fails his first attempt at the JEE—the IIT entrance exam—and goes to Kota at his father's behest for a year of coaching to prepare him for a second attempt. There he encounters an entire ecosystem, with its own rules and hierarchies, that exists in response to an annual cycle of competitive examinations.[56] Many students in Kota live with a variety of pressures. Not all students want to be there in the first place, and for some, the demands of studying, financial concerns, homesickness, and the personal anxieties of adolescence become unmanageable.[57] In October 2015, the news media reported that 72 students had committed suicide in Kota in the five years to date. Twelve of these students died in the first ten months of 2015, and five in June 2015 alone, prompting the Rajasthan government to introduce guidelines to moderate stress among the 150,000 students living in Kota for coaching.[58] The perceived necessity of coaching acts as another barrier to progress along the path to AIIMS.

Reflecting on his own experience, Sushil said:

> These are coachings only for . . . who can afford from middle class. A guy from a poor family can't afford all these things. He first goes to Hindi-medium school, then he has to pay 50,000 for coaching, it's not possible for them to come here . . . so always, like, people who are above middle class, only they can make it up to here.[59]

Coaching is another augmentation of the cultural capital demanded by a process that impedes or excludes aspirants already disadvantaged by oppressive social structures, and it lays bare the entrance exam as less a measure of achievement than "a proxy for ascription."[60]

Of all the students I spoke with, Anjali, the latest of five generations of doctors, was the most candid about the ways her personal and family privilege—her inherited capital—had smoothed her route to AIIMS. Getting into AIIMS was almost inevitable, she said: "very comfortable circumstances, good schools, the best coaching." Her family and friends thought she was "amazing" for getting admission, "but I've never really had to fight," she said. And besides, she added, the entrance exam was largely about memorization: "The test doesn't really test how smart you are. It tests how hardworking you can be." Nor does the admissions process discern the potential of future doctors on the basis of anything other than the result of a science exam, allowing for the scenario in which Tashi could secure a place at AIIMS despite a professed lack of interest in medicine. Satish Deshpande notes the indexical quality of most competitive exams, meaning that "they claim to measure something more than (or other than) what is established by the actual tasks they set."[61] Deshpande takes the example of the rather spurious implicit link between scoring well on papers in, say, geology, philosophy, and general knowledge, and the potential to be a good civil servant. In the case of AIIMS, the potential to be a good doctor is indexed to achieving an almost-perfect score on a series of multiple-choice questions about biology, chemistry, and physics. In Anjali's view the exam measured a capacity for the hard slog of preparation. No doubt true, but the narrow criteria also suggest that AIIMS is less interested in the potential of medicine as a social profession and more concerned with reproducing its elite character by restricting access to those possessed of sufficient privilege to even consider taking the exam. I return to this theme shortly and in the next chapter.

At the time of writing, the computer-based MBBS entrance exam takes place during three-and-a-half hours in morning and afternoon shifts at over 150 centers around the country. The exam comprises 200 questions and is divided into four sections: physics, chemistry, biology, and general knowledge, and it can be taken in either English or Hindi, although very few people choose this option, reflecting Sushil's point about the necessity of English-language education to entering AIIMS.[62] Of the 200 multiple-choice questions, 60 are "reason assertion" based, wherein the candidate has to ascertain the correspondence, or lack of, between a stated assertion and the reason provided for it. This aspect differentiates the AIIMS exam from other medical entrance examinations and gives it a reputation for being more challenging.[63]

I met Vivek, an intern, at the AIIMSonians' picnic on an unseasonably warm day in February. The picnic is a boozy annual event held by the AIIMSonians president at his "farmhouse" in a very affluent part of South Delhi, during which current interns are celebrated and encouraged to join the alumni association. On this occasion, the picnic coincided with the Cricket World Cup, and a screen had been erected to show the India–South Africa match. "The process of selection is completely flawed," and getting into AIIMS is "a matter of chance," Vivek said. He felt that the admissions process should include an interview in order to recruit students who would make the best doctors. Dilip, a fourth-year student, agreed:

> As far as the exam is concerned, in India, getting selected into a medical or
> an engineering college is purely on academic basis. They don't look at your

CV, extra this or that, work experience . . . nothing. It's purely academic. So for most families it also becomes a prestige point for their children to get into a prestigious institution. It's like a social . . . they get respect. That's why they push their students to work hard, get into this college, go to IITs, go to AIIMS, this and that. Not thinking, not realizing that the student might actually not have an aptitude for medicine per se. Just for job security and not actually thinking what the child wants to do. So maybe that's the reason why most students after getting into AIIMS, studying hard, getting into this college, now when they are given the freedom to do whatever they want, they realize, "OK, I am not meant to be here, it's not what I want to do." So then they go and do their MBA, do their IAS [civil service exam], et cetera.

Both Dr. B and Dr. D, senior faculty members who had studied at AIIMS several decades earlier, recalled that the entrance exam used to require short narrative answers and was later changed to entirely multiple-choice questions. For Dr. D, the newer format coupled with the introduction of more reserved seats for disadvantaged groups, while not offering a completely level playing field, was an important means through which the student body at AIIMS had become more diverse and less exclusively the domain of students from privileged backgrounds.

For Dr. B, the format of the current entrance exam as the sole means of admission to AIIMS was informed by its gatekeeping function in response to overwhelming demand, but it also reflected a broader social discomfort with the "subjective":

Our demand and supply difference is so much, that there is an inherent mistrust of everything. So anything that has got a slight amount of subjectivity is not acceptable. It has to be something that is totally objective, it can be marked, it can be assessed, and there is a number there. I achieve that number, I get it, somebody else who doesn't achieve that number doesn't get it. It's immaterial whether I don't have the skills and somebody else has the skills. I don't have the aptitude, somebody else has the aptitude. "Aptitude," "skills," these are all subjective terms, so not acceptable in our society as of today.

Dr. L, another senior faculty member, strongly opposed the narrow method of the entrance exam and claimed that it had detrimental consequences for the selection of students. "The stumbling block to good quality learning is the quality of entrants," she said to me, complicating the standard perception of AIIMS students as India's brightest and best trainee doctors. Subramanian found a similar concern among IIT administrators, who feared that, as a result of the coaching industry, the entrance exam was unable to distinguish "what candidates *are* from what they have *learned to do*."[64] Recognizing the shortcomings of the admissions system does not necessarily lead to resolution about an alternative method, however. As Deshpande notes, mass examinations are easy to criticize but hard to replace, mostly for reasons of money and labor, and particularly where large numbers are involved on the scale of those in India.[65] Dr. L echoed Dr. B's comment that any effort to measure aptitude would be met with charges of biased subjective judgment and could lead to court action by disgruntled parents. Shankar, in his intern year, agreed that the narrow focus of the admissions process inevitably excluded some talented and highly motivated candidates, but he also felt that India's social context precluded any alternatives:

> It's not possible. Some psychological tests can be there, about why are you joining this and all; interviews can be there. But India is very corrupt. So if someone has power, then he can say, "give him more marks." It's very subjective. Whereas the system that we have now is more objective so nothing can be done. I mean no one can manipulate it. In US they have these recommendation letters and interviews and all. But if it happens in India then it will all be manipulation.

Shankar's thoughts confirm a distrust of the "subjective" and a faith in the "objective" as an entity that cannot be manipulated and is devoid of social content. Or, to return to Bourdieu, the perceived objectivity of the entrance exam is divorced from the influence of social structures on candidates' chances of success and thereby protects the interests of those who are advantaged by it. This discourse of trust in "objective," measurable data takes us back to the imposition of standards through the colonial examination system that were held to be impartial while reflecting the elevation of particular epistemological norms. "The examination is a technique for exercising hierarchical and normalizing judgement," was the view of Michel Foucault, as noted by Deshpande.[66] For Shankar, of course, the current order of things worked very nicely—few people from groups who benefit from the status quo have any interest in challenging it in the interests of greater equality. As well as serving these vested interests, Subramanian writes of IIT alumni who consider the "fairness" and "objectivity" of the entrance exam as a hallmark of the "incorruptibility" of the institutions and their "transcendence of Indian conditions."[67] We find a similar narrative of excellence and exceptionalism deployed in objections to affirmative action policies, which we will encounter more directly in the next chapter, which are claimed to undermine true equality by betraying the principle of merit.

"MY DREAM COME TRUE!"

Rahul took the exam at a government school that acted as the testing center in Chandigarh: "I looked at the question paper and I thought it was so-so—you know a few, you don't know a few." He recalled attempting around 180 questions, of which only 4 were from the general knowledge section. "Because I didn't know anything!" he said. "They were asking pretty tough questions. Like this singer belongs to which *gharana* [house of classical music] and things like that. I didn't know anything about that!" Rahul later learned that he had secured 33rd of 37 general category seats, but at the time he had no idea how he had fared, having taken the exam only to please his father (also a doctor). He had achieved a national rank of 128 (of around 400,000) in the All India Pre-Medical Test (AIPMT), and he was happy with the prospect of attending medical college at home in Shimla:

> So that was the plan. And next day was AIIMS. I was like, "Why give AIIMS, I'm not going to get selected in it, I'm not such a brilliant child, I'm 128, and the top 30–40 will get selected in AIIMS, that's it." So [my father] said that you just give one paper for me, this I'm requesting you, just give it for me. I had also applied for JIPMER and all, so I said, I'm not going to give JIPMER, and he said, but you should give AIIMS.

Rahul was relaxed when he took the exam. He remembered that it was a beautiful morning after heavy overnight rain. He and his father went for a walk as they waited for the test center to open. Several students suggested that the main reason they got admission was that they were relaxed during the test, having already secured a place at a college they were happy with. In a similar story, Priya told me that she was pleased with her place at Lady Hardinge Medical College in Delhi and took the AIIMS exam only to satisfy her mother:

> I just gave it with a very cool mind because I knew I am already selected. Maybe that worked . . . there was no pressure at all. I got into the bus at night, overnight I did my journey, morning I gave my exam and came back. And I was not even waiting for the result, then the result came and I was like, oh my god! It was the best gift.

Rahul and his father were about to collect the admission letter from the college in Shimla when a call came to confirm his AIIMS admission. "So my father was so happy! And I was like, a face-palm thing, like that! I was banging my head, what the hell did I do?! Because I didn't want to go." But Rahul had made a twofold deal when his parents had agreed not to send him away from home for coaching during class 12. First, that if he didn't get selected for a good college on his first attempt he would drop a year after class 12 and leave home to attend a coaching center in preparation for a second attempt. And second, that he was free to reject offers of admission from any college in favor of Shimla—except AIIMS. "So I realized: now I have to leave," he said.

Rahul's reaction to his admission was more ambivalent than most. Surprise and delight were more common, reflecting the special place occupied by AIIMS in the imaginations of these high-achieving students, all of whom had already secured places at respectable alternative colleges given their ranks in the AIPMT. As Ashish said:

> It's miraculous I cleared it. I never expected to clear that exam. And my parents just said, give it for sake of giving it. Because my rank in AIPMT was 58. Here there are 37 seats, so it was kind of dicey.

Despite being ranked first in the AIPMT, Neha—the first medical student in her family—was still stunned by her acceptance to AIIMS: "I was not at all expecting it! I just cried when I got to know the result!" For Nikhil, the joy he felt on news of his admission was still tangible when he spoke to me about it four years later: "It was amazing! I was thinking like, it's AIIMS! My dream come true!"

Sushil had already begun the semester at a medical college in Ahmed-abad when he learned that he had been offered a place at AIIMS, having been on the waiting list:

> I was, like, praying the whole week that I should get cleared. I was praying a lot. When I got cleared I was very happy. My family was very happy. . . . When that letter came to my home, that my waiting is cleared, it was in English. Then they called someone, my dad called his friend, they had to read out the letter [for translation]. That guy told my relatives that my waiting is cleared and they should call me back to Delhi.

Krish was reflective when I asked if the thrill of admission—the sense of being special—had endured through his time at AIIMS: "Yeah; I mean, not always, but sometimes I get the feeling that why have I got selected, why in the 72 I got selected and [I was] not among the one lakh students who didn't."

This moment of admission, and the reactions it produces, recalls Long and Moore's description of such achievements as events, the experience of which "is both material and semiotic; concretely embodied and affectively charged, yet also known and elaborated through the work of fantasy and the imagination." The accomplishment of such a feat, and the recognition of possessing the necessary capacity, generates a "new knowledge" about the achiever, in relation both to herself and potentially to others, "who either have or have not enjoyed the same achievement, either in the present instance or in the past."[68] The impact of this achievement on a student's understanding of self has consequences, not only for immediate decisions upon leaving AIIMS but also for the foreseeable future, in which they will always be AIIMSonians, no matter the path they choose to follow.

RANK AND THE BIOGRAPHICAL
LIFE OF NUMBERS

Following the entrance exam, candidates are ranked on the basis of their results. Talking to students about this, I became interested in the influence of exam rankings on self-perception. I began to think of rank as a "biographical number," which I situate here as a bridging concept between the literature on the historical bureaucratic use of number in India and the work of scholars on numbers and contemporary "numericized narratives."[69] Interrogating the deceptively complex function of rank illuminates another important dimension of the AIIMS admission process, with consequences that outlive the achievement of "getting in."

Arjun Appadurai writes that in nineteenth-century India: "Numerical tables, figures, and charts allowed the contingency, the sheer narrative clutter of prose descriptions of the colonial landscape, to be domesticated into the abstract, precise, complete, and cool idiom of number."[70] Number, he continues, was a means of taming India's overwhelming sociocultural diversity. The clean whole integer, the "cool idiom" of numerical rank assigned to thousands of AIIMS applicants, does similar obfuscatory work in one sense, but it also does the opposite, suggesting diversity where there is homogeneity. Consider five people who have scored 63, 76, 87, 93, and 98 on an examination. A letter-grading system might attribute grades C, C, B, A, A, splitting the five into three categories and grouping students accordingly. The ranking system, by contrast, ruthlessly individualizes, precluding any shared identity: five people become five separate ranks, no matter how similar their marks.

In the case of the AIIMS MBBS entrance exam, the difference between ranks is miniscule. In fact, identical results in the 2018 exam meant that the top 1,188 candidates produced only 306 aggregate scores between them and tie-breaker formulas were applied to differentiate them into individual ranks.

Rank fuels a protest among upper-caste candidates that Other Backward Classes (OBC), Scheduled Caste (SC), and Scheduled Tribe (ST) candidates who benefit from lower cutoff scores are less "meritorious" than those in the general category (GC). As table 1 shows, the ST candidate who got the eighth of eight reserved seats in 2018 had an overall rank of 2,090, and the candidate with overall rank 51 was a GC student who missed the admission cutoff. This might inform GC candidate 51's feeling of having been unfairly denied a seat in favor of someone less capable—a common emotional reaction and understandable in its simplicity, even by those who support affirmative action. When we look at the percentile marks, however, we see that the lowest-scoring ST, SC, and OBC admitted candidates are all well within the 99th percentile, and the ST candidate ranked 2,090 still outperformed 372,430 people. The difference of ability in a biology, chemistry, and physics multiple-choice exam between all admitted candidates is negligible. And as table 1 also shows, in 2018, the highest scoring SC and OBC candidates were ranked overall 5 and 18 respectively. But it is the difference of 2,040 ranks between GC 51 (excluded) and ST 8 (admitted) that becomes weaponized in an ideological argument about merit that serves to protect and maintain the structural privilege of upper castes.

Through the ranking system, "every individual is illuminated in the harsh light of a hierarchical evaluation."[71] Ranking thus acts as a management tool, suggesting a warranted differentiation of achievement that disguises the homogeneity of marks among top-ranked students and implying that OBC, SC, and ST candidates who score lower than the GC cutoff lack the necessary aptitude to study at AIIMS. As a former director of AIIMS noted when we spoke about the factors that set the institution apart from other medical colleges, this is far from true: "it is not only the 35 who join are good; the 3500 who are after this are equally good candidates." In Deshpande's terms, "the guillotine of the cut-off point [creates] two internally homogeneous but mutually exclusive groups" one considered "meritorious" and the other "without merit."[72] Ranking, Deshpande explains elsewhere, is considered "a moral-ethical ordering."[73] We will see in the next chapter how this plays out through upper-caste objection to affirmative action.

Aside from demonstrating the spurious grounds of the merit argument, the AIIMS exam results reveal two critical factors that warrant urgent political response. First, that discussing OBCs and STs as though they experience affirmative action policies in the same way is confused and misleading: ST candidates as a whole continue to score significantly

TABLE 1 AIIMS MBBS entrance exam results 2018.

	RANK	BIOLOGY %	CHEMISTRY %	PHYSICS %	GENERAL KNOWLEDGE* %	OVERALL PERCENTILE	TOTAL CANDIDATES WITH LOWER SCORE
Highest overall	1	100	99.9404672	100	97.8752192	100	374,519
Highest GC excluded	51	99.8566216	99.9679004	99.9358007	98.7887737	99.9871601	374,469
Highest OBC	18	98.4718781	99.9978732	99.9883025	99.0695152	99.9957464	374,502
Highest SC	5	99.9323739	99.9788668	99.9978867	99.4928042	99.9989433	374,515
Highest ST	522	99.3754465	99.5681164	99.8625333	94.2004200	99.8636157	373,998
Lowest selected OBC (OBC 27)	188	99.9818102	99.2766882	99.9283108	98.4538675	99.9507806	374,332
Lowest selected SC (SC 15)	655	99.3754465	99.9328903	98.9533046	94.2004200	99.8311432	373,865
Lowest selected ST (ST 8)	2090	99.3783370	99.3751271	99.1536396	57.6702083	99.4468163	372,430

Source: https://www.aiimsexams.org/info/archive_result2018.html

Note: The general knowledge component of the exam, which students I spoke with considered inconsequential for the overall result, is the only area where marks varied by more than a few decimal points.

lower than SCs or OBCs, suggesting that the enduring marginalization of ST children requires more attention. And second, that the urgent issue is not one of merit being denied, or the admission of less capable students, but of an overwhelming demand for higher education that India simply does not have the institutional capacity to absorb. The competition that continues to swell as a result fuels a virulent casteism and simultaneously sustains the reputation of elite institutions as "the best" by virtue of the numbers of candidates they turn down via the spurious justification of rank.

Bernard Cohn's now-classic 1987 paper on the role of the colonial census in objectifying Indians to themselves and the administration through caste categories is an essential starting point for an exploration of the role and significance of numbers in the emergence of modern India.[74] Cohn inspired several scholars to pursue this line of thought, evolving an argument that, as Norbert Peabody puts it, "the British collection of numerical data on caste in India was not simply referential but was, in fact, generative."[75] In a different context but with similar implications, Ian Hacking's work on the history of statistics and specifically the concept of dynamic nominalism takes inspiration from Foucault in its interrogation of how new categories of people are brought into being through the very application of new labels.[76] Arjun Appadurai combines these implications in an effort to extend analysis from colonial classificatory logics to the ways in which quantification was employed as a tool of social control:

> Though early colonial policies of quantification were utilitarian in design, I would suggest that numbers gradually became more importantly part of the illusion of bureaucratic control and a key to a colonial *imaginaire* in which countable abstractions, both of people and of resources, at every imaginable level and for every conceivable purpose, created the sense of a controllable indigenous reality.[77]

Appadurai extends this argument to suggest that while numbers always served a pragmatic referential purpose for the colonial administration, their rhetorical purpose was often at least, if not more, important.[78] This insight resonates with my interest in contemporary exam ranking as both a social tool and as a biographical number—a form of shorthand for understandings of self and others beyond the simple reflection of academic aptitude that it purports to indicate.

In Charles Stafford's terms, I consider how rank might be used as a means of "narrating the self numerically."[79] Reflecting on the apparent wariness of anthropology to tackle the lived experience of numbers, Stafford notes the tendency to view numbers as reductionist (we balk at the idea of being "reduced to a number"), at odds with imagination and the narrative description inherent in autobiography.[80] While things have begun to change for the better in recent years, I recognize the suspicion with which many anthropologists have been accustomed to apprehend numbers. A suspicion of the neat simplicity they impose on a messy world—the tendency of statistics to "flatten and enclose."[81] Challenging the sometimes suspect hygiene of number—revealing the myriad social, cultural, political influences digested by digits—is a valuable endeavor.[82] It is, after all, what I am attempting to do in this book by asking what it means for AIIMS to be ranked number one—to be "the topper" among Indian medical colleges. My simultaneous effort, however, by extending Appadurai's work in the direction of Stafford's, is to recognize that some numbers have meaning for those to whom they are applied—that as well as words, numbers, including rank, even after we have revealed its empirical absurdity, work upon subjectivity, as Guyer and colleagues note:

> What do ordinary people do when they are drawn into emotional states as well as cognitive maneuvers by numerical terms? Once number moves out of technical life and into domains of culture and power, quantitative anthropology becomes no longer about how *we* should quantify the world, but about how *people* inhabit worlds that they already apprehend numerically.[83]

In his work on "numerical lives" in Taiwan, Stafford writes about one interlocutor, Mrs. Chen:

> It is interesting . . . that although social scientists might think of numbers primarily as a way of aggregating the (otherwise unmanageably diverse) experiences of individuals, for Mrs. Chen numbers are one way of differentiating *her* story from everybody else's. To put this differently, although numbers appear to aggregate things, restricting the scope for what can be said (because

they simply tell us "how things are" once everything is added up), in reality numbers may equally help *disaggregate* individuals from collectives and may also help them to see (and to say) something new about their lives.[84]

Rank has a social life and significance that long predates the entrance exam. It compresses into single numbers not only a student's most recent exam result but also that student's position within a classroom, within a school, within a state, within a nation. It has consequences for personal and family reputation, and it contains assumptions about all that can or cannot be expected of the student's future. For example, Anjali told me:

> I am definitely very, very sure that I am never ever going to get a medal! Like, I know that is beyond me. I am usually in the top 15, but I am, like, never in the top 5. Being 7th or being 14th doesn't make a difference, to me at least.

As we have seen, in an exam with large numbers of candidates, the numerical differences hidden behind ranks 1–15 are barely distinguishable, and in some cases may be nonexistent, with tie-breaker formulas necessary for individualizing the results. But even as she hinted at an understanding of this through her equivalence of ranks 7 and 14, Anjali was convinced she would never be a topper. Similarly, while Rahul's anxiety about not getting into AIIMS was well founded given the competition, it was partly informed by having been ranked 128 out of around 400,000 candidates in the AIPMT, leading him to conclude that he wasn't sufficiently "brilliant."

A perception of potential based on rank was also embedded in the calculation by Purush to leave a college in Jaipur after a few disappointing months in order to retake the AIIMS entrance exam (to the horror of his parents), which was based on the following information:

> That time I was rank 36 and 11 people were to be selected, from the Scheduled Caste category—I come from that. So 11 people were selected and I was 36 . . . so I thought I should give it one more chance.

When I raised the question with friends in Delhi, they were often able to recall their rank from classes at school more than 20 years earlier. One friend described visits by an aunt and uncle who would demand to know their nephew's rank in maths (and it was always maths), even if they had met just a fortnight earlier—a salutation that didn't so much break the ice as ensure an ever deeper freeze. As Patricia Jeffery notes in her reflections on grading and assessment, rank as a numerical repository of so much meaning ensures the individualization of both failure and achievement, even while "the profiles of the successful and the unsuccessful largely reflect the fracture lines of previous privilege, of wealth, language facility and social contacts."[85]

While India's numerical scale can only be matched by China, Bourdieu considers a very similar phenomenon from the perspective of the cultural capital bestowed by success in the highly competitive French civil service recruitment examinations, which

> out of the continuum of infinitesimal differences between performances, produces sharp, absolute, lasting differences, such as that which separates the last successful candidate from the first unsuccessful one, and institutes an essential difference between the official recognized, guaranteed competence and simple cultural capital, which is constantly required to prove itself. In this case, one sees clearly the performative magic of the power of instituting, the power to show forth and secure belief or, in a word, to impose recognition.[86]

The exam, and therefore rank, is thus a means of justifying the rejection of huge numbers of candidates by producing, via the cool idiom of number, an "objective" difference in capability. Deshpande observes that the enormous demand for places also allows top institutions to rest on the assumption that admitted students will require few additional interventions to ensure they pass the final exams.[87] In the next chapter I show how this approach can lead to the neglect of students, particularly those with weaker English, who *are* in need of extra support. This informs my discussion about the way that merit both bestowed and withheld by rank becomes inextricable from a discourse of caste and the politics of affirmative action.[88]

Thoughts about biographical number need not be confined to the students in this book, of course. Biology provides us all with (auto)biographical numbers: age, weight, height, blood pressure—all dimensions imbued with sociocultural meanings that influence the way we think about ourselves and others. Stafford writes of the various ways Mrs. Chen's life is permeated by numbers: the income from her tea stall becomes a narrative device connecting various parts of her numericized life, including gambling, religious worship, and fortune-telling. In India, the Aadhaar scheme, administrated by the Unique Identification Authority of India, is a technological intervention that enfolds an individual's biometric data within 12 randomly generated digits, acting as a digital authenticator of identity.[89] Rank operates differently, however, as a number that ascribes value in response to individual efforts to pass an exam, and which unavoidably, and enduringly, encodes that individual's place in a hierarchy.[90] The incorporation of rank into (auto)biographical narrative might be understood as a strategy for taking an inescapable—public—signifier and imbuing it with personal meaning.

In *RevolutionTwenty20*, Chetan Bhagat's Gopal ranks 52,043 of almost 500,000 candidates, a position that informs his self-definition as a "loser" despite having scored better than hundreds of thousands of others. Karthika, a junior resident in community medicine at AIIMS, explained to me how personal rank maps onto the prestige ranking of particular medical fields and laughed at her prospects of securing a coveted place on an internal medicine course, which required a top 10 rank in the postgraduate exam. And that, she confidently stated, was "not possible." Here, rank informs a self-perception that is considered indisputable and quite possibly immutable. A senior resident at AIIMS recalled falling short of the cutoff for the MBBS by two ranks over 10 years earlier, and a public health professional immediately told me the exact number of ranks by which he had missed a place at AIIMS a decade ago. These particular memories were not recalled with regret, more commonly with a wry smile. An AIIMS rank below the cutoff does not necessarily threaten an individual's sense of self-worth in perpetuity, therefore, but it may remain a feature of an autobiography, reflecting its consequences for subjectivity and experience. Nor is rank a necessarily stable identity, as Azam explained:

> When everybody reaches here, the very first two, three months, it will be like everybody, almost all the students are competitive, because whoever reaches AIIMS was a topper of his batch. I was a topper of my school, then in the coaching institute also I was the guy who got the best result out of my class, even though 10–15 students got admission to AIIMS, and when we come

over here we feel like we should be competitive, [because] it's like a dream of the whole nation.

There were other reasons for ranks to shift around. Mihir's psychological argument demonstrates the power of rank to impose differentiated identities on candidates with virtually identical marks and confirms the exclusion of candidates in reserved categories from what is considered truly "meritorious" competition:

> You see, even when you analyze our rank list, there are around 35 seats for the general category. Among the 35 seats you will see that the people who are in the top ten to 15 ranks, they are generally those sort of people who had a bit of talent for solving questions or reading a particular thing and extracting . . . so they didn't work hard that much to get into AIIMS. But the people who are from 30 to 35, generally those are the ones who by the skin of their teeth have got here, so when in our first [internal exams] you see the rank list, the toppers are those who were [ranked] 30 to 35 [in the entrance exam]. They are in the habit of working hard from the start. Those are the people who generally come here and then are on top because they know they can study for six hours a day, or eight hours, whatever is required. We aren't in the habit of working that hard, at least in academics, so we don't take it seriously.

Reflecting on her conversations with IIT alumni, Subramanian notes the tendency former students had to distinguish between "the gifted" and "the coached" as a means of articulating concerns about the changing profile of IITians and the threat posed to the exceptionalism of the institution (and, implicitly, themselves).[91] Reflecting the complex and interrelational nature of biography, then, it is not only one's own rank that has the power to influence identity, self-perception, and how one is perceived by others. Nor is this influence static or confined within a single generation. Recall, for instance, the story of Rahul, whose trajectory toward medicine was largely informed by his mother having missed the cutoff for acceptance into medical college by just 11 marks. Rank by association also ripples beyond the individual to inform other relationships. Anjali had dated the previous year's AIIMS postgraduate topper for several months, and she smiled as she told me of her parents' disappointment when the relationship with someone they had considered so suitable for their daughter came to an end.

Our students have made it into AIIMS, thanks in part to historical and contemporary mechanisms that have contributed to these particular young people, and not others, being invited through the gates. And thanks in part to luck, which plays its own role when overwhelming demand means that so many candidates score in the upper echelons of the 99th percentile. The event of admission guarantees the continued accrual of social, cultural, and economic capital. As we will learn, however, the lived social and educational experience of AIIMS has more nuanced consequences—for students' understandings of themselves, for their relationships, and for the politics and practice of Indian healthcare.

CHAPTER 4

BEING IN
"Freedom"

The thing is, AIIMS is not a hospital or an island in isolation.
It's like a whole society, so already what are the problems
in this society as a whole are ingrained in AIIMS also.

—Purush

AIIMS is an island—people don't relate to the outer world.

—Purush, during the same interview

HAVING EMERGED TRIUMPHANT (if exhausted) from the ferocious
competition for admission, many of the students I interacted with used
a discourse of "freedom" to characterize their time at AIIMS. The precise
nature and extent of this freedom, however, depended on particular aspects
of students' experience, not least whether their place at AIIMS was one
of those reserved for students from Other Backwards Classes, Scheduled
Castes, and Scheduled Tribes groups. I did not, as it were, go looking for
caste at AIIMS. Yet without denying the analytical salience of other in-
tersectional determinants of student experiences (class, in particular), the
simultaneous centrality and obfuscation of affirmative action on campus—
the semispectral presence of reservation-based difference—made its scrutiny feel particularly urgent. The politics of affirmative action counter any
idealized vision of AIIMS as an institution transcending oppressive social
structures in the pursuit of a universal humanist medicine. The lives of
students are permeated by the consequences of structural inequalities both
in the clinic and on campus. The institute, and medicine itself, is not set
apart from but is emblematic of the social unease that is characteristic of
modern India.[1]

"I THINK AIIMS IS LIKE HEAVEN"

In 2015, attendance at classes had only recently been made compulsory for MBBS students, and the ruling had yet to be taken seriously by fourth-year students.[2] The choice of whether or not to attend classes was considered part of the freedom that made life at AIIMS so appealing:

> We have 100% freedom in AIIMS, compared to other medical colleges and all; we are free to do anything. In our hostel also we can come any time, we can leave any time, we can do anything. No one is there to control. It's a very good opportunity for people. . . . [L]ike if I want to study, I can study 100%, if I don't want to study, I can enjoy 100%. In AIIMS that's like that. We can study freely, we can enjoy freely, we can do anything freely. I think AIIMS is like heaven.
>
> —Krish

> This hostel is like the best hostel in the whole of Delhi, because I can go out at 2 a.m. in the morning in my car and no one will ask me anything about it. While even in Delhi University, arts students, they cannot leave after 7–8 p.m. . . . [A]nd I can do pretty much anything I want to. Besides that, the facilities are great. I have a room with an AC and a heater, and a fridge, which no one else gets.[3] And then there was no attendance, when I came . . . now it's changed: now the attendance has become compulsory. But when I came, like my seniors had attendances of 23%. So yeah, they were pretty much free to do anything with their lives. They didn't even have to be medical students! The independence and the freedom is overwhelming.
>
> —Anjali

AIIMS is considered special precisely in comparison with other institutions that are understood to be lacking in important ways. Hearing about friends' experiences at other colleges fed students' perceptions of AIIMS as a unique environment that was insulated from external realities. Talk of freedom at AIIMS stands in stark contrast with the "timepass," or the passing of time, described by Craig Jeffrey in his work with young men in Meerut, Uttar Pradesh. Among students at a college where standards of teaching and infrastructure have declined in recent years, timepass is imbued with frustration and melancholia, and is used "to signal [students'] removal from spaces of relative 'modernity.'"[4] Students at AIIMS, conversely, experience the exhilaration of an existence at the heart of Indian modernity, both in terms of urban life in South Delhi and as part of the country's most prestigious, highly technologized medical community. "Timepass" in Meerut is about killing time, whereas "freedom" at AIIMS is—for some—about wanting time to stand still.

Karan had left AIIMS a year before I arrived and had spent several months working at a community health center in the Himalayas. We met on one of his periodic visits to AIIMS—which he described as "coming home"— when he spoke earnestly about the onus the institute placed on independence:

> AIIMS is the most liberal institute in India. You have choice. If you want to go down this path it's your choice. So no one is going to force you. If you want to learn medicine, you can learn. If you don't want to learn, no need to. It's your call. You have to decide where you have to reach, what you have to achieve.

Karan extended the freedom discourse further and credited the AIIMS environment with facilitating his personal development and growth into adulthood:

> That was extraordinary for me. You know I belong to a very narrow, say orthodox, family. I came out of my home and I really enjoyed it. And rather, I have evolved here. I have evolved at AIIMS. I was this tiny, and I have evolved into a human being. It really nurtured my perspective.

Sushil echoed this sentiment:

> AIIMS molded me completely. Before coming here I was a different guy. I never used to think about anything else, I was a self-centered guy. I was not a bit worried about the world, about what's going on around me. But here I have improved. When I was at home, I was in my cocoon. But after coming here I saw the world, where I am and where the world is and where the people are. I saw YouTube videos, learnt what I am . . . I learnt everything from YouTube. Dance, English . . . I used to dance, during our fest [Pulse]. This is because I saw people around me, they are better than me. So it gives like a competitive environment. AIIMS is like very . . . it has changed my personality a lot for the better.[5]

Liminality usually marks a period of transition from one state to another—young people becoming adults, or students becoming doctors, for example. For some students, AIIMS itself seemed to be a liminal space, where social norms, though not absent, were less rigid, less determining of whom a person was allowed to be and more accommodating of whom she might choose to become.[6] As neophytes, students exist "betwixt and between all the recognized fixed points in space-time of structural classification." In this "interstructural" position, Turner writes, the subject is made "structurally, if not physically, 'invisible,'" present in "a realm of pure possibility whence novel configurations of ideas and relations may arise."[7] Turner continues: "Neophytes are withdrawn from their structural positions and consequently from the values, norms, sentiments, and techniques associated with those positions. They are also divested of their previous habits of thought, feeling, and action. During the liminal period, neophytes are alternately forced and encouraged to think about their society, their cosmos, and the powers that generate and sustain them. Liminality may partly be described as a stage of reflection."[8] Both Karan and Sushil described AIIMS as a world that was simultaneously a great expansion of that which they previously inhabited, and also sufficiently removed from that reality to allow them to explore opportunities. To "evolve," in Karan's words. Other students described freedoms afforded them at AIIMS that they had not previously encountered at home or heard of at other institutions—whether freedom of movement (particularly for women), self-directed learning, or the relaxation of taboos around socializing and sex.[9]

Following the stress of the admissions process, students' embrace of these freedoms might be a logical reclamation of an adolescence suspended during the competition for a place at AIIMS. But student life also offers the opportunity to enact an adolescence out of reach while living at home. And a sense of liminality was particularly pronounced for those students conscious of how dramatically some freedoms—of both action and thought—would be curtailed upon their graduation back into a deeply conservative society.[10]

In his original description, Turner states that while a strong social structure is imposed on the liminal period through the authority of instructors over neophytes, the liminal group itself, composed of people, whose "condition is one of ambiguity and paradox, a confusion of all the customary categories," "is a community or comity of comrades and not a structure of hierarchically arrayed positions."[11] To the extent that a shared AIIMSonian identity endures beyond graduation, this is certainly true. However, for the very same reasons that AIIMS as an institution cannot be understood as entirely insulated, the student body cannot be understood as an undifferentiated entity with a shared liminal experience.

The freedom that AIIMS offers students suggests conversely that a high degree of self-direction and institutional navigation is required to extract the greatest benefit from the MBBS. Not all students arrive equipped with the resources this demands. For some whose childhoods have not afforded them the necessary privileges, "freedom" has a darker side that can lead to tragic outcomes. The politics and experience of affirmative action demonstrate both the possibility and the frailty of AIIMS as a liminal space, as this chapter goes on to explore.

"THE COASTERS": THE SOCIAL LIFE OF AFFIRMATIVE ACTION AT AIIMS

From where I was sitting in Anjali's small single room in the women's hostel, I couldn't see what she was pointing to. "Look in the mirror," she suggested. When I did, I saw a list of words written in green pen reflected from the wall behind me. The mirror writing made little difference to my comprehension—even when I twisted to see the long list of revision topics made legible, many of the scientific terms remained mysterious. The list was a visual reminder of the looming final professional exams, or "profs," for MBBS students that take place in October and December of the fourth year, before the internship. A sense of dread begins to mount during the summer that follows the comparatively relaxed third year, which is free of major exams. In Anjali's view, however, that dread, and the pressure it expressed, was not evenly distributed. "There are two types of students," she said. "Competers and coasters."

I was told several times by students that AIIMS was not as competitive an environment as they had anticipated. The pressure of the entrance exam and the place of AIIMS in the popular imagination combined to conjure an imagined cohort of superstudents who spent every waking moment at their desks in an effort to outdo all others. This expectation was, on the whole, confounded on arrival. As Rahul put it:

> You come here expecting, like, it's AIIMS, everyone will be just studying and studying. Because you are thinking it's a top medical college, top hospital of the country and everyone will be just into books and everyone will be wearing big thick specs! But it definitely was not that.

"Competers" were the exception—those who studied to the exclusion of everything else, including close friendships. In the background of these conversations about competition, and sometimes explicitly acknowledged by students, were the looming postgraduate entrance exams that face all those who plan to continue medical training. Most students anticipated a more competitive environment as they approached the end of the MBBS, particularly during the internship year. The "coasters," in contrast, were, in Anjali's words, "the ones who are always relaxed," those who studied after watching a movie or a game of football. Either, she explained, these are students who intend to leave medicine for an alternative career, or they are those "who don't have to bother because they know they've already got a PG [postgraduate] place." This was not a reflection of a particular genius for memorization and test taking, according to Anjali. Rather, it was an indication that these students had it easier because they were at AIIMS "on reservation."

Before continuing with the experiences of students at the contemporary institution, I pause here to offer some historical context for the politics of affirmative action in Indian higher education with specific reference to medical education and the position of AIIMS.

The Mandal Commission

The Mandal Commission, so called for its chairman, B. P. Mandal, was established in 1979 by the short-lived Janata Party government, with a mandate to "identify the socially or educationally backward." Policies that reserved a quota of jobs and college seats had been in place in various forms in parts of India for many decades by this point, beginning under the influence of social reform movements in the state of Maharashtra.[12] Since independence in 1947, 27% of all jobs in central government services had been reserved for SC and ST candidates. The Mandal report recommended extending this quota to 50%, to include OBCs—a category incorporating other lower-caste and marginalized groups. The report was submitted in 1980 but ignored by then prime minister Indira Gandhi, and her heir Rajiv, neither of whom had an appetite for further political turbulence in the wake of the Emergency that the prime minister had recently imposed, suspending democracy in the nation between 1975 and 1977. Rajiv Gandhi is reported to have said in response to a question about the report: "It's a can of worms; I won't touch it."[13] It was the non-Congress coalition government of V. P. Singh, ten years later in 1990, that implemented OBC reservations in an action popularly known as "Mandal I."

The reaction to the extension of reservations to OBCs was dramatic: upper-caste protesters took to the streets. Whereas the existing SC and ST reservations had been understood as a means to improve equality of opportunity for undeniably oppressed groups, extending reservations to OBCs posed an unprecedented threat to the status quo, adding momentum to a new subaltern politics that was already under way.[14] The change in policy occurred amid rising levels of education and greater competition for jobs, particularly the prized positions in government service that represented the pinnacle of achievement and security for middle-class families. The Mandal Commission had also recommended the introduction of affirmative action, or "reservations," in centrally funded higher-education institutions—a prospect that brought young people onto the streets too. For upper-caste children and their families, increasing demand meant that possession of the capital necessary for admission to elite institutions did not necessarily translate into easy access—a vision of their chances becoming even slimmer was a frightening one. Delhi University student Rajiv Goswami became a famous symbol of this potent milieu following his self-immolation attempt in Delhi. During the subsequent agitation in 2006, student protesters referred to the intersection outside AIIMS as Rajiv Chowk (Rajiv Square) in remembrance.

The 1990 protests subsided once the Supreme Court heard a petition against the proposed policy.[15] In 1992, the Court upheld the validity of the OBC quota contingent on the exclusion of the most affluent, or "creamy layer," and the policy was enacted in 1993.[16] The reaction was muted, reflecting resignation by protesters but also the changing socioeconomic landscape. By 1993, private-sector careers in the newly liberalized economy were proving more attractive to young upper-caste Indians than the careers in government service coveted by their parents and grandparents. By 2006, following the most transformative decade of independent India's socioeconomic history, the primacy of the private sector over the public in the career aspirations of the country's young elites had taken on the mantle of conventional wisdom, making public-sector job reservations less threatening. The introduction of reserved seats for OBCs in centrally funded institutes of higher education, however, remained contentious.

Youth for Equality
In early April 2006, a group of students at Delhi's University College of Medical Sciences (UCMS) held a meeting to discuss the announcement by Human Resource Development Minister Arjun Singh that the Congress-led United Progressive Alliance government intended to introduce a 27% quota of reserved seats for OBCs at centrally funded institutes of higher education. Combined with the existing 22.5% quota of reserved seats for SC and ST students mandated during the original drafting of the Indian Constitution, the new policy meant reserving 50% of seats for those from historically disadvantaged groups.

Following their initial meeting, the UCMS students allied with peers from four other medical colleges—Maulana Azad Medical College, Lady Hardinge, Vardhman Mahavir Medical College, and AIIMS—to establish a forum they called Youth for Equality (YFE). By late May, YFE was known nationwide for its central role in protests that demanded the proposed OBC quota be scrapped and the existing policy providing reservations for SC and ST students also be reviewed. The agitation led to a 19-day medical strike in several cities, supported by the Indian Medical

Association. AIIMS became the national hub of the protest, referred to as Kranti Chowk (Revolution Square).

AIIMS hosted a rolling hunger strike by students that led to at least one person being admitted to the hospital, where emergency services were compromised as part of the protest. The strike was supported by "the corporate sector, traders associations, chambers of commerce, industry lobbies, the Indian Medical Association" and voices in the media.[17] An editorial in the *Hindustan Times* lauded medical students for their "heroic role in resisting the irrational government policy of enforcing quotas for the OBCs in institutions of higher learning."[18] The agitation ended on June 3, 2006, when the Supreme Court stayed the reservation law in order to submit it to judicial review. The law was implemented in 2008, with amendments that expanded the number of "general category" seats to maintain the existing proportion and rendered the "creamy layer" of the OBCs ineligible.

The more pernicious objections to affirmative action have always been imbued with the residue of nineteenth-century eugenicist thought that naturalized intellectual ability, or its lack, as a feature of racial type.[19] In India, this is tightly bound up with a historical social hierarchy that locates intellectual superiority within upper castes, specifically Brahmins, who occupy the apex of the caste order.[20] A petition to the Madras High Court in 1950, challenging state-legislated reservations in education, claimed: "It would be strange if, in this land of equality and liberty, a class of citizens should be constrained to wear the badge of inferiority because, forsooth, they have a greater aptitude for certain types of education than other classes (para 54)."[21] In his 1983 report on the institution, the director of IIT Madras reflected on the legislation that protected seats for SC and ST students by establishing a dichotomy between "the socially deprived" and "the talented," "special privileges" and "rights," and "Indian" versus "international" standards. The same individual took the Government of India to court in 2011 in an effort to dismantle the 2006 reservations for OBCs.

Where they still exist in contemporary narratives, these prejudices are often disguised within a discourse of merit.[22] One of the writ petitions filed in the Supreme Court in 2006 stated: "The statute has lost sight of the social catastrophe it is likely to unleash. The products [of the educational institutions, if the OBCs had reservations] would be intellectual pygmies as compared to normal intellectually sound students presently passing out."[23]

During the 2006 agitation, while YFE declared its allegiance to an equitable, casteless society, particular methods of protest were rich with caste symbolism. By sweeping roads and shining shoes at traffic lights, upper-caste students enacted a vision of the demeaning future that awaited them should institutions be made more accessible to members of caste groups traditionally associated with such occupations.[24]

The Thorat Report

Even though the 2006 agitation was smaller and more circumscribed than the 1990 protests, it forms an important chapter in the story of AIIMS. In 2007, a government-appointed committee headed by Professor Sukhadeo Thorat submitted a report into caste discrimination at the institute.[25] In the section about the 2006 agitation, it states that the protests at AIIMS took place with the encouragement and facilitation of senior faculty, including the director at the time:

> The involvement of the administration in supporting the agitation was alleged on the grounds that the same administration had strictly applied a court order banning agitations within 500 meters of the AIIMS on previous occasions when workers went on strike. But this time, the striking students and resident doctors had parked themselves in the central lawns. A tent was installed at the site to protect the striking doctors and students. The striking-persons also stayed at this site during the night. At any time, 50 to 100 persons were on hunger-strike at this venue. The erection of a *shamiana* [marquee], provision of electricity for coolers and other comforts such as mattresses and pillows, they allege would not be possible without the support of the administration.[26]

Those faculty members and students who supported the proposed policy reported harassment by their peers and complained about the behavior of the medical superintendent who demanded that faculty "report for hunger strike." Dr. R. Deka, then a dean of the institute who would go on to be director from 2009 to 2013, testified to the committee that he had been harassed and humiliated by the leaders of the agitation, to which he was opposed.[27] Dr. Deka alleged that such events could not have proceeded without the sanction of the director, Dr. P. Venugopal, and that some of those involved in the harassment were residents working under him.[28] SC and ST students told the committee that they had been pressured by the dean of examinations, Dr. T. D. Dogra (who became interim director from July 2007 to March 2008), into withdrawing complaints of harassment or discrimination, and they spoke of wanting to attend classes during the strike but being ignored by faculty.

The Thorat Report was rejected in its entirety by the AIIMS administration. An eight-member review committee concluded that "the Thorat Committee acted with a clear prejudice to deliver a misleading report that relies on imaginary facts, flawed methodology and baseless conclusions apparently with the sole purpose of discrediting the AIIMS."[29]

During Nepal's revolution in 1990, doctors at Tribhuvan University Teaching Hospital in Kathmandu went on strike in protest against the state's violent reaction to pro-democracy rallies. This politicization of members of the medical profession occurred as leaders of the movement saw an opportunity for a biomedical epistemology to contribute to the shaping of a nascent democratic process.[30] In India in 2006, by contrast, a medical strike took place as a means of demonstrating a profound dissatisfaction with events occurring under the auspices of a democracy that was approaching 60 years old. As Subramanian writes in her work on upper-caste consolidation at IIT Madras, doctors and medical students were able to render the outcome of Mandal Commission as illiberal as well as unjust.[31] Venkatesan points out that, although the YFE protest claimed to espouse democratic, egalitarian ideals, the movement actually betrayed contempt for parliament and the political system.[32] This distrust cannot be divorced from the evolving political and socioeconomic scenario in which these students had come of age. The discourse of privatization, economic growth, India's rising geopolitical profile, and a general disillusionment with the state all permeated the 2006 protests, together with the political assertion of lower-caste groups.

Satish Deshpande writes that, in the transformation of caste capital, caste itself becomes elusive: "it appears to be a story about something *other than caste*, like the story of nation-building for example, or the story of a great and ancient tradition modernising itself."[33] Against this new socio-economic backdrop, YFE could claim that reservations were not only a violation of equality motivated by vote bank politics but also, by undermining "efficiency," they posed a threat to India's national development and its burgeoning status as a global superpower.[34] This theme surfaced in my conversations with students about caste and reservations at AIIMS. As I will discuss, encoding caste in a discourse about medicine as a moral endeavor not only reveals feelings about who warrants the status of an AIIMSonian. It also disguises within a purported concern for life and death opinions about who should—and should not—be permitted to become a doctor at all.

"Caste doesn't matter here"

AR: Is there any caste discrimination at AIIMS?[35]

MIHIR: No, no. If I have to say as a blanket statement, I'd say that in AIIMS there is no . . . it's totally nonexistent, any segregation, or any politics on basis of caste. Me personally, I wasn't aware of any of my colleagues', say, status for the first year. I only got to know that in the second year when there are SC Student Union elections going on. So at that time, yes, these things may come up sometimes. But those are only closeted discussions, not in the public. So yeah, I won't say it is existent any more.

AR: Are you aware of the categories that other students are in?

PRIYA: Yeah, we did know because there is a list of all the selected people, so you get to know. It's written in front of the name, that this is general category, this is this, like category-wise there are names written. So we get to know. But in AIIMS I didn't personally get any such different treatment as such, because I myself am a reserved . . . but I have heard, in other colleges, especially in Rajasthan and Madhya Pradesh there is a lot of such discrimination going on, because the general people have this problem that the people get reservation, so they don't find it fair enough, so they have their own community. In AIIMS, it's not at all like this, not at all in AIIMS. But then, yeah, in other colleges, in periphery of India, I have seen, there has been a lot of discrimination, there are fights going. There are these groups you know, gangs, general people and ST people, like that.

When we continued our conversation on another occasion, Priya said:

But then . . . there were friends of mine who were kind of jealous because, in my coaching times I had my competitors, like friends and all, and we used to get good ranks, like top ten or something. So they knew that we were good, same level as each other, then later on I got selected in AIIMS, and they got a random college . . . of course I got some benefit, definitely. So they would not have liked it, I know that. They might have you know, talked behind . . . so it's like that, people might be jealous or something, but they won't tell that on my face. That's what I am saying. In Delhi, the scene is less bad, as compared to other areas, where there is a lot of discrimination going on.

The juxtaposition of comments by Mihir, in the general category, and Priya, in the Scheduled Tribe category, exemplifies both the common denial by general category students of any awareness of caste identity or reservation-based differentiation among their peers and the way this purported casteless worldview is denied to those whose access to and presence at AIIMS is contingent upon their association with a particular category.

Priya was unusually candid in acknowledging that students could learn the category affiliations of their peers through the official admissions sheet. In June, AIIMS releases results of the MBBS entrance exam: the list is disseminated through the media and includes full names, ranks, and reserved category affiliation. A blank space implies general category, which emphasizes the erasure of denoted caste for those at the top of the hierarchy. In my conversations, it was more common for students to narrate an initial ignorance followed by a gradual realization of who was who, revealed either through a concrete method such as student union elections, as in Mihir's case, or assumed—not necessarily accurately—through behavioral observations, as in Anjali's example about competers and coasters. Priya was not alone, however, among students in reserved categories in denying any experience of overt discrimination among peers at AIIMS. "We talk amongst friends and we all feel that there is no discrimination on the basis of caste," Sushil said.[36]

AIIMS, while predominantly North Indian in its composition, does not cleave tightly to a regional institutional identity, and thus does not reflect the sort of local caste dynamics that Subramanian describes at IIT Madras, or that Purush and Priya described at Rajasthani institutions. There are, however, regional—and therefore linguistic—allegiances within the student body, and it was common for students to tell me that these took precedence over caste groupings, as Priya said:

> Yeah, actually, that's very true. We have a group of Keralites, and they talk in some language we don't get at all! So we feel out of place like that . . . but . . . caste is very less, it comes down and, yeah, language goes up.

Anjali pointed out the factional dynamic when she mentioned a party being organized by the interns. Only the North Indians would go, she said: "The Keralites are invited, but they won't come." Malayalam-speaking students from Kerala did form a group—Hari told me he was reassured to find so many fellow Keralites at AIIMS—but not to the complete exclusion of their North Indian classmates, with whom they spoke more Hindi than English.[37] Santosh agreed that regionalism trumped reservation in a way that distinguished AIIMS from peripheral colleges, and he explained how the regional fractures became visible in student politics. The Keralites and Punjabis were "enemies," he said, but, in an apt microcosm of national politics, they formed a coalition to win control of the student union—an outcome that made the national news in 2015.[38]

Purush argued that linguistic divisions were "quite natural" and that not everyone cleaved along regional lines. There was, he said, a variety of "chaotic confrontations" that diluted caste and reservation as the main differentiator of students: region, language, those going to the United States versus those not—these were all themes. But he considered class and upward mobility the most significant leveler among the student body. "Now there are no binaries," Purush said, suggesting that there was a shared middle-class habitus that the majority of AIIMS students had in common, regardless of whether they had a reserved seat or not. It is a revealing argument, begging the question of whether the primary reason for less overt caste discrimination at AIIMS than elsewhere is that access is denied to India's more disadvantaged students. On the one hand, this allows AIIMS to unjustifiably claim superiority over other institutions more troubled by caste conflict while on the other suggesting that much greater scrutiny is required of the discrimination that *does* occur in the elite institution.

"Discrimination" in the form of overt bullying or exclusion may not have been common in the experiences of the students I worked with, but that does not mean that they were not made aware of their caste status in other insidious ways. Sushil and Purush were both well aware of the perception of students with reserved seats as, in Anjali's words, "the ones who are always relaxed." How did that make them feel? I asked. Purush grinned and gestured at Sushil. "It makes him angry," he said. Sushil shook his head and smiled patiently. "Not angry," he said, but at the back of his mind he felt like he should work harder, "even though I'm working as hard as they are." A general category friend had recently told him that he would get a PG place more easily. "I understand their position," Sushil said. "I take it as motivation." This tussle between shrugging off and being hurt by accusation was evident in Purush, too. After teasing Sushil about being sensitive, and telling me that the assumption that reserved seats came easily was "not hostile," Purush added that he was not aiming for the lower marks required for an SC seat. "I am not studying for five hours, while general people study for ten," he said. Toward the end of our conversation he mentioned that he had conducted an informal study and found that Facebook status updates confirming PG admission got more "likes" if they were posted by GC students than by SC or ST students.

The 2007 Thorat Report reported systemic discrimination against students and faculty. During my research I was often told that while things had improved for students, faculty members in reserved categories continued to experience overt discrimination at AIIMS. Dr. N was a long-serving faculty member in the general category known for his efforts to expose caste discrimination and for his extracurricular discussions with students about the politics of health and inequality. "There is a deep-rooted hatred" at AIIMS for lower castes, he told me when we met. The Thorat Report condemned systemic discrimination against faculty in reserved positions, including the denial of promotions and opportunities for research, student supervision, and international conference participation in favor of colleagues, sometimes more junior, in the general category.[39] It is the outright denial of employment to SC, ST, and OBC candidates, however, that continues to attract public attention.[40] When I raised this issue with a senior member of the administration, he acknowledged that caste discrimination in recruitment used to be a problem—quotas were "misused," and it was often claimed that there were no suitable candidates from reserved categories in order to allocate posts to unreserved applicants on an ad hoc basis. This was "no longer possible" he claimed, given the fixed and "very transparent" nature of the present recruitment mechanism.

A letter written by members of the Forum for Rights and Equality at AIIMS,[41] which exists to expose caste discrimination at the institute, suggests otherwise. The six-page note was written in January 2015 to the secretary of health, following a meeting at the Ministry of Health and Family Welfare to discuss a petition submitted to the health minister (and president of AIIMS). The petition demonstrated how the AIIMS recruitment procedure was manipulated "to undermine the representation of SC/ST/OBCs" among the faculty. Following a court case about the same issue in 2003 (following that year's recruitment round, of 13 posts reserved for SC or ST and 46 for OBC faculty, all but 8 in total were filled by general category candidates), when the government declared that all ad hoc appointments of upper castes to reserved category faculty posts should be quashed, AIIMS filed an affidavit claiming an administrative mistake. At the time of writing, the case is still pending with the Supreme Court.

Students I spoke with acknowledged the history of caste relations at AIIMS but said that times had changed. For example, Nikhil said:

> Not now, a few years back it was bad. Not now. At that time there was very much a big struggle in AIIMS, like politicians came, everyone came, it was a big issue. It was like a kind of fight. But now it's a wonderful environment, everybody is so friendly and eats from the same plate.[42]

Deepak offered a more cautious assessment than Nikhil and suggested that discrimination persisted to some extent but that things had improved significantly since the days when the student hostels reflected a de facto system of segregation enforced through the bullying of SC and ST students.[43] It seems, then, that what remains most salient for an understanding of AIIMS as both insulated from and permeated by social norms is the tension between the statement by Santosh (OBC) that "caste doesn't matter here" and the multiple instances when it appears, in fact, that it does.

"It all becomes about caste"

As we have seen, rankings on the AIIMS entrance exam serve both classificatory and rhetorical purposes. Individual ranks obscure miniscule differences in marks: the top 2,000 ranked candidates in the 2018 exam all scored in the 99th percentile, making clear that rank is more a means of managing demand and reproducing prestige than of differentiating aptitude. It is nevertheless true that an SC, ST, or OBC student can be admitted to AIIMS with a lower absolute score on the entrance exam than a candidate who misses the general category cutoff. The rhetorical purpose for which admission data are most often marshaled, therefore, is the fueling of upper-caste resentment. This appears to exist independently of absolute marks and rests largely on the argument that having three cutoff points for success in the exam is unfair and denies opportunities to upper castes whose "meritorious" achievements are subordinated to the political expediency of serving the interests of less capable candidates. What this also does in the process, as Subramanian describes with regard to IIT Madras, is to consolidate the association of merit with upper casteness.

During Pulse in 2014, I spoke to two brothers from Bihar. The younger brother was studying for an MBBS at a college in Nepal; he was visiting his elder sibling who had graduated from the same college and was a junior resident in anatomy at AIIMS. They had both been inspired to pursue medicine by their father, a surgeon, in whose footsteps they hoped to follow. They were joined in our conversation by a friend from the private boarding school they had attended in the northern Indian hills, whose alumni include figures in the Indian Foreign Service, academia, and entertainment. "We are from a school in which we never knew what was caste," the friend said. The brothers agreed, and the younger sibling expanded on their anxieties about the impact of affirmative action on upper castes:

> We need reservation for upper-caste poor . . . they are very poor and they don't have any reservation. In my entrance exam for MBBS, I had got double the marks of a guy who was Scheduled Caste, and that guy got through and I couldn't get through. So even if you are not believing in the caste system— when I studied in school [the] system [was] like, you should not believe it— when you go through that you start believing. Because it all becomes about caste, when you give an entrance exam.

The student's suggestion of reservations for poor members of upper castes speaks to the enduring critique of structural discrimination rather than economic deprivation as the basis for affirmative action, which in turn reveals an understanding of reservations as a mechanism for ensuring "fairness" rather than addressing the outcome of historical structural inequalities. It also demonstrates how reservations have become a naturalized dimension of Indian social and political life.[44]

Subramanian notes that one of the reasons protesters could present the Mandal Report as "regressive" was that it compelled "students who previously thought of themselves purely as individuals or as part of modern institutional formations . . . to enter into caste consciousness."[45] During our conversation, the three young men seemed to exemplify this unwelcome confrontation that Deshpande has described:

> Long accustomed to a comfortably homogeneous environment populated almost entirely by people like themselves, this group is unsettled by the recent arrival of hitherto excluded and therefore strange and unknown social groups in their vicinity. It is the double coincidence of the maturation of a sense of castelessness and the arrival of caste-marked strangers in hitherto upper caste social milieux that confirms and amplifies this response.[46]

The biographical number of the younger brother's rank was imbued with a grievance that his "meritorious" achievement had been subordinated to a political intervention based on an unjustified and outmoded argument of caste advantage. His statement was a precise illustration of Subramanian's description of the "back and forth movement between the marking and unmarking of caste" she observed among general category students at IIT Madras.[47] The expression of casteless identity in fact disguises the reinscribing of upper-caste identity "as an explicit basis for merit."[48]

In this discourse, given the upper-caste ownership of "open competition," only those students admitted without reservation can be truly meritorious. The visibility of the role of caste identity and the central government in enabling SC, ST, and OBC student admissions is at odds with the invisibility of those agencies in accruing the capital that propels admission via the general category, allowing for a discourse of innate superiority and ensuring that the rhetorical weapons of merit and equality remain firmly in the hands of society's most traditionally privileged groups.[49] Part of this obfuscation work is done by the very terminology of a "general category," which is dominated by upper castes but works to sustain a myth of an Indian "general population" that will eventually absorb even the most disadvantaged groups, as Susie Tharu and colleagues have described.[50] The general category supports a narrative of castelessness espoused by upper castes in relation to the "hypervisibility" of lower castes.[51] Membership of the general category may be an implicit indicator of a likely caste bracket, but it does not elicit the specific identification made clear in the articulation of membership of the OBC, SC, and ST reserved categories. On the AIIMS entrance exam results table, students have ST, SC, OBC, or a blank space next to their name. The latter suggests not a category membership but a default belonging to the norm, from which reserved groups are set apart. Reservations and their categories, then, reify caste for everyone, but only those at the lower end of the spectrum are forced to give it voice.

The professed allegiance of many upper-caste young people to "modern" citizenship and universal ideals is often sincere, even as it reflects the "naturalised equation of the register of democracy with the institutionalised dominance of a minority."[52] The student from the college in Nepal offered a narrative in which modernity had been liberated from considerations of caste, only to be compromised by what he considered the regressive politics of affirmative action. In being taught "not to believe" in caste, the pupils of the elite school in the hills are crafted into cosmopolitan citizens who espouse universal ideals of democracy, equality, and rationality, as well as the myth of a common Indian subjectivity. Within this is embedded a particular interpretation of hard work and merit simultaneously detached from caste histories and entrenched through the contemporary manifestation of caste capital that ensures that upper-caste children begin life from a position of structural advantage. Competitive entrance exams confirm this dual process, Subramanian notes in her work building on that of Bourdieu and Passeron, by formally certifying the achievement of individuals while tacitly endorsing "ascriptive forms of caste belonging as the basis of intellectual ability." This relationship between the tacit and the formal is important, she notes: it is critical that structural advantage remain implicit, "in order for caste claims to merit to appear as legitimately modern and consistent with democratic principles." The role of caste in underpinning merit must remain "unspoken."[53]

For a student to deny caste as a defining aspect of his or her identity is not necessarily to deny the instrumental role of inherited privilege, however. Anjali openly acknowledged the ways in which her path to AIIMS was sufficiently smoothed to make admission feel almost like a foregone conclusion. Her generation is "distanced from the process of the conversion of traditional caste capital into secular modern caste-less capital that previous generations effected," Deshpande argues.[54] In Anjali's understanding, her family unit and its class position had a much more explicit role in bestowing social capital than caste did.[55] Nor is this perspective necessarily confined to upper castes. Priya joined AIIMS through the ST category and told me that discomfort about her eligibility made her question affirmative action policies. I asked her why; she responded:

> I don't [support reservations], because then people think this seat is given out of pity or something. Me getting one is not my fault. And I guess I can anyway fight for it. Me being a backward caste, but still my dad is earning the same as a general family, so financially we are good enough, so I guess that way the people would be . . . like my friends in the general category would

be thinking that she's getting all the same facilities, then why is she getting reservation. I guess it might be true on their side, but people who genuinely need it, because there are still people who don't get facilities and they really try hard to get into AIIMS . . . they also don't get much exposure. General people study in good schools, have good personality development, unlike SC/ST people and other OBCs, so that way it's good. But then I guess fair distribution should be there also, like I don't think I needed one. The creamy layer should be I guess removed . . . but the deserving should get it.[56]

"Efficiency suffers"

Although Anjali wasn't entirely opposed to reservations when the policy was enacted, she had become "concerned by the consequences." "Efficiency suffers," she said, when less capable people were promoted purely in order to conform with policy. "People should be enabled" and given more support during their schooling, she suggested, but reservations should cease at the graduate level.

Akin to the narrative that presents a concern over merit as a concern for national development, a discourse of efficiency is the default defense against reservations within the private sector in particular.[57] Studies have challenged this stubborn perception in India, demonstrating a lack of evidence for a detrimental impact of affirmative action and mounting tentative arguments that greater diversity in the labor force actually boosts productivity.[58]

During an interview with me in Delhi, two directors at the corporate healthcare chain Max Healthcare described the private medical sector as happily unencumbered by affirmative action and its presumed negative consequences. The section of the interview I reproduce here began with a reflection by one director (D1) on the decline in standards he had observed at his alma mater since the introduction of reservations. He went on to say that AIIMS was likely to be the top choice for aspiring medical students for the foreseeable future, and that "quality of human resources" was what enabled the institution to maintain high standards despite the pressure of an enormous patient load:

> D1: So by default they would get the best people. And when the starting material is good, exiting material has to be good. So it's a selection

bias, which hasn't been really purposely created, but over the years when competition has gotten to that level, then the best of the lot . . . would get selected at AIIMS. And once you are doing your graduation there, by default you are preferred for post-graduation. And by default, if you have [studied there for] 10 years, you are given preference for faculty. So you keep going up the stream, up and up. You come as a best student and you remain there as the best student until you leave. What is causing this change of mix is a very controversial issue, which I don't want to really discuss too much, is the reservation. Which is the main reason why institutes like these are getting diluted. AIIMS also will ultimately fall prey. Other institutes have already . . . like the ones I'm talking about—Maulana Azad and all. This is something which is sad.

D2: So like he said, as long as the best and the brightest go there, there is no problem. But you start fiddling with that fundamental—

D1: By doing reservation you are changing that mix.

D2: You are changing that mix. Then you have a problem. And it's going to perpetuate over a period of time. It's not a political statement by either of us; it's a statement of fact. That's the way it is.

D1: And the effect of that policy change you see only after about a decade or two decades. That's the stage where most of the hospitals presently are, the public hospitals.

AR: And the private sector is wholly exempt from the policy?

D1: Yes, luckily. So far. The government keeps changing, keeps talking about pressurizing or doing something about it. So far no one has . . . they have been talking about encouraging private organizations also to hire people like that. But there has been no law as yet.

While the medical context of this conversation was clear, the directors did not articulate a specific impact of reservations on medical practice. It was Mihir, back at AIIMS, who raised this point:

AR: If you were a policymaker, and you could make one change to health policy, what would you do?

MIHIR: *Yaar* ["mate" or "friend"], I don't know. What we generally discuss is that because right now we are students and we are more in sync with what [policies] are at the academic level, so what we would like is actually maybe the amount of reservation there is . . . maybe I'd decrease it. I don't know, I mean this is a very controversial point. Generally what we have seen is that at least for a profession in which you are handling people's lives, you shouldn't allow someone with less merit to be before someone with better merit. So that is one thing which we discuss a lot of times.

AR: You discuss this with your friends?

MIHIR: Yeah, yeah. This is a sort of thing which we can't discuss in public right now, because this is a very sensitive issue, people take offense very easily. And the other thing is that it's not like everyone in the reserved category is incompetent, but the percentage who are incompetent, if you compare general and the reserved, it's definitely high. At least in my eyes. So that is one thing we would like to be not there.

AR: Is that your own observation? Have you observed that at AIIMS?

MIHIR: At AIIMS too, yeah. And sometimes it's from other people's experiences also which they have told me. So yeah that's one thing, definitely.

As we saw in the previous chapter, Deshpande has written about how exam ranking becomes a "moral-ethical ordering" used to construct a narrative of deserving versus undeserving students. He expands that this description stems from the sociologist Max Weber's framing of competitive examinations as "oriented towards the 'cultivation' of the student as part of a preparatory process that trains him/her to inhabit a particular moral-ethical world and to practice prescribed forms of conduct."[59] The world in question at AIIMS is that of medicine. In his comments, Mihir positioned affirmative action—and therefore those who are enabled by it—as a threat to the morality of this world. In Mihir's reasoning, the perceived sanctity of medicine itself was privileged over the messiness of social relations, from which it is considered distinct. (On a note to which we will return in subsequent chapters, this conceptual separation of medicine and social life illuminates the glaring absence of the humanities from the educational experiences of young Indian doctors.) By invoking a doctor's responsibility for human lives, Mihir introduced an emotive discourse of moral panic that rendered medicine as an ethical domain that must be protected from infiltration by people without merit—not because they threaten the supremacy of upper castes, but because they pose a literal threat to life. Recall Deshpande's description of how casteism gets disguised by narratives deemed to be morally unimpeachable, such as that of nation-building or development.[60] In Mihir's account, it is not an abstract vision of national development that is imperiled by reservations, but the actual lives of citizens. This is not about the interests of individuals (or, worse still, "politics"), this narrative insists; it is about humanity itself. Crucially, the inheritors of structural privilege expect to be the moral arbiters of these narratives; upper castes consider themselves the rightful "owners of the nation," in whose hands should rest the responsibility for enacting and distributing "development."[61]

The anthropologist Sarah Pinto describes the "deceits" that underpin discourses about medicine and development in contemporary India and how these are revealed when the "wrong people" attempt to enter these spaces. "The first of these deceits," she writes, "is the idea that universal knowledge (of medicine and development) precedes power and legitimacy, and that power (economic, political, self-mastery) and authority in a modernizing world come from correct understanding instead of being mutually constitutive."[62] In other words, the lie suggests that if disadvantaged groups would only get the answers right and behave appropriately, they would be welcomed as equal "owners of the nation" and imbued with equivalent power. Second, Pinto goes on, comes the deceit that associates education with equality: "This includes the notions that medicine and development embrace a politics that is separate from the interests of particular groups or individuals . . . that the legitimacy of development is available to all who enter into certain universalized ways of knowing by participation in authorizing structures; and that universal knowledge manifests itself in the same way and is equally available to all who seek it out."[63] Responsibility lies with the individual to seek and obtain universal knowledge, then, say those whose power to set the order of things is determined by their very existence as the inheritors and reproducers of a collective structural privilege. Further, by participating in "authorizing structures," anyone can be legitimized as an actor in the modern developmental state. But as we have seen, even those who participate in the nation's most elite medical college are immediately differentiated into "right" and "wrong," "meritorious" and "undeserving," according to the general category's "casteless" gatekeepers of universal legitimacy.

Mihir's characterization of a "high percentage" of medical students in reserved categories as "incompetent" points us to three themes that I discuss in the next sections. First, just how determinedly general category students deploy the rhetorical power of exam ranking to insist on their superiority, despite the undeniable empirical absurdity of differentiating between candidates all with results in the 99th percentile. Second, that rank is used as a cipher for judgement of inferior ability on the basis of skills that the exam does not test, particularly facility with English. And third, that extreme competition guarantees the homogeneity of exam results across categories, which in turn allows AIIMS to neglect attention to equality of student experiences (as distinct from broadening opportunities for entry), without threatening either its own institutional brand or that of elite medicine.

"You have to fight your fight"

In our discussions about caste and reservations, Priya told me that "general people" had "good personality development, unlike SC/ST people and other OBCs." This notion of good personality development alludes to the ways in which disadvantage can be coded through a person's habitus, or way of being, and it becomes another way of discussing merit from within the unmarked general category. Usha Zacharias remarks on the imagery used in the *India Today* college rankings report: "The majority of the images presented fair-skinned, upper middle class, Westernized students radiating confidence, positive energy, and a general sense of 'fitness' to confront the world of opportunities."[64] This sense of fitness speaks both to Priya's description of personality development and also to the efforts Sushil described having made during his time at AIIMS to change his personality "for the better."[65]

Although difference is also expressed through clothing and eating habits, it is language and communication that have the greatest influence on how an individual experiences an institution and on how they are perceived.[66] Bourdieu describes linguistic competence as "a dimension of bodily hexis in which one's whole relation to the social world, and one's whole socially informed relation to the world, are expressed."[67] At AIIMS, as in aspirational India more widely, the language that matters most is English, as Zacharias describes:

> English . . . is a whole set of intervening cultural apparatuses, knowledges and filters that separate out circles of peer networking and social circles in college. Far more than a language, English on campus represents a set of cultural competencies and idioms of interaction that finely differentiate students based on the kind of schooling one had: not just between private and public, but of hierarchies within the private and within the public.[68]

These hierarchies were not confined within the student body. When I asked Anjali if she thought reservations were an effective mechanism, she shook her head immediately. She had slept through a class that afternoon, she said, because she couldn't understand the lecturer: "He couldn't talk sense." On a previous occasion she had told me: "When you come here half the professors are speaking in an accent of English you can't really understand. And you are like, OK, I am going to waste the next hour just sitting here, and not really understanding anything." In this case, the traditional hierarchy of the teacher-student relationship is undermined and reversed through an implicit narrative of merit, or its lack, as defined by an upper-caste undergraduate.

While reservations enable access to a previously closed domain for some, they guarantee neither full inclusion nor equal access to the resources necessary to succeed. The Thorat Report condemned the failure of the AIIMS administration to provide support to SC and ST students who arrived without the breadth of academic experience required to excel during the MBBS.[69] Poor English skills were cited as a particular concern. Sushil had spoken to me about the necessity of English-medium schooling for AIIMS admission. He had attended an English-medium school himself but spoke no English at home (recall his anecdote about his admission letter arriving in English and being translated into Hindi for his family by a friend), and he told me that he improved his language skills at AIIMS through YouTube. I asked Sushil if he had ever been offered institutional support for improving his English. He shook his head and said: "No. You have to fight your fight." My notes read: "And then he laughs, but there is weariness in there too."

In 2012, a first-year batchmate of Sushil and Purush hanged himself from the ceiling fan in his hostel room. The son of a farming family in Rajasthan, he had reached AIIMS through the ST category (and came second in the ST group of the AIPMT) following a Hindi-medium school education— achieving precisely what Sushil considered impossible. While he had enrolled in private English lessons, his friends and family blamed a lack of institutional support for the poor exam results that they maintained led to his suicide. The 2015 film *Placebo* documents the aftermath of his death, including angry student protests outside the bungalow of the director, who remained silent. But while purporting to expose the darkness of the institution, the film rather enhances it, fueling the myth of a homogeneous student body by making no mention of caste or reservation. In reference to an earlier suicide, a student in the film explains how strange it feels that he didn't know the individual in question. "He was just some Hindi guy," he says.

Also in 2012, AIIMS responded to the growing concern about caste discrimination first articulated in the Thorat Report by establishing a two-week orientation program for incoming students run by the Centre for Research and Education for Social Transformation (CREST).[70] The program is intended to support students from disadvantaged backgrounds by connecting them with faculty mentors. Given the timing, the main student protagonists of this book had no such orientation and weren't very familiar with the CREST program other than vaguely approving of its intentions. Rahul told me that in his observation it was common for new students to register at AIIMS and then return home for the CREST fortnight before the semester began. In August 2015, a young woman hanged herself in her hostel room. She was the fourth student from a reserved category to commit suicide at AIIMS since 2010.

"Pull him up, pull him up, pull him up"

Dr. T, a senior faculty member, told me that the nature and extent of additional support afforded to students depended entirely on individual teachers. Dr. T was motivated both by a concern for the AIIMS brand and by her own reputation: "I would like them to know without telling my name; everybody should know that this student has studied under me. It should be that good. Nobody need ask, 'Who trained you?'"

When I asked whether she perceived any particular threat to the AIIMS brand, Dr. T began hesitantly, and when I realized she wanted to talk about reservations, I reassured her of anonymity in anything I might write about our meeting. We laughed: a common and uncomfortable deployment of humor in an effort to create a secure space for sensitive opinions:

DR. T: Because like, you know, I have a student who has entered with rank 12, and I also have student who has entered with rank 83, so when we don't have the equal type of caliber of students then no matter how much we try to take this fellow from 83 level to level of 12 . . .

AR: So you notice that difference, between ranks 83 and 12?

DR. T: Too much difference. Earlier too much difference was not there. Now too much difference is there because of the quota system, in the entry. So someone entering from general category has a higher rank, somebody is entering from another quota category is a lower rank. So when we keep these two together it is very difficult to bring this student up to that level. So sometimes they become impatient. And the person who is with higher rank, we are giving less attention to that person. And we are giving too much attention to this person who came in with lower rank to pull him up, pull him up, pull him up. All our energy is going in that. Earlier I had students all with 12, 13, 14, 15, 16 rank. So I could just give instructions—10 minutes— they will bring the output, and then 10 minutes next instructions, excellent output. So I could just claim that all the students under my hand are the best in the country, but now in order to maintain that feeling I have to keep on pulling the one who came from lower level, and neglecting the one who is from upper level because there are only 24 hours in a day. And how much work you can do in a day? So I feel the superior students are getting neglected. I have this view.

AR: Can lower-ranked students access extra tutoring at AIIMS?

DR. T: Every teacher has to put extra hours. Like I do that so many times—put extra hours—but sometimes I feel students are feeling harassed, tired, and frustrated that I am giving . . . They may realize that I was after them for a particular purpose, but that is after leaving they may realize. But when the process is going on, at that time it may hurt them. Today morning, that student with 83 rank, I expected that she will do something. Yesterday I sent two, three mails to her. I sat in my home at night and did more than 30 reviews of literature. I mailed her, I only wanted her to read them and come today. She said she couldn't read them. She printed them in the morning and she didn't read and come. So that is too much for me. I am sitting and doing review for them, which I am not supposed to do, but she didn't even read and come. So this is my frustration, but she started showing me crying eyes and red face, so I felt bad. Early morning I spoilt her mood. But my expectation is too high because her speed of reading is not that good. Or maybe language ability is not that good. Or whatever is the reason I do not know. So commitment is not there or the ability is not there. Maybe ability is not there, because when you don't have ability only then you feel like crying. So I am really trying to pull them up. Too much, I feel. Some of them are saying that in very less time I want them to pick up a lot. Because they are postgraduate students. I want them to at least come up to the level of my undergraduates. So then only they can go forward. So I am very tough in the beginning. I am very tough.

AR: So do you sometimes have postgraduate students who you feel are performing at a lower level than your undergraduate students?

DR. T: [Nodding] Because they come in through a very difficult screening system, but still because of quota and other things they have entered the system, but now we really push them, push them, push them.

Dr. T was speaking of her postgraduate students, all of whom had been through yet another highly competitive admissions process with extremely tight differentiation in results. Nevertheless, Dr. T's experience of the difficulties her student faced was understood through the prism of rank. The significance of rank in the exam is exaggerated as a means of encoding disadvantages that have relatively little bearing on exam performance but become visible when students are expected to perform tasks—such as speed-reading and English comprehension—that their home environments, schooling, MBBS, and exam coaching have not prepared them for.

In her individual effort to compensate for the cumulative disadvantages that stymied some students in their effort to learn, Dr. T evinced a sense of responsibility that AIIMS appeared to shirk as an institutional principle. There was no comprehensive investment in helping students fulfil their potential, Dr. T said, because with a pass mark of 50%, there was little concern about anyone failing altogether:

> Fifty percent is not a difficult thing. I don't think it is difficult because we have a lot of opportunities, lot of classes, lot of seminars, lot of conferences, library is very good. They can attend any program, anytime, anywhere, so that way 50% I think everybody will get, because already the cream of the country is here. Fifty percent all of them will get but it is our problem that we want all of them to be in a really good bracket. Very good bracket. "Good" does not satisfy. "Very good" only satisfies us. Very good and excellent.

By including all AIIMS students in her reference to "the cream of the country," Dr. T specified that this was a conversation specific to a unique institution with a long pedigree: in Madan's study of AIIMS doctors in the 1970s, a faculty member told him that "the very strict admissions procedures" allowed for pedagogical experiments on "the finest guinea pigs you could get."[71] The competition for entry, and the tightly clustered results, means that most students pass their internal exams without much trouble, even if they feel little institutional compulsion to study. This points to Satish Deshpande's argument that the enormous demand for higher education in India allows elite institutions to minimize their pedagogical and pastoral responsibilities by minimizing the number of students they accept through a narrow process focused on aptitude for test taking and thereby ensuring that students are virtually guaranteed to pass their final exams with a minimum of institutional support.[72] For an institution that prides itself on cultivating doctors who will go on to pursue highly specialized medicine in private hospitals (often emigrating to the United States) and that knows that all graduates benefit from the AIIMSonian affiliation, there is little incentive to address internal inequality. Further, the prestige of AIIMS and the elite regime it promotes is maintained precisely through the reproduction of inequality. "Prestige" connotes social and cultural capital *convertible* to economic power, to return to Bourdieu. Institutions are not deemed "prestigious" because of their commitment to the substance of affirmative action; the effort they make, in fact, is to retain their reputation in spite of their adherence to the legal obligation to reserve a portion of seats for historically marginalized groups. Nothing more than that. Medicine, as we saw earlier when we looked at Mihir's comments, also provides a unique moral excuse for an institution like AIIMS to focus on the students denoted "the best" by virtue of caste consolidated through exam rank. This makes clear a dissonance in which the noble profession of medicine cannot in good conscience participate in this particular movement toward social justice, because it is obliged, in Deshpande's words, "to cultivate 'excellence' to the exclusion of all other objectives (such as those of equity)."[73]

Dr. D (who studied at AIIMS in the 1970s and went on to join the faculty) told me that he was pleased the introduction of the OBC reservation had led to a more diverse student body, but he also observed the hurdles faced by students who found themselves in a more challenging academic, and social, environment than they had previously been exposed to:

> Though they come on the basis of reservation, they have to have a certain level of performance in examination. So when they come from . . . in their own milieu they are probably fairly high on scholastic achievements, but once they all land up in AIIMS the people who are coming from general category are far more, their performance is much better than the other ones. And therefore there is a constant stress upon those who have come through reservation to prove themselves. Some of them have not been able to deal with it

and I know a few who left in between, others who wandered into substance abuse and such things.

The hypervisibility of caste is again pertinent here, with students in reserved categories understood as a group with generalizable characteristics and occasional individuals who may defy type and expectation. As Dr. T told me:

> It has happened. I think it has happened with the effort of the teacher only. Teacher has pulled them so much so they have outshined, they have outshined the 12th rank. It has happened. But a lot depends on the . . . both sides. You are pulling up but the student is also equally running with you. Both are running. If both are running then it is possible that they will outshine the higher rank person. They can outshine. They have done it. They have done it. Two of my students are doing PhD now, and everybody wonders what we did to them that they became so good. And they were lowest ranked people. But they were also running with me—only then. Like I am pulling, pulling, so they also work that much harder.

This trope, in which a member of a reserved category defies expectation by excelling on par with a general category student deflects suggestions of institutional casteism or the naturalization of attributes associated with a particular social group. When I spoke to a former senior member of the AIIMS administration, he pointed out that SC and ST candidates often "become better than others," and that "many are already brilliant on arrival." He cited the SC identity of a highly respected former head of department as a case in point, as did others I spoke with.

"There's no equality in the country," Dr. A, an OBC faculty member, said when I raised the subject of caste with him. "How can there be equality in the institution?"

Of all the students I interacted with, it was Purush who most embodied the ambiguity of AIIMS as a liminal space. In his original conception, Turner noted that in a liminal situation neophytes are relieved of the responsibility of specific social roles and are able to "confront one another, as it were, integrally and not in compartmentalized fashion as actors of roles." "For a while," he goes on, "there was an uncommitted man, an individual rather than a social *persona*, in a sacred community of individuals."[74] Reflecting from a contemporary standpoint, Thomassen writes, "Turner realized that liminality served not only to identify the importance of in-between periods, but also to understand the human reactions to liminal experiences as they shape personality, suddenly foreground agency, and (sometimes dramatically) bind thought to experience."[75]

I observed some of these reactions in Purush over the course of our conversations, as he tussled with questions of identity and allegiance. "It is important to find your individuality," he told me. He didn't feel responsible for the SC community, he said: "I was just born into it." When we spoke of suicides at AIIMS, he said that they weren't necessarily linked to reservation and that individual students had personal issues for which they lacked support. Then he paused before echoing the words of the Dalit anti-caste activist and architect of the Indian constitution B. R. Ambedkar: "caste will always be a factor, until it is annihilated."[76] If he had to choose a dividing line, Purush said, he would split people into "stupid versus non-stupid." At AIIMS, he said on another occasion, "ideas matter more than identities." For doctors in particular, "identity matters less," he said, because "everyone is a potential patient." And in an exquisite allusion to the transition in which he and his peers were engaged, he said that "doctor" itself was a new identity, with its own status and reputation, which would supersede all others. With this vision, Purush presented the potential of the liminal state at its most ideal and powerful. He also signaled a movement toward accessing the "universal knowledge" that Sarah Pinto, earlier in this chapter, describes as a deceitful promise. Mihir's comments about the "incompetent" doctors produced by reservations illustrate this, as well as the power of those with structural privilege to determine the life chances of others. There is a poignancy about this distinction between the experiences and expectations of Purush and Mihir that Turner recognized:

> Liminality is the realm of primitive hypothesis, where there is a certain freedom to juggle with the factors of existence . . . But this liberty has fairly narrow limits. The neophytes return to secular society with more alert facul-

ties perhaps and enhanced knowledge of how things work, but they have to become once more subject to custom and law . . . they are shown that ways of acting and thinking alternative to those laid down by the deities or ancestors are ultimately unworkable and may have disastrous consequences.[77]

When I arrived on the AIIMS campus in 2014, four students from reserved categories had committed suicide since 2010. While denied meritocratic recognition, their aptitude and determination was made clear by their painfully brief presence at AIIMS. For many students in reserved categories, a middle-class upbringing with a decent standard of English-medium schooling equips them with the cultural capital and habitus necessary to thrive at AIIMS. In a few instances, where these prerequisites are lacking, a faculty member might be willing to invest time in helping a student fulfill her or his potential. And in others, met by an indifferent institution, a struggling student might resort to the ultimate erasure of ascribed identity in the shadow of the country's most highly regarded public hospital. The tragedy of these extreme cases, where the pursuit of knowledge to preserve life ends in death, throws into sharp and disconcerting relief the reality of how reservation-based difference is experienced by some students. The transformative possibilities of AIIMS as a liminal space are denied these students; their deaths expose a dark and lonely underbelly of a celebratory discourse of freedom. If the moniker "coaster" has any relevance at AIIMS, it begins to seem applicable not to a particular group of students, but to the elite institution itself.

CHAPTER 5

WAYS AND MEANS OF LEARNING
Impressions from the Clinic

AIIMS IS CONSIDERED SPECIAL for a variety of reasons, some justified and others less so. Students benefit from access to good academic and clinical infrastructure, nationally respected faculty, research opportunities, and the social advantages of decent accommodation and an absence of curfew. During my time at AIIMS, it also became apparent how student doctors benefited from another, very visible and very human resource, overwhelming in number and presence: patients.

In the course of our conversations, students regularly offered a dual narrative about the large numbers of patients at AIIMS, casting them simultaneously as a burden on limited time and resources and as an educational resource. Patients become an educational asset by virtue of their "bioavailability":[1] by seeking treatment at AIIMS, they make their bodies available to the institution for teaching and learning. This form of exchange is not unique to AIIMS—it is a fundamental feature of medical education in any teaching hospital. But what makes patients at AIIMS particularly valuable, according to students, is not just the large number of them but also the diversity—and often complexity—of the conditions they present with. This is another way in which enormous demand, in part a consequence of inadequate infrastructure elsewhere, contributes to and maintains the institute's reputation as the best place for medical training.

During an interview, a long-serving member of the AIIMS faculty recalled his time as part of an early MBBS batch at the institute in the late 1950s. While the main AIIMS hospital was still under construction, students were partly taught at Safdarjung Hospital, a government institution across the road. It was interesting, the doctor recalled, because it was a busy hospital with "lots of clinical material." I take this concept of patients as clinical material, or bioavailable resources, as a way to approach what MBBS students are not explicitly taught but what they are exposed to in clinics and on wards: that is, the social lives of patients and doctors, and their implications for health and medicine.

The power asymmetry between doctors and patients has long been the focus of social scientists.[2] Medical consultation and treatment is not only a clinical interaction between a doctor and a patient. It is also—and always—a channel through which pass the determinants of social and medical power that inform the doctor-patient relationship. Four decades ago, anthropologist Michael Taussig urged us to pay attention to how human relations are "embodied in signs, symptoms, and therapy." In the clinical encounter, he writes, social categories are confirmed and made real. "In any society," he goes on to say, "the relationship between doctor and patient is more than a technical one. It is very much a social interaction, which can reinforce the culture's basic premises in a most powerful manner."[3] At AIIMS, this encounter is an instruction to students about what constitutes the exemplary medicine for which the institution is renowned. In this chapter, I use ethnographic material from clinics and wards to illustrate how the interaction Taussig describes plays out at AIIMS and the implications it has for students learning how to be doctors. In the process we will see that what students are *not* explicitly taught during the MBBS can tell us as much as what the curriculum *does* include about how AIIMS defines excellence in medicine.

"YOU CAN BUILD YOUR OWN BRAIN AFTERWARDS"

During my first conversation with Dr. E, he posed a question: "Is AIIMS a university with a great hospital attached, or a hospital with a medical college attached?" Dr. E had first arrived at the institute as an MBBS student several decades earlier; when we met in 2015, he was a highly respected member of senior faculty. His personal lament for "the loss of university character" at AIIMS was laced with sadness and frustration, even as he acknowledged that standards of clinical care had improved. "Ours was a period of romance," he told me in his office. "It was all about the students." As we learned in chapter 2, India's first health minister Rajkumari Amrit Kaur emphasized in her speech to Parliament in 1956 that AIIMS was intended to enshrine an ethos of *guru-shishya* at the heart of the institution—an educational tradition based on a close relationship between student and teacher. The wife of the first director would invite undergraduate students to their campus bungalow for dinner, Dr. E recalled. The third director made an impression by assuring undergraduates that they could "walk into his office at any time." And in the early days, Rajkumari Amrit Kaur herself would stroll around the campus, interacting with students and observing the institution that she had been instrumental in creating.

According to Dr. E, expansion had led to depersonalization, with detrimental consequences for students, and had also, through a growing emphasis on individual departments, led to an erosion of institutional cohesion. The variable commitment to teaching was a concern and stemmed, he suggested, from the tendency of the institute's senior management to rest on the laurels of reputation, at the expense of self-assessment and strategic vision. Other faculty members shared this view. Reflecting on a period as director, however, Dr. V complicated it somewhat:

> I was not able to do the things that in hindsight I should have done because I didn't have the management skills. If I had the knowledge to fight the bureaucracy I would have done much more. But whatever I had was my own intuition. Even if I had a vision, I didn't know how to execute the vision because of a lack of skills to fight the bureaucracy.[4]

Nevertheless, Dr. E said, "Now the MBBS program is on the fringes."[5]

Students tended to agree. For those who compared AIIMS with the idealized image that fueled their application, and which Dr. E alluded to, the institute regularly fell short. Neha implied that the newfound freedom so many students spoke of had ambivalent consequences for learning:

AIIMS is better than other colleges I think . . . it depends. Actually in other colleges they spoon-feed you, they teach you all the stuff, they make you write the notes. Here we are very independent. We can study any of the books we want. In other colleges they have some prescribed books . . . Here we can experiment . . . that way I find AIIMS very nice . . . but . . . mixed. I think that they don't give that much attention to the undergraduates. And some of the professors are not very interested in teaching us. And I think whatever we study, we study on our own. The practical experience is very nice, you can go to wards and you can learn about new cases. But I find the class is not that interesting. I think that in my school days, the classes were more interesting. And medicine can be very boring if you don't teach it right.

Several students were disappointed by a lack of engaging practical train-ing. "It's OK, but I expected more than this. I wanted to learn more, like more interactive sessions, case discussions with the professors . . . This is not going well," Ugyen told me. Ashish agreed; he felt that the standard of instruction had deteriorated during the course. "I find it quite theoretical," he said. "So it would be better if we would have more case studies to discuss and all. We had it in our second and third years. But this year so far has been quite uneventful. Not uneventful, it has been . . . I don't know, dull." Not everyone was dissatisfied, but the most glowing assessments of the AIIMS academic experience came from students who compared it with less prestigious colleges. Nikhil exemplified this perspective:

Our pattern of teaching is so good. When I compare with my friends, who are doing MBBS in peripheral colleges, our college is so focused on the practical things; along with theory, yes, the lectures are there. In third year, it was very good, I would attend my seminars, and seminars were so nice. Like there they give one topic, like coronary artery disease and the faculty from surgery, pediatrics, they all come . . . and it is so wonderful. I ask all my friends and there is nothing like that in the peripheral colleges, no such thing is happening. It is still very exciting and I think I am not even able to use all resources at AIIMS. I am doing well but I still think I should use more opportunities.

Several students expressed frustration that mugging up, which was so crucial for getting into AIIMS, remained so throughout the MBBS. The reliance on memorization, while necessary to an extent, was deemed excessive. Mihir summed this up:

> Sometimes you feel like pulling all your hair out because the textbooks are like that. . . . [I]t's not conceptual, in the end you have to memorize as much as you can. And whatever concepts they say there are, actually it is that you have memorized this much, now you apply. . . . It's a bit tedious. I'd say that the expectations which I had when I entered were quite academic in nature. I thought that there would be more stress on academics and teachers would be teaching us around the clock and that we would be learning things that no one else does in the country. But the academic culture here is not that good.

Deepak explained how the legacy of intensive preparation for the entrance exam had continued to influence his approach at AIIMS, until a senior student advised him to read only the portions relevant for the exam, saying, "You can build your own brain afterwards." While this instrumental approach to assessment didn't sit comfortably with Deepak, when I asked if he passed similar advice on to his juniors, he nodded: "But it's not like I mark it for them. I say that if you are reading a book, try to analyze that information rather than, you know, mugging up all the sentences." Deepak's advice to junior students to think about the information they were reading seemed an effort to inject into the MBBS experience the intellectual stimulation he found lacking.

Shankar's concern was about the emphasis placed on book learning at the expense of clinical experience, and the consequences this had for students graduating from the MBBS. It was seen as symptomatic both of a lack of pedagogical commitment, and of the structural flaws in a system that incentivized preparation for postgraduate study at the expense of the clinical experience that would prepare students to be confident doctors:

> It should be more of, you know, more from books to patients. We are mostly reading books and it is not experiential. We obviously see patients when we go to wards and all but . . . from books MCQs will be asked . . . and so people

give more importance to each line of a book. [But] it is not important, because if you know the basic things you can always look up in MedScape . . . So more of going to the wards [is needed], so that we can actually practice, we can actually become primary care physicians at the end of the MBBS.

In chapter 6 I discuss the fact that none of the students I interacted with could imagine becoming a primary care physician, or general practitioner, following the MBBS. This was primarily to do with prestige and the expectation of specialization inherent in the AIIMSonian's status. It was also true, however, that several students described general practice as being beneath them as an AIIMSonian while simultaneously feeling unprepared for any kind of clinical practice precisely because of the pressure to study for postgraduate entrance exams.

Students acknowledged the pressures on faculty too, citing the huge number of patients and the demands of research as reasons why they did not prioritize teaching. Mihir suggested that a reluctance to teach was informed in part by the reluctance of students to attend classes. This seemed to have become self-fulfilling, at least among the senior students, who had not internalized the new requirements and remained confident that they would pass as long as their attendance didn't drop below 50%. Anjali thought that the neglect of undergraduates was inevitable given these pressures but suggested that assigning teaching to faculty members committed to education might ensure a more reliable standard. "Because I'm sure a lot of professors just take teaching as an add-on which they don't really want to do, but they have to do, and [they] do it in a very . . . there is a special word for it, it's called *jugaad* [a form of improvisation, or making do, with whatever resources are to hand]."

It was not only students who complained about the uneven quality of teaching and unimaginative pedagogy at AIIMS. Some of Dr. E's concerns were shared by faculty members who published regularly on the need for curriculum reform and the impediments that prevent it, both at AIIMS and in India more widely.[6] During my time at AIIMS, the Centre for Medical Education and Technology (CMET) organized a voluntary three-day faculty workshop on teaching methods. Those in attendance were mostly junior faculty who had recently joined the institute, although an enthusiastic deputy head of department also attended, and at least one person had come from another medical college in Delhi.

The workshop involved discussions of medical education, teaching, and assessment methods. During the final feedback session, participants expressed their appreciation of the workshop, but they also shared their anxiety that for all the encouragement to be innovative, the capacity of junior faculty to instigate change was constrained by hierarchical departmental structures. Without the support of their heads of department, people had very little room for maneuver. In the workshop setting, the additional constraints of caste discrimination went unspoken. I wondered to what extent institutional transformation was an eternal waiting game, as young faculty members were encouraged to innovate by a few of their seniors, while knowing that challenging embedded practices was unlikely to be the route to approval and promotion.[7]

What was the answer to this, I asked Dr. E when we next met. He shook his head. "We need good role models at this stage," he said. "Very badly."

PATIENT LABOR

The pressure exerted by the sheer number of patients is blamed for many challenges at AIIMS: overcrowding, time constraints, doctors' impatience, the neglect of MBBS students, and reduced opportunities for research. Most of my interlocutors held North India's inadequate public healthcare infrastructure responsible for the number of patients, coupled with the cost and variable quality of private treatment. Some students and faculty also cited a growing demand among patients for specialist treatment (which I discuss further in chapter 6), but on the whole there was a sense that most patients were propelled through the AIIMS gates by circumstances beyond their control.

The challenges that 10,000 outpatients a day pose to the functioning of the institute is often discussed, but a parallel narrative exists among students that the sheer number and variety of patients they are exposed to during their training is an asset that distinguishes AIIMS from other medical colleges. Krish encapsulated the way in which these dual narratives coexist:

The crowd is not useful, but the type of patients is really useful. We are exposed to various rare diseases, and common diseases are also coming, but the rare diseases. . . . All these things they are just learning from books in our state, they have the diseases but it is not diagnosed there. But here I have seen almost 40 to 50 patients with SLE [lupus] in 3 to 4 years. Many patients are here. All rare diseases are coming in, many syndromes are coming in. From a student's perspective it's good actually.

Ashish agreed: "Because you get a lot of cases, you get exposed to a lot of rare diseases, you get the whole spectrum of diseases."

Students I spoke with during Pulse also cited patient diversity as a unique attribute that contributed to the superior reputation of education at AIIMS. A young student from Bihar suggested that state hospitals tended to see more locally prevalent diseases, such as *kala-azar* (visceral leishmaniasis) in the case of her college, whereas AIIMS doctors treated a greater variety, with beneficial consequences for students. And in the sociologist Rama Baru's interviews with retired AIIMS doctors, those who spent entire careers at AIIMS speak of being motivated not by money but by the opportunity to be part of "the premier institute of the country" where one could "see medicine in its full spectrum."[8]

This treatment-for-education transaction has long been at the heart of medical education around the world. In *Birth of the Clinic*, Michel Foucault writes about how the unity of the hospital and the teaching domains became central to the development of clinical observation, citing the French psychiatrist Philippe Pinel from 1815: "What a source of instruction is provided by two infirmaries of 100 to 150 patients each! . . . What a varied spectacle of fevers or phlegmasias, malign or benign, sometimes highly developed in strong constitutions, sometimes in a slightly, almost latent, condition, together with all the forms and modifications that age, mode of life, seasons, and more or less energetic moral affections can offer!"[9] Writing about the socialization of new doctors, Hafferty and Franks note how patients "are cast concurrently as victims of disease, objects for learning, and subjects for research."[10] In his reflection on Foucault, Turner writes that "the hospital transformed the sick patient into an object of medical training. The sick were to become useful as illustrations of disease. Since the sick were typically the poor, they also became useful in the fulfillment of science."[11]

What is so stark at AIIMS is both the scale at which this dynamic operates and the unabashed way that the institution encourages students to take what they have learned from AIIMS patients and apply it to the pursuit of prestigious careers treating more affluent people, usually in private practice and frequently outside India. Balraj emphasized why it was important for his education that many of the patients he saw were poor:

> Yeah . . . actually useful in the sense that most of the diseases you see, I don't know why, but those diseases occur among poor people. I mean those who are rich and well furnished [*sic*], they just have those lifestyle disease, like diabetes, hypertension or all these type of diseases, or this excess fat. But most of the diseases, infectious diseases, malignant cancer, you see most of the times among these poor people. So it's better to see these people.

Vipul alluded to patients as "clinical material" when he explained that exposure to live human anatomy in place of synthetic dummies gave AIIMS an advantage over Western medical colleges: "In the West they mostly have dummies, they don't have real patients. Here we do get a chance on real patients and more exposure. That way it's an advantage, yes."

Reflecting on this theme during my time in Delhi, I began to see in patients' treatment seeking at AIIMS not only their own biological claim upon the state but also their contribution to it.[12] By making their bodies available for teaching and learning at a government medical college, patients augmented scientific knowledge and contributed in the process to the fulfillment of the institution's original purpose. What my conversations made visible was the way in which "patient labor" informed the exceptionalism of medical education at AIIMS—a description within which is encoded an urban, technological, and thoroughly modern medicine. The value of an AIIMS MBBS is produced, at least in part, by patients who do not have access to the type of healthcare environment in which an AIIMSonian is ultimately expected to practice.

THE HIDDEN CURRICULUM

In the clinic (1)

Eleven people fill the 10-by-10-foot consulting room (including me, tucked into a corner of the room on a plastic chair, beneath a tiny opaque window that suggests a distant external world), with an assistant trying to contain the hustle around the door.[13] Dr. B maintains an unruffled calm. His long experience reveals itself in an ability to stay focused on a patient while reaching without looking for the relevant form and ticking off the tests required, keeping the patient informed about his decisions, and re-assuring them if necessary, before gently but firmly encouraging them to make room for the next person in the queue. This is the instinctive cho-reography of a veteran doctor.[14] I can see Gaurav, the most experienced of Dr. B's senior residents, beginning to learn a similar technique. He is able to continue writing instructions for his own patient while glancing up to comment on the shade of jaundice in the eyes of a colleague's patient. The contrast with the rabbit-in-headlights demeanor of the MBBS interns is striking—their bodies have not yet learned. On the opposite side of the shared desk, another senior resident commands an elderly male patient to move seats. The brusque use of the informal register *tum*, rather than the honorific *aap*, emphasizes how class, professional status, and environment combine to confirm the power differential between patients and doctors. *Tum* can also connote affection in the clinic, but I hear this only in Dr. B's voice, and usually only when he addresses a patient he has established a relationship with over a significant period of time.

As we have seen, the MBBS admissions process is based on multiple-choice questions about biology, chemistry, and physics. It builds on a school system that segregates sciences and arts as incompatible, and as such, the exam entails no social science or humanities component, no expectation that students will have thought about the human interaction at the heart of medicine, and no opportunity for students to articulate their motivation for becoming a doctor. By extension, the study of human interaction in the clinic and the social life of medicine it reflects is not part of the AIIMS

MBBS curriculum. Students are not given the opportunity to reflect on doctors as social actors with their own values and interests who are imbued with enormous power over human beings who seek their help.[15] At AIIMS, that fundamental power differential is made all the more striking by the gulf between the everyday reality of middle-class clinicians at an elite institution and the poverty and marginalization of many of their patients. Other than a cursory glance during the community medicine module, the structures that maintain and reproduce social inequality, and its impact on health, are paid little attention during the education of students who are told that they are the country's most promising young doctors.

Given its absence from the MBBS curriculum, students learn about interaction with patients through either implicit example or overt instruction by individual faculty members. Learning in this manner entails a subtext about why certain styles of communication are deemed appropriate to certain patients and not others, and by extension, what it means to be a good or bad patient. It also reveals, without addressing, each doctor's own location in the social world of the clinic and the values they hold. This is an example of the workings of a "hidden curriculum": "that which the school teaches without, in general, intending or being aware that it is taught."[16] The hidden curriculum has particular implications for medical students:

> Most of what the initiates will internalize in terms of the values, attitudes, beliefs, and related behaviors deemed important within medicine takes place not within the formal curriculum but via a more latent one, a "hidden curriculum," with the latter being more concerned with replicating the culture of medicine than with the teaching of knowledge and techniques. . . . Sociologically, medical training is the pathway by which lay persons are transformed into something other than lay persons—in this case, physicians. Neophyte students are taught what is valued by this new culture, along with strategies and techniques to organize these values. They are also provided with opportunities for internalizing these values.[17]

Kenneth Ludmerer describes the hidden curriculum as "noncognitive," in contrast with the knowledge and reasoning emphasized by the formal curriculum.[18] For others, the concept of a "null curriculum" refers to areas that are not attended to, or "lessons that are conspicuous by their absence."[19] Ad hoc efforts notwithstanding, language and communication are part of the AIIMS null curriculum. As Taylor and Wendland note, this is made particularly complex by virtue of communication being at the heart of medical practice: "The hidden curriculum in medical education, although it is right there in plain sight, remains effectively hidden because of the patterns of unseeing characteristic of medical education. In other words, the hidden curriculum helps create the blind spots in which it then hides."[20] One consequence of such absences is the conclusion by students that particular issues are not sufficiently important to warrant direct attention or are somehow unrelated to the practice and experience of health and medicine.[21] Nevertheless, all the students I spoke with considered language and communication an important dimension of medical practice and felt that it should be integrated into the formal curriculum. The Centre for Medical Education and Technology held occasional communication workshops, but these were voluntary and required students to miss or rearrange other commitments in order to attend. With friends, Shankar had conducted a study among students during the previous year's Pulse and found that a majority of participants responded that communication should be taught and assessed and that they needed better role models. While Shankar understood communication as a set of skills integral to a doctor's "professionalism," along with ethics and teamwork, others hinted at their discomfort with the way in which communication revealed the power dynamics inherent in the clinical encounter. Rahul was unhappy about the impatience of some doctors and the way the patient load was blamed for this inadequacy:

> [They should] teach people how to talk properly to a patient, that should be improved. I have seen a lot of doctors talking very . . . angry . . . I am not able to express myself. . . . [T]hey don't talk to a patient as a human being, they just come and write. I know there is a lot of load, but still some time should be given to talk to the patient politely. History-taking is taught, like what you need to ask to a patient, but *how* you are going to ask the patient, that's the thing.

"THE LEAST YOU CAN DO IS LISTEN TO US"

In the clinic (2)

Dr. B repeatedly asks an elderly man to explain his trouble in his own words. *Aapko kya takleef hai?* (What's the problem?) he asks, then shakes his head as the patient proffers a sheet of test results.[22] *Nahin—kya hai takleef?* This continues until everyone in the room, patient included, is smiling. There is a palpable ripple of achievement when the patient mumbles a few words about his stomach; Dr. B nods in satisfaction and pats the man's shoulder, communicating through a form of touch distinct from that of the medical examination.

Aggressive behavior toward patients by doctors is integral to perceptions of public healthcare in India.[23] At large hospitals in particular, poor and minimally literate patients are often confused and intimidated by administrative procedures and documents before they even reach a doctor, whom they then find is impatient and unwilling to "hear" them.[24] That said, during my interactions with patients at AIIMS, their complaints were predominantly about administrative inefficiency and long waiting times. Patients rarely criticized doctors directly, and they often expressed sympathy for the workload generated by the large crowds.[25] According to most of the patients I spoke with as they waited at various spots around the hospital grounds, the generally courteous behavior of AIIMS doctors distinguished them from those at other public hospitals. A man from Delhi who was accompanying a patient said, "The doctors here are very well behaved. There are some problems here, there is a lot of crowd that comes. . . . But mostly it's excellent." A young man who had accompanied his aunt on her journey to AIIMS from Bihar spoke along similar lines:

> The doctors are fine. They are good in every respect. They talk nicely. Here crores of patients come, and someone might get cross with the patient but that is not the case here. They give their time and are compassionate. Every single person says that, "Yes, we went to AIIMS and the doctor behaved very well, and treated very well." That is what the patient remembers after everything. Everything else is in the hands of god.

Nandini, a young woman who had brought her toddler to AIIMS from Bihar for an operation, had only positive things to say about her experience. In particular, she emphasized that she felt comfortable asking the doctors questions and that they were happy to explain things multiple times if need be. In an interesting parallel, among the students I spoke with there was a general consensus that the best teaching took place in the pediatrics department.

Some people challenged these accounts, however. Sharmila, a young woman who was at AIIMS for a consultation following a kidney transplant, pointed out that most patients would be comparing AIIMS doctors with those at other government hospitals. There was no question of their superiority on that front, she said, and on the whole she found the behavior of AIIMS doctors fine, particularly if one discounted the occasional impatience provoked by overcrowding. In comparison with the private practitioners she had seen, however, Sharmila found some AIIMS doctors wanting.[26] She recalled one incident in particular that vividly illustrated the porous boundaries of an institution through which leak attitudes at odds with any idea of the hospital as a biomedical island untouched by "culture":[27]

> It happened once. I'm a Muslim and my kidney donor was Hindu. She was my friend. Repeatedly the doctor would say to me, "How come there is such friendship between a Hindu and a Muslim?" He used to torture me with this. He was not a senior doctor, he was just a junior. One day I got really angry and I said to him, "Do you also need a kidney? I'll get you one, I have other friends." I was very angry, and I said, "Despite being so educated why do you have such discriminatory behavior?" He apologized and said, "No, aunty, why are you getting angry?" I said, "A person jokes once, not ten times about the same thing." After that day, that poor doctor was also embarrassed and then behaved very well with me. I think he got scared that I would take it up with the higher authorities. He left here eventually.

Sharmila went on to praise the senior nephrologist who had treated her at AIIMS and with whom her family continued to exchange greetings on Eid, Holi, and Diwali. I can't say from Sharmila's testimony whether the junior doctor had observed and taken a cue from senior clinicians expressing disquiet about Muslim-Hindu relationships during his time at AIIMS. Perhaps not, in which case the anecdote serves as a reminder that students do not arrive at medical college as completely blank slates upon which new knowledge and experience is impressed. Rather, they arrive having been conditioned in different sociocultural and economic contexts and in ways that they may not always be aware of.[28] The behaviors they witness in clinical encounters may work to confirm or challenge preexisting conceptions of relations pertaining to religion, caste, class, and gender, with implications for their understandings of themselves as professional doctors and for their future medical practice.[29]

Gita, a middle-aged woman whom I met sitting outside the main outpatient department (OPD) one afternoon and later visited at her two-room home in western Delhi along with my research assistant Preeti, was the most irredeemably dissatisfied of all the AIIMS patients I spoke with. Gita had been receiving treatment at AIIMS for 15 years, and she told us that the behavior of doctors had deteriorated in that time. Their refusal to conduct an operation that Gita deemed necessary had left her feeling neglected and misunderstood. Her positive recollection of her original AIIMS doctor was associated with the fact that while he spoke respectfully, Gita had also benefited from his treatment. This reflects Das's findings among low-income Delhi residents that effective treatment depended on a combination of harmonious relations with a doctor, and that the prescribed medicine "take" on a person (*unki dawai mujhe lag jaati hai*):[30]

> The doctors that used to be there 15, 16 years ago were good. The present batch isn't so good. They scold nowadays. I go and complain that I have body ache, joint pains, and I have difficulties walking, they just say that "What can we do? We have prescribed the medicines, go home and rest." They refuse to operate, saying it isn't a big deal. Many times they behave very badly. I sometimes addressed them as "beta," seeing that they are younger than me. But they immediately retaliated saying, "We are not your children." They scolded me. They don't talk nicely. Only [my first AIIMS doctor] used to talk nicely; he understood well. His prescriptions also worked well for me. It's difficult. They should behave well and should behave the same with the rich and poor

alike. We are anyway in pain; the least you can do is listen to us, irrespective of whether we are rich or poor. If you talk politely, the patient will be reassured. They shout and scold a lot, even at the slightest mistake in diet. They scold. That is the biggest shortcoming, their manner of talking.

On two separate occasions we met a young woman, Sunita, in the main OPD. She was very distressed about her sister's deteriorating kidney condition and offered a complex assessment of her AIIMS experience. As she spoke she seemed torn between sympathy for doctors and a tentative assertion of the rights of the patient and her family:

> Too many patients come here. When there is an overload of patients, then they deal accordingly. But overall it's fine. The doctors are compassionate, their behavior is good, and they are also thorough. But [in the Emergency Department] I was pained because the doctors work so hard, look at you, treat you compassionately, but they also think, how can we treat so many patients? But when a patient is coming to you, then you are responsible for them, right? They don't respond. If you ask them they get irritated at you talking too much, asking too many questions. They say they don't have time to answer useless questions, they say, "look, we are treating the patient, OK? The treatment is underway, so it's all fine." It's also probably our fault that we ask too much, to clarify things or to ask their opinions. But sometimes we need to.

TAKING ADVANTAGE

For some students the socioeconomic composition of the patient body inevitably—and necessarily—informed the nature of interaction in the clinic. For example, although the diversity of diseases encountered may have been useful, Ashish was concerned that he would leave AIIMS at a disadvantage if he wanted to pursue a career in private practice because he hadn't learned how to communicate with well-off patients, who, implicitly, he understood as a different type of patient regardless of the diagnosis or treatment he may be administering:

> Patient demographic here is mainly people from low socioeconomic background. So we don't get access to, we only know, I don't know how to say this,

but you know we talk to different kinds of people in different ways? So we only learnt how to talk to people of low socioeconomic background.

When we spoke, Shankar had recently returned from a semester as part of a research group at UCLA's medical school. Several students I spoke to had undertaken research fellowships at US institutions. Although these visits were not officially part of the MBBS curriculum, there was a tacit understanding between students and administration that allowed for a manipulation of the system, provided that all compulsory examinations were still taken. AIIMS did not provide any financial support for these visits, some of which lasted for three months, so they were limited to students whose parents could afford them. The differences between the clinical encounters Shankar had observed in the United States and those at AIIMS were fresh in his mind:

> So the main difference was like the doctor [at UCLA] spends more time, 10, 15 minutes. In the OPD for example, here everyone is there. But there [they have] patient rooms, so a patient sits in there. And then a nurse first takes the vitals and all, and then the patient is comfortably seated in the room and then the doctor knocks and asks what have you come here for, what are your problems. He explains to the patient in a very nice manner, spends around 10, 15 minutes there. So that's what I think is different. And here we have more patients.

As Shankar spoke, the generic defense of time pressure compromising an ideal standard of behavior revealed a more complex argument about the nature of the patient demographic at AIIMS. He was making a similar point to Ashish, it turned out:

> Given the practical scenario where the patient's educational status is low, they are not able to understand, and then they ask lots of questions. So if you speak to them in a very polite manner then they will not leave . . . *sar pe chad jaate hain* [they will take advantage of you] and you have very less time. If you spend 5, 10 minutes with everyone, you will end your OPD at night. And you have to end your OPD at 1 p.m. Because they are not, educational status

is so low. So [doctors] can be more courteous but it also has drawbacks, the patients will say all this . . . but still I think [doctors] can be more courteous.

From this perspective, paying excessive attention to patients poses a risk to order in the clinic, suggesting that the hospital not only reflects but also works to actively maintain the unequal social status quo.[31] While anticipating that patients with little education might seek clarity from doctors if given the chance, and recognizing that these two social facts were interrelated, Shankar argued that time constraints meant doctors could not indulge patients' efforts to "take advantage" of an opportunity to better understand their situation. The limits of a doctor's responsibilities in Shankar's eyes are made clear here. Maintaining communication at a tenor deemed appropriate becomes a means of disciplining a potentially unruly patient, in the guise of temporal exigency. Sarah Pinto found a similar dynamic in her work on psychiatric practice in North India, in which an ethos of pragmatism was understood as both "a requirement in strained conditions and an ethic derived from *material* context" and "a matter of *cultural* context."[32]

As exemplified by Sunita above, "pragmatism" by doctors can provoke a complex response from patients. What they object to is not necessarily the brevity of the encounter, which is anticipated and does not in itself preclude a detectable ethos of care. Many patients also tolerated a degree of impatience by doctors and were discomfited only when this crossed a line to become insult and degradation. At that point, tolerance became muddled with anxiety about whether the chastisement was warranted and further complicated by the doctor's failure to acknowledge the importance of a patient's questions about what was taking place in, and being enacted upon, her own body or that of her relative.

What Shankar's scenario ignores, however, is that, if anyone, it is patients of higher social status who "take advantage" of doctors at AIIMS. We know that social mobility into and within India's middle classes sees people exiting public services for the private sector, particularly in education and health.[33] The exceptional status of AIIMS among Delhi's public institutions in particular is emphasized by the fact that those who have access through personal connections continue to seek second opinions from

AIIMS doctors, even as they receive actual treatment in more salubrious surroundings. This additional burden is rarely referenced as part of the "patient load" AIIMS has to manage.

At the extreme end of this spectrum are those whose access is so highly privileged as to allow a direct phone call to a doctor's office (such calls were often made in search of what Dr. E referred to as a "big-ticket second opinion," as he apologized for cutting short our conversation to answer the phone to the solicitor general) or being ushered in front of a head of department for a private consultation part way through an ongoing meeting.[34] Then there are those who put their heads around the door of the consulting room during an OPD and plead in English with the doctor to add their card to the pile. In my observation, while Dr. A tended to accept such requests with an air of resignation, Dr. L had no patience with these methods, including when they were deployed by AIIMS colleagues as was common. Her dismissal of such requests was usually blunt and accusatory and her disruption of a system of tacit privilege caused visible confusion. Even Dr. L, however, was unable to insist that a senior faculty member join the queue like any other patient, however palpable her frustration.

Kalpana Ram has written about how the class confidence of middle-class patients in Tamil Nadu informs the doctor-patient encounter.[35] She employs Bourdieu's concept of habitus as a means of understanding "the ways in which the past flows through individuals, absorbed as a part of their repertoire with which they meet the challenges of the present, without necessarily being aware of every element." At AIIMS, it is these queue-jumping middle-class English-speaking patients who engage the doctor for as long as possible, deploying biomedical vocabulary to signal shared literacy and seeking opinions until the doctor succeeds in encouraging them out of the door. In one example during an OPD I was observing, a smartly dressed middle-aged woman persisted for several of Dr. A's precious minutes in trying to convince him that her status as a public figure meant that refraining from coloring her hair as instructed was not possible. "Not even a little bit of henna?" she tried, as Dr. A shook his head and reached determinedly for the next patient's card.

Ram suggests that beyond the use of biomedical language, patient confidence is also observable in the way that they regard biomedical environments as an extension of their own class habitus.[36] For such patients at AIIMS, the doctor's authority stems predominantly from medical knowledge; the power to discipline and diminish is therefore, while still evident, at least challengeable in this encounter. By contrast, as Bourdieu also reminds us, the combination of biomedical knowledge and social authority often act as a silencer of patients of lower social status, reifying the power of the doctor.[37] In her work on communication and medical education in South Africa, Berna Gerber argues that the endurance of this dynamic, and its transmission to students, rests on the fact that clinical medicine persists with inaccurately defining itself as a positivist science which maintains that statements must be empirically verifiable to be considered "true or meaningful."[38]

In the clinic (3)

It is February and already hot.[39] The fan is on a month too early. A glass paperweight stops papers fluttering from the desk to the floor. I remark that the pile of patient cards in front of Dr. L is smaller than usual. She replies that the hospital feels relatively quiet and wonders if people are staying away because of the publicity around Delhi's swine flu outbreak. A middle-aged woman is led into the consulting room by her husband and son. They are concerned about a tremor in her hands. Dr. L teaches her students to involve the patient's companions in a conversation if it might be helpful for diagnosis. Accordingly, she asks the men to describe what they have observed in the patient and they both respond with *kamzori* (weakness).[40] Dr. L shakes her head and pronounces that this is a subjective feeling, not an objective judgement. She proceeds to voice her suspicion of Parkinson's disease. Cowed, the family sit in silence.[41]

"THE CLOSED WORLD OF WORDS"

On the wards, case discussions take place at bedsides among professionals who rarely involve patients other than to ask an occasional question for clarification. When I shadowed Dr. B on his rounds, patients' relatives who had been made to leave the ward before the doctor and his entourage arrived would cluster around the entrance, waiting to offer a namaste, trying to catch his attention for a word about their relative's condition. Dr. B's patients were all either pre- or post-operation, and all were severely ill. They lay on beds covered by white sheets with "AIIMS" stitched into a red border; the sheets were sometimes stained and sometimes had holes in them, and were occasionally supplemented with a blanket or two brought from home. Many patients wore their own loose clothing rather than a hospital gown, and on the cabinet beside the bed there might be a packet of milk from the Mother Dairy shop on the hospital compound, or a bottle of Miranda orange, or, rarely, a more expensive carton of pomegranate juice. Occasionally, a lone fly traced shapes in the air above the beds, embodied proof of the permeable hospital boundary.

Conversations took place above a patient's head in both Hindi and English; a patient might hear confusing fragments of speech about her condition or miss altogether the news that she was to be allowed home the following day. The learning of medical language is central to the process through which new doctors are created. Foucault notes the perpetuation of a "medical esotericism" through a language into which a student must be initiated and that is inaccessible to others: "one now sees the visible only because one knows the language; things are offered to him who has penetrated the closed world of words."[42]

This speech "can be understood only by those initiated into true speech," those initiated "into the truth of things," Foucault goes on. This esotericism is different from that which historically compelled elite French doctors to speak in Latin. That, Foucault says, was simply a deliberate effort to protect professional privilege through a language that the patient could not understand. At AIIMS, however, both facets of esotericism are at play. For the patient without English, learning what he or she is to be treated for, and how, demands an act of double translation—a form of "cognitive comfort" in Kirkpatrick's words—for which the patient is entirely dependent on the doctor providing treatment, whose translated words the patient has no choice but to accept as truth.[43] Take this example from Dr. L's OPD:

In the clinic (4)

An elderly man enters the consulting room alone, which is unusual.[44] We are in the midst of Delhi's annual dengue fever outbreak and I have come to appreciate the surgical mask that Dr. L insists I breathe through. Having elicited a complaint of breathlessness from the man and read his notes from a previous appointment, Dr. L proceeds to discuss the case in English with an intern and a junior resident. The man sits frail and diminished on a stool in a well-worn cotton shirt and trousers, his eyes flicking anxiously between the three doctors standing above him. They occasionally gesture toward his sickened body as they discuss it in a language he cannot comprehend. Is it worse than he thought? Does he need an operation? Are they discussing his impending death? "Please explain to him," Dr. L instructs the resident and the intern who go on to explain the conclusions the doctor has reached, without any of the reasoning behind it.

What are the implications for trust here, and for how the role of medicine is understood, when the clinical encounter is mostly conducted in a language inaccessible by the least powerful party?

Dr. B's manner tended to be more brusque on the wards than in the clinic. Patients often struggled to sit up as they saw the doctor approaching or at least to make some acknowledgment of his approach—folding hands in greeting, or quickly covering the head with a dupatta. Dr. B did not always acknowledge the person in the bed, whose skin yielded beneath his fingers. Patients watched mostly in silence, as though from a distance, while their bodies were palpated, the viscous contents of tubes extending from their flesh examined, and their charts scrutinized by Dr. B and his small flock of senior residents, nurses, and me.

Occasionally he appeared uncaring. He continued speaking over the wails of a middle-aged woman distressed by her nausea, leaving her to be soothed by a young nurse. The nurse whispered to her and stroked her hair in a gesture more intimate than anything I had yet observed at the hospital, demonstrating both the qualitative division of labor between doctors and nurses and its starkly gendered nature.[45] One young man remained on the ward 21 days after his operation. He wore white cotton pajamas, and from where I stood at the end of his bed I could see the dry scaled skin on the soles of his feet. A senior resident took the man's X-ray films from the bedside cabinet and held them up to the light for the group to see. Dr. B pulled up the patient's pajama top and palpated his abdomen; he asked a question to which the patient shook his head. Then the group moved on, leaving the young man to pull down his top and cover his exposed skin.

But there were other moments when Dr. B seemed to intuit that touching a patient's knee, or lingering to offer a reassuring word, would provide comfort. One morning in the intensive care unit, I joined Dr. B's group beside the bed of a man made prematurely old by disease. So emaciated that the contours of his skull appeared sharp beneath a fragile layer of skin, he was agitated, repeatedly tapping the metal bar at the edge of the bed. His lower jaw trembled as he moved it in an attempt to speak, but he made no sound. "*Araam se saans lo* (breathe gently)," Dr. B said, and put out his hand for a stethoscope, which was immediately proffered by two residents. He listened to the man's chest, but the patient was still panicking, shaking his head. Dr. B tapped his hand steadily. "*Koi dikkat nahin hai* (there's nothing to worry about)," he repeated, and kept his hand still as the man began to calm down, and then gradually began to smile until he appeared almost to be on the brink of laughter.

"GO FOR A WALK"

In their discussion of the hidden curriculum, Hafferty and Franks write that "the overall process of medical training helps establish and reinforce a value climate that explicitly identifies matters of rightness and wrongness within the overall culture of medicine. From these perspectives, a significant component of medical training involves the development of a medical morality and supporting rationales within its initiates."[46]

In the following few pages, I use ethnographic material from Dr. L's OPD clinic to illustrate these dynamics and how the clinical encounter at AIIMS acts as a lesson to students about what it means to be a doctor at the country's most well-regarded public hospital.

Over several months, I witnessed Dr. L interact with a changing cast of students and patients in her OPD. There was always an intern assigned to her clinic, and she was candid about her efforts to teach a more comprehensive approach to medicine, stressing the importance of communication and regularly drawing students' attention to the types of questions they should be asking and how to elicit information by making enquiries relevant to patients' lifeworlds. More tacitly, Dr. L's interaction with patients demonstrated her expectations of herself as an AIIMS doctor, her expectations of patients' behavior, and the nature of power in the clinic. This all contributed to MBBS students' experiences of clinical interaction, informing their perceptions of a form of medical practice that they may (or may not) go on to emulate.

In the clinic (5)

Sometime after 11 a.m., a woman wearing a colorful polyester sari sits down on the small plastic stool beside the desk.[47] She appears to my eyes to be in her 60s, but she estimates her age as between 53 and 55 years old. She is accompanied by a younger couple, probably her son and daughter-in-law, or vice versa. The man sits quietly against the wall while the woman takes explanatory charge. When the patient herself speaks of her pain and discomfort, she looks at me.[48] She comes from Jalandhar in Punjab, and the family has brought her to AIIMS from Sir Ganga Ram, a private hospital in northern Delhi. The younger woman presents Dr. L with various pages of test results from multiple consultations. After conducting her own examination, Dr. L decides to admit the patient, even as the patient herself says that she is worried it will prove useless. "They haven't been able to give her a diagnosis and she needs one, so we give priority to such patients," Dr. L says.

Although Dr. L was frequently frustrated with what might have been medically unnecessary visits to her OPD, I didn't see her refuse anyone attention, even if she didn't always offer treatment. During one OPD, a man in his 40s sat in front of Dr. L wearing a mint-green hand-knitted sweater vest and a gentle smile. He asked Dr. L to check him over because he had a cough. Dr. L listened to his chest then gently chastised him for coming to the hospital. He had been coming to her OPD for the previous

15 years, she told me, and she considered it a case of "somatization disorder" stemming from a childhood history of TB. Perhaps he felt a sense of safety in the medical environment that was denied him in wider society, Dr. L mused, offering a brief example of how she imagined the lives of her patients beyond the clinic.

On another occasion, a woman in her 50s, with a ready smile, turned her face between Dr. L and me as she explained her feelings of weakness (*kamzori lagti hai*). A local doctor had told her she had low blood pressure. In Dr. L's opinion, this had exacerbated her symptoms and spurred a search for remedy at AIIMS. "The standard of general practice is very low," she told me. Neighborhood practitioners in poor areas often conflated symptoms with diagnosis, as anthropologist Veena Das has studied in Delhi.[49] Rather than dismissing the woman's complaint as groundless, in her manner that managed to be both brusque and humane at once, Dr. L said that postmenopausal osteoporosis was a possibility and ordered some blood tests that would be conducted by the AIIMS laboratory at no expense to the patient.[50]

The access to functional on-site laboratories is a reminder of the resources AIIMS has at its disposal, the normalization of which has consequences for the behavior of students. On one occasion Dr. L berated a junior resident for filling in the tests form incorrectly. Rather than ticking the specific tests required, the student had drawn a large bracket encompassing all of them. Dr. L told him off for both the generalization and the unnecessary load such a demand would place on lab staff. I watched, embarrassed for the sheepish student, as Dr. L crumpled up the form and reached for a fresh one. "I'll do it myself," she said. Communication in the clinic is not only between doctors and patients; it also is a means of directly impressing upon students what is expected of them as AIIMS-trained clinicians.

Dr. L also ensured that students appreciated the importance of thinking through a case meticulously and of eliciting a range of information needed for a diagnosis. Questions needed framing in language appropriate to the reality of the patient, and in this sense the doctor tried to enter into the patient's lifeworld.[51] In one instance, Dr. L criticized a student for recording a young male patient's place of work simply as Mother Dairy, a state-run dairy company. The man complained of breathlessness (as did so many patients in heavily polluted Delhi); recording only that he worked at Mother Dairy gave no information about the job profile and tasks involved. Was it a sedentary position, or did it demand hours of heavy lifting? Did time and posture have any bearing on the man's difficulty breathing? Such symptoms were often described as feeling worse at night, Dr. L explained, but in some cases that could be explained by a heightened awareness of discomfort during quieter periods or a more audible rasping of the breath. When the student had asked whether the patient experienced "wheezing," he had said no. But when Dr. L enquired whether he experienced "noisy breathing" (*saans lene mein avaaz aati hai?*), he nodded without hesitation.

Dr. L's approach to patients was also a means of making students more aware of the consequences of the unreliable and often punitive healthcare landscape beyond AIIMS. During an OPD one morning, an intern instructed a frail elderly man to attend a local clinic twice a day to have his blood pressure and blood sugar checked. Dr. L immediately intervened, explaining that a clinic would "fleece him for checking twice a day." She conveyed other lessons to students that alluded to the poverty of patients, such as regularly reassuring patients that particular powdered medicines could be consumed with water and did not require the purchase of milk.

At other times, however, an impression of empathy was confused by Dr. L's impatience. Patients were regularly told that they were wrong. Their answers to Dr. L's questions were wrong, their understandings of their bodies were wrong, their lifestyles were wrong. This recalled for me Kalpana Ram's assertion that "the scolding lecture" that takes place in the Indian clinic should be considered a genre of its own given its ubiquity and particular dynamics.[52] The "patient labor" that informs medical education, as discussed at the start of this chapter, does not preclude the criticism and correction of these same patients by doctors. Rather, it forms part of the same educational project: informing students not only of appropriate diagnoses and remedies but also of the shortcomings of certain patients' ways of being.

In the clinic (6)

A woman and her son enter the consultation room.[53] Speaking on his mother's behalf, the son explains that they have been sent from both gastroenterology and endocrinology following a series of investigations into his mother's "swelling." He presents Dr. L with a sheaf of test results that she leafs through, finally looking up to declare that there is no apparent illness and that the swelling is most likely the result of sedentariness. "It is not money that will buy health"—she suddenly says—"it is lifestyles." She looks at the slightly bewildered mother and son. "*Dawai* [medicine] is not the solution for everything."

This assertion, and the accompanying command to "take responsibility," seemed an almost willful denial of the reality of patients' lives beyond the hospital, at odds with the impression Dr. L had given on other occasions. Medical technologies have never been so central to perceptions of health and healing in India given the unprecedented exposure (if not access) of patients to these purported solutions. The "biotechnical embrace" that Mary-Jo DelVecchio Good has described, or the association of "health with *things*" in Sunil Amrith's analysis, is as encompassing of patients as it is of medical students.[54] An AIIMS doctor's rejection of this order of things (however warranted in principle) would seem to challenge both patients' and students' understanding that medical technologies hold the key to a modern state of health.

Dr. L combined her identification of an epidemiological trend that saw an increase in symptoms associated with inactivity with a discourse of individual responsibility, to produce instructions to patients that took little account of local context. "Go for a walk," she would say, generally recommending five kilometers a day. While the poorest patients are anyway unlikely to suffer from symptoms related to inactivity given the exhausting demands of daily life, it remains the case that walking as a form of exercise demands infrastructure, specific footwear, time, and freedom of movement, all of which are precluded by the conditions of many patients' lives, particularly those of women.[55]

On another occasion, Dr. L belittled a father and son for not "taking responsibility" by failing to ask their previous doctor for the boy's most recent chest X-ray. This appeared to be institutional insulation at its most myopic, where it refuses any recognition of the power relations that inhibit patients from taking such actions. As anthropologists have pointed out, it is often the case that "the symbolic content of health-related messages is less important than the social hierarchies such messages reassert."[56] At AIIMS, such communication not only reasserts hierarchies in the minds of patients but also acts as a pedagogical performance, impressing upon students a relational dynamic in the clinic that they can only assume they are expected to reproduce in their own practice.

Taylor and Wendland argue that "the curricula of medicine—formal, informal, and hidden—rigorously schools practitioners in individualism as a habit of thought and practice, in ways that discourage, or even disable, social and cultural analysis."[57] Among urban consumers in India, a discourse of individual responsibility and the crafting of a new form of citizen-patienthood is well under way, in a privatized landscape increasingly augmented by (literal) technologies of the self, including apps through which a patient can self-monitor and purchase tailored treatment on demand, and air purifiers that insulate privileged homes from the indiscriminate threat of particulate matter.[58] The demographic most able to consume this new form of health management is far less visible among patients at AIIMS than it is among its trainee doctors. For many AIIMS patients, personal responsibility for health and care has long been the default mode of being, in the absence of reliable public services.[59] We might understand some patients' journeys to AIIMS as expressions of a biological citizenship that demands a neglectful state take responsibility for the provision of decent, affordable medical treatment. This does not mean, however, that patients are equipped to subvert hierarchies by challenging clinical power. It is from this perspective that a lecture on personal responsibility by an AIIMS doctor might seem perplexing to a patient while also encouraging a student to understand affliction and patienthood as determinedly individualized states of being.

Despite her demands that patients be more autonomous, Dr. L could also be affronted by assertiveness. During one outpatient clinic, a young woman around 25 years old entered the consulting room accompanied by her sister. The patient was confident and self-possessed; she spoke firmly and fluently in English, articulating her understanding that a benign tumor was growing in her brain. She continued speaking as Dr. L interrupted her but gave up as Dr. L persisted. Dr. L asked about a particular test while looking down at a sheet of paper from the patient's file. The sister responded politely that the test had been done. Dr. L snapped back, "Obviously she's had it done if it's here in front of me." Ram suggests that, "in the spaces of clinics and hospitals, didacticism is, if anything, further accentuated as a mode of authority."[60] These moments when Dr. L seemed determined to inhabit the traditional didactic mode of the doctor were at odds with her efforts on other occasions to acknowledge the realities that informed and influenced patient behavior, and to adapt her own accordingly. In such instances of transparent rudeness rather than a brusque efficiency, I was unsure what was going on. Was a patient's self-assertion, or command over her own body, received as a threat to medical authority, exposing a limit to Dr. L's demand that patients take responsibility for their own health? Was this particularly the case when the patient demonstrated the same class habitus as an AIIMS doctor used to a greater power differential, or did Dr. L object to this middle-class patient seeking treatment at AIIMS when the demand from the poor was so overwhelming? Dr. L's students were exposed to conflicting messages, which there was no space or opportunity to discuss as part of medical education or, I suspected, of a doctor's own reflective practice. This brings to mind the work of the medical anthropologist Arthur Kleinman, who urges us to consider the "particular people" who produce and uphold cultures of medicine, as social actors with values that inform their practice but which often remain unspoken. "The physician," Kleinman reminds us, is "simultaneously a professional and a particular person with his or her own deep subjectivity." A "hidden conflict" exists, he argues, "between what the professional persona seems to demand and what the personhood of that professional actually feels but cannot or will not speak."[61] Bringing the hidden curriculum into the light at AIIMS would mean interrogating this conflict and creating space for attention to the subjectivity of both established and trainee doctors.

In the clinic (7)

A middle-aged man enters the small consultation room with his son; he is bloated and a large vein throbs visibly in his neck.[62] On sight of him Dr. L immediately begins shouting that she will not take responsibility for him if he refuses to take responsibility for himself. The son's sheepish smile quickly fades beneath the doctor's barrage of words. Dr. L turns to me and explains that the man had been admitted to the hospital last year with congestive heart failure and was decongested and discharged with a management program. He had not returned to AIIMS until now, however, when he is once again in a state of advanced congestive heart failure, with a pulse of 48. Dr. L immediately admits him. When he and his son have left the room, she tells me that she knows that many AIIMS patients are "so preoccupied with making a living" that they only return when they are very ill and it seems absolutely necessary. "I understand it from their point of view, but sometimes as doctors we feel so helpless." Her anger appears, on this occasion, to be a manifestation of distress.

BALLABHGARH

The hidden curriculum doesn't operate only at the hospital in Delhi. The AIIMS Centre for Community Medicine is responsible for the Comprehensive Rural Health Services Project in once rural, now peri-urban, Haryana. A 45-minute drive from the South Delhi campus, the project comprises a community hospital in Ballabhgarh and primary health centers in two local villages. All MBBS students are posted to Ballabhgarh for a seven-week community medicine module during the fourth year and for three months of the internship. For many of the students I met, Ballabhgarh was their first experience of life beyond a city. In chapter 6, I look at students' experiences of community medicine and why for many it was considered incommensurate with the type of career ambition befitting an AIIMSonian. Here, I reflect on two examples from my visits to Ballabhgarh to illustrate how the Comprehensive Rural Health Services Project acts as another arena in which the hidden curriculum works in different ways to establish and reproduce power relations between doctors and patients.

As part of the community medicine module, the group of fourth-year students I observed during my visits were tasked with devising short sketches about the importance of sanitation for health (or the WASH—water, sanitation, and health—approach, in public health language). The students then performed these sketches to three different audiences: an all-women group of accredited social health activists (ASHAs), children in a secondary school, and a group of local people in an open space beside a stream that bisected this particular village. The ways that practices around medicine and development jointly authorize particular forms of knowledge and its transmission have long been the focus of social scientists.[63] In each of these scenarios the audiences were cast as passive recipients of scientific knowledge that they were expected to put into practice in order to improve their health, irrespective of the sociopolitical determinants of ill health that students were ostensibly in Ballabhgarh to learn about. What these local communities actually were was another type of educational resource whose presence worked to confirm the incipient authority of MBBS students performing the role of doctor by telling poor people to wash their hands. This hidden dimension of the curriculum was made unavoidably explicit when several of the ASHAs in attendance told me that they were regularly part of the audience for these performances by changing casts of students.

On another of my visits I was struck by how the behavior of a faculty member implicitly confirmed the social hierarchies that an effective community medicine syllabus might be expected to, if not explicitly disrupt, at least reveal to student doctors as part of a discussion of health inequalities. I was sitting with several students in the minibus that would take us back to Ballabhgarh, following a visit to one of the village primary health centers. The faculty member who had led the excursion arrived and occupied a seat at the front, placing his laptop bag on the vacant seat beside him. It was hot; he wiped his brow and signaled to one of the center staff waiting beside the bus. A couple of minutes later, a young man stepped on to the bus with a glass of water on a tray. The teacher took the glass, drank the water, replaced the glass on the tray, and dismissed the man with a wave of his hand. The bus filled up. The last students to arrive asked the teacher if he could move his laptop bag so that they could sit down; he shook his head and we drove off as students perched on the edge of their classmates' seats.

I had already interviewed this faculty member and heard his thoughts about the need to resuscitate primary care in India, and I had observed him reminding students in a group discussion to bear in mind the influence of local politics on village sanitation practices. I didn't know him well enough to ascertain whether his actions in the bus were informed by caste, class, or his position in the AIIMS hierarchy (or a combination of the three factors). But his actions that day were a striking example of how the hidden curriculum could extend beyond the classroom, working to undermine the ostensible ethos of community medicine by sanctioning a social status quo that works to the detriment of the health of marginalized communities.[64]

"WE'RE NOT CONSIDERING THE PERSON AS A PERSON"

In March 2015, in conjunction with the Centre for Medical Education and Technology, the Department of Psychiatry organized a communication skills workshop. The workshop was voluntary; while the organizers had expected 25 to 30 students, they began with 6 and ended with 13. Two junior residents in attendance told me that even if people wanted to attend, they would find it difficult given the various academic and clinical demands on their time. A resident I recognized from Dr. L's OPD confirmed the need for faculty support—Dr. L explicitly encouraged her students to attend such workshops.

The workshop began with an introduction to the importance of communication in medical practice. When students were asked to imagine themselves as patients and to articulate what they expected of a doctor, they agreed that a doctor should listen carefully, explain the method of investigation and diagnosis, give treatment options, and explain their pros and cons. Throughout the afternoon, those present demonstrated a capacity, and often an enthusiasm, for self-critique and discussion of behaviors and protocols that at times felt at odds with the institutional context in which we sat.

A young member of the psychiatry faculty spoke with conviction to the small class as he explained that patients were viewed as collections of symptoms rather than as human beings. "We're not considering the person as a person," he said. Doctors failed to listen properly and were too focused on the symptom-diagnosis-treatment trajectory to look up and engage with the human being in front of them. He urged empathic listening and a vigilant awareness of the trials the patient has already gone through before he reaches the consulting room: he has come on a train from Bihar to queue at AIIMS from 3 a.m., he may not have eaten, and he is ill. "He has so much to say, for heaven's sake give him half a minute to express himself," the faculty member told them.

A later session guided students through an ideal doctor-patient interview. Language was central, the instructor explained. "Why" questions often sounded accusatory and threatening, and rarely had straightforward answers. Students were told they should impart reassurance by telling the patient that they understood their condition. Actions and examinations should be explained: a doctor should invite a patient to the examination table by explaining that she would like to examine her rather than using the standard command, *let jao* (lie down), which echoed through the hospital corridors. A consultation should end with the doctor asking if the patient had any questions, the instructor said. I could not recall having observed this at AIIMS. Rather, consultations tended to end with a rhetorical *theek hai?* (all right?) and a dismissal often signaled by the doctor's selection of the next card from the pile, or by telling an assistant to call the next patient. During one of Dr. B's busier OPDs, when 12 people occupied the small consultation room, an elderly man sat on a stool and watched as the senior resident who had been speaking to him left the room. He remained sitting patiently until the doctor returned, looked at him, and asked why he was still there.

Preparing for a role-play, when one student said he wasn't sure how he should address patients, he was told to always use *aap* as the default mode of address and to employ "culturally appropriate terms" that took into account age, gender, and relationships between people. This led to an exercise in which students had to grapple with a tension between "culture" and a patient's agency. Two groups were asked whether a doctor should request the presence of a female patient's husband before breaking bad news about her condition. The scenario reminded me of several occasions in Dr. B's OPD (which saw a significant number of patients at a terminal stage of illness), when I was briefly confused about who the patient was, as information was conveyed to the husband of a female patient, or an elderly parent was sent out of the room before the gravity of his condition was explained to his children.[65] Responding to the scenario, one group said that the husband should be called, reflecting normative values around kinship and patriarchy that they felt should be respected. The spokesperson for the other group disagreed and cited bioethical literature to argue that the woman's autonomy must be respected.

These different answers illustrate two different ways in which AIIMS is permeated by prevailing and sometimes contradictory social currents. In the first case, the group that decided to wait for the husband presented a clear example of how doctors' behavior is influenced by the web of social norms within which they also exist; these go unchallenged by the overt curriculum and are regularly affirmed by its hidden component. The second case contained echoes of the institute's founding mandate, as social norms were superseded by a supranational discourse of bioethics suggesting adherence to a tale of "culture-free medicine" independent of the context in which AIIMS operates.[66]

In the absence of attention in the core curriculum, such workshops have the potential to open up a space at AIIMS in which the determinants of power that are reinforced in the clinical encounter are recognized and interrogated. In this case, however, the focus was predominantly on the effective utilization of communication as another medical instrument. Berna Gerber has noted that this tends to be true of approaches to communication methods at many medical schools. And while learning to ask open-ended questions and listen attentively is critical, this instruction is insufficient for preparing trainee doctors to effectively engage in what Gerber describes as "a very *human activity*, namely attempting to identify and treat disease and to lessen the suffering that comes with it."[67]

Empathy for the human other was certainly promoted at the workshop, and the default discourse of pragmatism as an excuse for disrespectful behavior was challenged. But the structures of difference that inform how communication influences the clinical encounter, the influence of positivist science, and the mutual perceptions of patients and doctors at AIIMS were not on the agenda. Communication was understood primarily as a tool to express sympathy and courtesy toward a human being who was differentiated not only by virtue of being a patient but often at AIIMS also by poverty and limited literacy. "Communication skills" were reduced to variations on etiquette, rather than stimulating an interrogation of the ways in which interactions in the clinic "both shape and reflect power relations, cultural identities, and social norms."[68]

Moving beyond this narrow approach demands greater recognition of clinical medicine as a fundamental and inescapable form of engagement with the human condition in all its wonderful and disconcerting complexity. In advocating for a curricula approach to clinical communication rooted in philosophy, Gerber stresses that "attention should be paid to the nature of patients as unique individuals who possess rationality and how this qualitatively distinguishes them from the relatively stable and simple physical phenomena, such as molecules, that are studied by certain natural sciences."[69] While this is undeniably necessary, I would return to Kleinman here and argue that the very same attention must be paid to clinicians as well. What Kleinman advocates is "a moral sensibility of critical self-reflection in caregiving," through which medical students can learn to consider "their own hidden and divided values and those of their patients and patients' families."[70] Without the committed integration of medical humanities (including anthropology, history, literature, and the arts) into a medical school's curriculum, Kleinman argues—as others have done[71]—this ethic of self-reflection is unlikely to be established. In the case of AIIMS, this is not a novel suggestion. In fact, the AIIMS Act, which founded the institution, contains a provision in its Article 14 to "provide for the teaching of humanities in the undergraduate courses."[72] This inclusion is likely to have been encouraged by the advocates of social medicine education involved in the original planning, but there is no evidence to suggest that such courses have ever taken place at AIIMS.[73]

Before concluding this chapter, perhaps it needs affirming that patients are by no means a passive entity whose own behaviors do not inform the clinical encounter. Nor has this chapter been an effort to "pit heroic patients against heartless doctors," as Veena Das puts it.[74] Where poverty and patienthood intersect, however, there is an inescapable power deficit vis-à-vis the medical establishment. It is telling, then, that in the wake of my time at AIIMS there was a wave of media appetite for stories about violent attacks on doctors by patients at hospitals across India, sparked by an incident in Maharashtra.[75] While I did not witness such violence at AIIMS, I was told of occasional incidents in which doctors were hurt. Following the initial media outrage, the attention offered an opportunity for the medical community to introspect and contribute to a sociological analysis of the motivations and potential remedies for physical violence in the clinic. It was also a potential teaching moment for colleges to take overt violence as a starting point for alerting students to the ways that power and structural violence operate in the clinic. Instead, the president of the AIIMS Resident Doctors Association responded in the media by announcing that doctors would be taught martial arts to defend themselves against patients.[76] The power differential between doctors and patients was interpreted in this case as a battle line.

In their discussion of the hidden curriculum in medicine, Hafferty and Franks note: "If surrounded by a medical culture that discourages certain feelings, introspection, or personal reflection, and buffeted by a basic science curriculum that emphasizes rote memorization, medical students may come to embrace . . . a reflexive myopia quite early in the training process."[77] Some faculty members at AIIMS place more importance on the communicative doctor-patient relationship than others, but no one has time, and few have the expertise, for in-depth attention to its implications for enduring social inequalities. Consequently, students learn through osmosis, by observing faculty members interacting with patients—experience that some students may supplement with their own reading and about which a few may reach critical conclusions of their own accord. They have no formal opportunities to reflect on the ways clinical encounters expose and reinforce the social structures that inform the lives of patients whose bioavailability, as students acknowledge, directly contributes to the value of an AIIMS education.

Patients at AIIMS are understood as simultaneously a hindrance to efficient practice and a bioavailable resource enhancing the institution's reputation for superior medical education. The result of this exchange of education for medical treatment, however, has little impact on the conditions that compel patients to travel to AIIMS for attention. As I go on to discuss in the next chapter, the large majority of students who benefit from this patient labor proceed to careers in private superspecialized practice rather than working in public primary or secondary healthcare that is endowed with little value, either by the institute or the society it reflects. Reflecting on my time at AIIMS once I had left Delhi, I realized that Dr. E's question about whether the institution was a hospital with a medical college attached or vice versa could be rephrased. I began to ask myself, "Who is AIIMS for?"

CHAPTER 6

GRADUATION
The Consequences of Excellence

FOR MANY OF THE STUDENTS I met at AIIMS, the end of the MBBS was already approaching. In Turner's sense, the students were on the brink of emerging from the liminal stage of their initiation into medicine and being reincorporated into society as doctors—in theory, at least. In reality, none of the students I met intended to practice medicine with an MBBS degree. In their work on medical education in South Africa, Pentecost and Cousins describe how "notions of vocation, political commitment, pastoral care, or even an entrepreneurial self" combine with "particular social, political, and professional histories of medicine" to produce competing values that trainee doctors have to negotiate as they consider their career paths.[1] This chapter is concerned with AIIMS students' perceptions of possible futures, which are shot through with discursive threads about achievement and reputation, family, the state, money, and technology. These threads combine to produce a hierarchy of biomedical practice that privileges a conventional wisdom about the devaluation of the MBBS degree and primary care and the logical pursuit of a career in urban, superspecialized medicine. Highly specialized medicine has implications: for the students compelled to pursue it, for the patients for whom it contains its own aspirational logic encouraged by the market dynamics of private healthcare, and for the role of medical education in training doctors to respond to the most pressing healthcare needs of a deeply inequitable society.

Not all medical students pursue medical professions, as we will see. However, whether a student aspires to a career as a superspecialist, a public health practitioner, a civil servant, or an entrepreneur, I argue that the choice is inextricable from the status bestowed upon AIIMS students at the moment of admission.[2] In her writing about young people in South India, Jocelyn Chua reflects: "Aspirational horizons are more than abstraction. They are the practical coordinates by which people locate themselves in the world, orient themselves to specific futures, and thus engage—and sometimes lose the capacity to engage—the present."[3] As I show in the following pages, the social life of winning a place at AIIMS, combined with the influence of norms around class, caste, gender, and kinship, produces expectations of the future and an individual's place within it, offering different but related impressions of what it means to be a graduate of India's most prestigious medical college.[4]

THE NEW CONVENTIONAL WISDOM

> Because familiarity is such an important test of acceptability, the acceptable ideas have great stability. They are highly predictable. It will be convenient to have a name for the ideas which are esteemed at any time for their acceptability, and it should be a term that emphasizes this predictability. I shall refer to those ideas henceforth as the conventional wisdom.
>
> —J. K. Galbraith, *The Affluent Society*

Of the 30 MBBS students with whom I conducted at least one in-depth interview during my time at AIIMS, 24 intended to pursue a medical career. Of these, all intended to study for a postgraduate (PG) qualification immediately after their MBBS. This intention contained a logic considered irrefutable: that to practice medicine with only an MBBS qualification was, if not an outright impossibility, certainly an act of professional self-harm:

> MBBS has become just like a preliminary examination, it's a "pre," so the actual doctor should at least do PG, otherwise you are not a doctor.
>
> —Nikhil

MBBS [alone] is considered nothing here; you are not considered a good doctor if you have only MBBS degree. You are supposed to do PG and then after that superspecialization. Even if you have done a postgraduation degree, you are not considered that good a doctor if you don't have a superspecialization degree. I guess that's the case all over now, not only in AIIMS. Everywhere people are encouraged to get more degrees. I don't like that trend basically.

—Neha

In India if you hold just an MBBS degree it makes no sense. I mean, you stand nowhere. Because no patient would want to go to a doctor who is not specialized. So everybody who wants to stay in medicine, everybody wants to do a specialization. No one can survive without a specialization here, with just an MBBS.

—Dilip

Dilip's statement echoed those of other students, but his particular reference to "survival" demonstrated its polyvalence, or multiple meanings, across contexts. Dilip's perception of survival was informed by his own socioeconomic milieu and his identity as an AIIMSonian. In a literal sense, his claim that specialization is key to survival is contradicted by moving around any but the most affluent urban neighborhood, and even more so beyond the city. The local MBBS doctor, for whom medical practice is a *means of* survival, remains a familiar figure in lower-income locales, occupying a space between the informal practitioner and the specialist. In the public health literature, MBBS doctors have tended to fare poorly in studies of accurate diagnosis and appropriate treatment.[5] This lends less credence to the perception that an MBBS doctor cannot survive at all than it does to the—still questionable—assumption that everyone practicing without a specialization is doing so because they were unable to secure a postgraduate seat.

Most students intending to study for a subsequent qualification planned to follow that with a superspecialization, a few weren't yet sure, and three intended to practice with "only" a PG. This seemed to reflect the sense that Krish and Rahul articulated of being on the cusp of a transition to the necessity of superspecialization; within a few years Krish thought medical students would have no choice at all:

[About] 20, 30 years back just MBBS doctors were doing all these things, no PG specialization or anything. But now PG is everything, without PG we can't do anything. It's becoming a trend that superspecialty is everything, without superspecialty we can't do anything. At present if I am postgraduating I will be just OK in medicine, but in my time in five-six years, I will be doing superspecialization.[6]

Krish's 20- or 30-year span encompasses the flourishing of India's corporate hospitals and the creation of a healthcare marketplace that not only purports to sell a "five star" experience to patients, but in doing so also influences the value of particular forms of medical practice in the eyes of both those patients and aspiring doctors:[7]

Nowadays all hospitals have become superspecialty hospitals, so they will need only one physician or something . . . and the work of the physician would be just to refer to other superspecialty. . . . [T]he physician will get only normal cases, no challenging cases, no system-wise cases, just infectious diseases or something like that. If you get any heart case, or brain case, or nephro case, you have to refer it. And he won't be getting that chance to treat a patient. But if you are superspecializing in something, you will be getting a particular group of patients . . . so I think after ten more years, the job of a physician will be just referring only.

—Agam[8]

Compounding this sense of the necessity of specialization was the fact that many students considered themselves insufficiently equipped to practice medicine upon completion of the MBBS. These anxieties become most evident during the final year internship, the function of which has become a point of contention among students and faculty alike.[9] With competition for a PG seat even tougher than that for the MBBS, there is a tacit understanding among students and faculty that the intern year will be used at least in part for entrance exam preparation, particularly the final eight-week elective posting.[10] Shyam blamed this situation on the theoretical emphasis of the PG entrance exam. He was attracted to the American system because of the greater attention paid to clinical skills:

[For] the competitive exam, which we have to clear for getting into a post-graduate program in India, we have to have a lot of theoretical knowledge. It's not the same as in the USA where you have to have good clinical skills too . . . if you haven't attended your clinics well, you are not bound to do very good in those exams. But in India it's much more of a theoretical paper. There is just one paper, one day, everybody gives that paper simultaneously. There are 200 MCQs, you solve those MCQs, the result comes on the basis of that. And boom, you are selected. So the person who sits in the room most of the time and reads the books instead of going to the college, he scores the most. So obviously, why would people want to go to the college?

The consequences of this are not unique to AIIMS—there is a broad recognition throughout Indian medical education that the development of clinical expertise among MBBS students is undermined by the pressures that the PG entrance exam places on the intern year. For some students, the study treadmill resumed long before the final year. Nikhil told me that one of his seniors had asked him at the start of his second year whether he had begun PG coaching yet: "I was like, no, not yet! I have just taken a prof examination, I want to take things coolly after so much studying."

The tension between these two imperatives is confirmed in an interview on a coaching website with an AIIMS PG entrance exam topper who notes the "mistake" of prioritizing the internship over exam preparation:

The mistake I did during my MBBS and internship days is to let the golden moments pass. I did not prepare during internship. I was enjoying my first days and first experiences as a doctor. My good friend . . . told me during my internship, "If you attend medicine postings too much, you are not going to get medicine in PG." While at the time I did not pay much heed to those words, but how true they were. It is very important to develop your clinical acumen during internship because after all, you are going to be a doctor. But for the unfortunate situation in our country, we need to devote the final years of MBBS and internship, which is better spent learning clinical skills, to prepare for PG entrance. I loved the internship, didn't read at all but it made me lose a year. I hope no one does the same mistake.[11]

Some students felt that this system had also been internalized by faculty, with the result that interns were not given sufficient attention. Shortly before we met for an interview, Shyam had written to the AIIMS director, complaining about his treatment as an administrative dogsbody and demanding that interns be given more opportunities to gain serious clinical experience; he had not received a reply by the time I left Delhi two months later. Anjali had little patience with faculty complaints about intern absences. "What do you expect?" she asked; few students could afford to take unpaid leave after graduating and so they had little choice other than to study during the internship. "That's the way the system is set up," she said. Deepak explained further:

> I'll tell you a scenario: if I am in AIIMS doing MBBS, my first goal is to get into the postgraduation. And when I am in postgraduation, my first goal would be to superspecialize. During that process, that patient interaction, that new learning from the patient, gets decreased. Because what an individual will tell himself [is], why would I waste my time? I can go to my room, read books, solve the MCQs and crack the superspecialization test—I can be a superspecialist.

The current situation appears to be self-perpetuating: MBBS graduates maintain that they have no chance of a viable career because they don't feel qualified to practice, which is itself in part because the time allocated for sustained clinical exposure is dedicated to studying for the postgraduate entrance exam. This argument doesn't hold in all circumstances, however, as we will see when students speak of wasting their skills in rural settings.

FRAGMENTED CARE

The journeys patients make through India's landscape of fragmented care are made visible through the documents that they are obliged to carry with them from appointment to appointment.[12] For all the faith invested in enhanced medical technologies, enormous power still lies in paper. Paper expresses a search for remedy through different letterheads, watermarks, the names of hospitals and doctors and laboratories around the country. The responsibility for papers on which illegible scribbles compress medical histories is expressed through care. An elderly couple produces a *parcha* that has been laminated for protection. Another patient's card is worn soft by touch, complete disintegration staved off only by shreds of yellowing tape. In Dr. A's OPD, a patient presents test results on a flimsy sheet of paper too damaged to be read with confidence; the process has to begin again. Documents are often kept in plastic bags with their origin stories in a clothes shop in Faridabad, or a wholesaler in Bharatpur, and in the plastic wallets stamped with monochrome flowers sold by an adolescent boy who can be found at the AIIMS gates in all weather. This legacy of protecting one's own medical records was visible during one of my ward visits, when a patient's husband pulled an envelope of CT films from beneath the mattress.

The fragmented body (1)
A middle-aged woman and her husband enter the consultation room.[13] The woman has been diagnosed with depression and multiple symptoms, including severe back pain. Her husband takes file after file from a plastic bag until a chaotic medical history narrated through test reports and records from different hospitals is spread across the desk. New test forms get mixed up with old reports as Dr. P leafs through the collection. He reads the last entry on each record, and it seems that only by meticulously combing the existing information is he able to find that the method of treatment he intends has already been prescribed by a doctor in another department. The husband seems to be aware of this. He asks Dr. P to give his wife an injection. Dr. P continues looking through the papers and finds a result that shows compression of the woman's spine. He sends them to the neurosurgery OPD. Dr. P describes this as one of a proliferation of cases of "reverse referral," whereby a patient goes directly to multiple specialists, before resorting to the general medicine OPD to seek clarification about the parallel courses of treatment, and even diagnoses, that she has been offered.

"PATIENT DEMAND"
An increase in patient demand was central to student narratives about the growth of superspecialization. I was frequently told that the ever-expanding private healthcare market, coupled with the internet, had

largely convinced patients of the expediency of consulting a specialist directly, leaving medical students little choice other than to pursue that career path. "Everyone wants to come to a superspecialist," a senior surgical resident told me. "If they have a headache, yes, let's consult a neurologist. For chest pain you consult a cardiologist." Krish explained to me how this worked in his home state of Kerala:

> What happens is that . . . if I get an MBBS degree from here and go to Kerala and if I sit in a clinic, patients won't come to me. That is the truth. We can't run a clinic with a mere MBBS degree. If I have a chest pain, if I am breathless, if I am having some breathing difficulty, what happens in Kerala is they will go directly to a chest specialist, who has not even MD medicine, rather DM in cardiopulmonology. They will go directly to the one with a DM. Even if you are a pediatrician, still you have to specialize in something, like pediatric cardiology. Earlier, surgeons used to do all the surgeries. Nowadays only the pediatric surgeons do the surgeries of children.

Much as the advertising of medical technologies is increasingly visible in low-income neighborhoods, so signs declaring the doctor within to be a cardiologist or dermatologist or fertility specialist have also proliferated. These small concerns exist in the shadow of the vast superspecialty corporate hospitals that have come to define the urban tertiary care landscape. It does not follow, however, that the direct pursuit of specialist care is universal. Veena Das asked residents of the low-income Delhi neighborhoods where she worked why they went to see specialist doctors: "It then emerged that there were 'normal' illnesses for which such remedies as indicated by the idea of the necessary harmony between doctors and patients worked, and then there were critical turning points in an illness—when, for instance, it became incomprehensible to their normal practitioners and then the 'big' doctors had to be accessed."[14] For the patients whom Das cites, direct resort to specialist doctors is precluded by both financial restraints and any assumed correlation between a headache and the necessity of consulting a neurologist. This doesn't mean that the information asymmetries of an unregulated healthcare market will not combine with aspirational consumerism to influence all parts of society in due course. At the time of my research, however, when explaining that no patient would choose to visit an MBBS doctor if the option of seeing a specialist directly were available, students spoke to the socioeconomic milieu from which they came and in which they intended to practice. They purported, however, to speak for all but the very poorest, and in doing so reflected Leela Fernandes's argument that "mainstream national political discourses . . . increasingly portray urban middle class consumers as the representative citizens of liberalizing India."[15] It is of these citizens, and the way in which the contemporary discourse of Indian healthcare increasingly frames them, that Baudrillard could have been writing in 1970, when he reflected: "Health today is less of a biological imperative linked to survival and more of a social imperative linked to status. It is less of a fundamental value and more of an 'assertion.'"[16]

Throughout this book I have illustrated different ways in which, as a living institution, AIIMS is both insulated from and permeated by the social and health inequalities beyond its gates. In the case of superspecialization, these dimensions interact to suggest that the institute is also *complicit* in that broader landscape. The observation that Indian patients who can afford it are increasingly going directly to specialists may be valid,[17] but students cannot confirm this hypothesis solely on the basis of their own experience. All AIIMS patients are by definition seen by a specialist, even if very many of them present themselves at the hospital unsure of which department they need to visit, having simply been directed to "go to AIIMS." Therefore, the narrative of patient demand is fueled within a particular socioeconomic reality, amid the increasing visibility of specialist services, and further consolidated by the confirmation bias lent by experience at AIIMS. What results from this is the new conventional wisdom that *all* patients have lost respect for the generalist, for reasons other than absent or inadequate care, leading to the hypervaluation of a career as a superspecialist.

In his work toward an anthropological theory of value, David Graeber describes the challenge of reconciling social structure and individual desire. The idea that value emerges through action points in this direction, by both understanding value as "the way people represent the importance of their own actions to themselves" and recognizing that "it can only happen through that importance being recognized by someone else."[18] For Graeber, "one might go so far as to say that while from an analytical perspective 'society' is a notoriously fluid, open-ended set of processes, from the perspective of the actors, it is much more easily defined: 'society' simply consists of that potential audience, of everyone whose opinion of you matters in some way, as opposed to those . . . whose opinion of you, you would never think about at all."[19] Value, then, becomes less exclusively about what someone wants, as the concept of desire expands to take into account feelings of obligation and perceptions of legitimacy. As Graeber puts it, drawing on the mid-twentieth-century anthropologist Clyde Kluckhohn: "[Values] are the criteria by which people judge which desires they consider legitimate and worthwhile and which they do not. Values, then, are ideas if not necessarily about the meaning of life, then at least about what one could justifiably want from it."[20] Max Weber described a dual process associated with the establishment of value—at one level, there is a tussle between members of a particular group (such as doctors), who vie "over their own peculiar notion of esteem," while at another "there is a larger struggle within the society as a whole to establish that particular notion of esteem, and the style of life with which it is associated, as the highest or most legitimate value."[21] In her work on psychiatry in North India, Sarah Pinto describes legitimacy as "an arrangement of ideas" that conditions postcolonial conversations about medicine.[22] The language of medical value also contains notions of legitimacy, of the types of medicine that are practiced and the types of people who practice them. This suggests why Dilip, quoted earlier, can speak about his career prospects in terms of "survival"—to survive in the milieu in and through which he and others consider the value of his actions is to thrive in a manner inaccessible by a neighborhood MBBS doctor.

Reflecting on her work on suicide among young people in Kerala, Jocelyn Chua notes the importance of understanding "how individuals and communities differently perceive and strive for a liveable life" as part of the larger project of interpreting the ways in which humans "discern possibility and encounter life's critical limits."[23] We can also connect these thoughts to Long and Moore's call to ground an understanding of achievement in a theory of human sociality.[24] Moore notes elsewhere that the self-other relations that achievement allows a subject to cultivate and transform, are

"set up in fantasy, based on a series of identifications and their circula-
tions . . . [and] shot through with social imaginaries and relays of power."[25]
Students' understandings of patients' perceptions of medical value, then,
combine with other influences to inform their own views and aspirations.

That said, some students were explicitly motivated to pursue superspecialization by an interest in a particular field. Vipul told me that the
more he learned about a subject the more interesting it became, which
motivated him to pursue particular fellowships during his MBBS studies,
and encouraged him to specialize. Balraj had developed an interest in "the
brain and spinal cord" at school and was more determined than ever to
become a neurosurgeon. Including a specific fellowship at Johns Hopkins
that he was aiming for, he knew that he would spend at least another decade training to reach his goal. The ambition to become a superspecialist
means that for a student like Balraj, the process of initiation continues.
Although this thought might be exhausting for some, for others perhaps
there is comfort in the prospect of the liminal period extending into the
future to become an almost permanent state of being.[26]

The emphasis on specialization, which is reflected in Indian health
policy more broadly, has troubling implications for a population that suffers so much for want of accessible and reliable primary care.[27] Students
were aware of this, and the personal logic of pursuing a superspecialized
career did not preclude critical thinking about the trend. Vipul's sense of
ambivalence was common:

> From the perspective of public health, it's not a good thing. Because the pa-
> tient has . . . a person specializing in a superspecialty like neurology will have
> to refer the patient for almost any other thing besides neurology. So from [a]
> public health perspective it's not good. But for patients who have a really bad
> intractable disease, for them, superspecialty is good. So it's like we need to
> balance these two things.

The dearth of seats for postgraduate medical training—approximately
14,000 for the country's 50,000 annual MBBS graduates at the time of
writing—was often cited as a natural counter to the specialization trend, a
logistical problem that also acted as a check on the number of specializing

graduates (although it was not considered a genuine threat to an AIIMSonian). This logical narrative stumbles, however, at the value question. Those
who fail to win a postgraduate seat do not necessarily accept the outcome
and enter general practice. A large number of graduates spend several years
sitting and resitting postgraduate entrance exams in an effort to join a specialist branch. When we met, Dr. Raman Kumar of the Indian Academy
of Family Physicians estimated in the absence of recorded data that India
had 300,000 MBBS graduates who weren't in full-time work. It is also
common for students unhappy with their allocated postgraduate branch
to resit exams in an effort to win a seat in their preferred specialization.
This regularly occurs in the Centre for Community Medicine at AIIMS,
which is used as a stopgap by junior residents seeking a different branch.

Here again we encounter the complicity of AIIMS in the wider medical landscape. As Dr. B said when we discussed this point: "not just AIIMS
graduates, *any* graduate—no one wants to be a general physician." AIIMS
has largely failed in its founding mission to systematically produce teaching
clinicians for the country, not least due to the lack of supporting infrastructure. It is, however, preeminent in the imagination of aspiring doctors and
is thus partly responsible for producing an idea of medical value not only in
the minds of its graduates, but also in the minds of those who would seek to
emulate the AIIMSonians they could not become for want of a higher rank.
In this sense, the "social knowledge," and the value, both produced and confirmed by the act of joining and graduating from AIIMS ripples far beyond
the gates of the institution to impact aspiring doctors across the country,
who look to AIIMSonians to demonstrate what it means to be the best.[28]

The fragmented body (2)

It is hot, and the fan is working hard; notebooks, pens, and a stethoscope
all act as paperweights.[29] A large man wearing a beautiful embroidered,
green-velvet hat shuffles into the room and dwarfs the plastic chair he is
guided into. He is aided by another man whom I initially imagine to be
his brother, but he identifies himself as a colleague. When they have left,
Dr. L says it is likely that the man is a paid attendant. The patient has
apparent neurological problems beyond a lack of physical coordination:

his speech is slow and slightly slurred, and he seems not to comprehend Dr. L's questions, even as she speaks deliberately slowly. The other man proffers a folder of carefully bound papers from various hospitals, including Apollo. He speaks a determined, deferential English to Dr. L and tries to offer clarification even though he clearly has little familiarity with the man's medical history. The patient's wife has cancer, the man says, and his children have "problems." The paper trail suggests diabetes, but Dr. L can't find a prescription, and neither the patient nor the man with him are able to tell her what medicines he is taking. Dr. L interprets the man's visible symptoms as pointing toward Parkinson's, compounded by the diabetes, plus hyperthyroidism and hypertension. But without any record of his current regimen, she does not want to risk any adverse drug interaction by writing a new prescription. She tells the attendant to take the patient to the neurology OPD and to return to see her the following week. I hope to see them again, but they don't turn up at the following week's OPD, which is also my last. According to Dr. L, this is a classic case of "episodic care," in which the absence of both a coherent medical record and a primary physician conspire to splinter a patient into a constellation of symptoms responded to differently by different specialists. For this patient, "treatment" seemed to be defined more as the act of presentation to a doctor than the receipt of dependable care.

REMAINING THE BEST

> I am doing MBBS from AIIMS, and after MBBS or PG,
> even in some community center or district hospital, I am not
> using myself as a whole. If I do superspecialty, I will become
> one of the few specialists, only for complicated diseases.
> If I am at AIIMS, so I should be like one of them.
>
> —Nikhil

In chapter 3, I showed that the trajectory for getting into AIIMS begins for many at a very young age and is informed by the possession of social and economic capital that determines educational opportunities and aspirational horizons. The reputation of AIIMS in the imagination of students, their families, and the public motivates the preparation demanded by the entrance exam and sustains expectations of what comes next. With this in mind, it was not surprising to hear AIIMS students imply that satisfaction was unlikely while there were still further, more competitive, targets in sight. Reputations are at stake:

> I think after coming here, your expectations are really high, so people expect a lot from you. They want you to become . . . you are not supposed to remain a MBBS. Even if someone wants to remain, there is a lot of pressure from parents, or from friends.
>
> —Ashish

> We can work, it's fine. You can be a part of a big hospital. But without specialization your name won't come anywhere. So the major thing is that there is some social stigma . . . other thing is that people are getting more and more degrees. So this is a competitive world, you have to cope up with that.
>
> —Azam

In this light, the achievement of admission is not so much a singular event with enduring consequences, as the first in a chain reaction of achievements, each of which is pursued in reference to the last. The state of constant achievement befitting an AIIMSonian is not always comfortable, however. Rahul's father had worked for several years as a general practitioner before pursuing a postgraduate qualification. But Rahul felt that for him, appealing though a break may have been, the challenge of resuming studying would have been too great. "I have been studying since school," he said. "It's a cycle going on." A senior resident told me that he felt his career had involved very little conscious decision making. "I never thought . . . I just thought that I have to do this, I have to do this, and things went on their way."

We have seen that families are often influential in students' decisions to apply to medical college. The certificates and newspaper articles proudly displayed on the walls of a home demonstrate the fact that a child's achievement amounts to more than "the successes of a lone striving individual," in Susan Bayly's words.[30] In her work on attainment in postsocialist Vietnam, Bayly describes "achiever collectivities," by which we can understand the families, teachers, and peer groups that contribute to the achievement attributed to an individual AIIMSonian and to whom that individual may feel a degree of accountability.[31] Anjali alluded to it, but only Azam explicitly spoke of stigma, of his "name not coming anywhere" if he didn't compete with those considered most successful. To exit that ecosystem is to go from having one's picture in the newspaper on entering AIIMS to rendering oneself invisible in front of the audience through which one's sense of value is confirmed.[32]

To pursue ever-greater specialization, then, is not only to continue achieving in and of itself but also to continue differentiating oneself (and one's family) ever more from the rest of an aspirational population. The accrual of greater and greater specific expertise—to be one of a handful of neurosurgeons in a country of 1.2 billion people, for example—is a route to an unassailable existential security in the eyes of a young person in the middle class of a social system in which everyone is perpetually jostling for status, reputation, and the reassurance of a decent life. For our students, this trajectory, and the privileged status the final destination connotes, begins with the letter of admission to AIIMS.

THE (SUPPOSED) DECLINE AND
FALL OF THE FAMILY DOCTOR

In his work on aging in India, Lawrence Cohen describes a popular narrative that laments the gradual dissipation of the joint-family living arrangement, and the relationships it connotes, at the mercy of the three impersonal and relentless forces of globalization, Westernization, and urbanization.[33] This discourse of transition from a golden age to a corrosive present expresses the anxieties of middle-class society grappling with the variable demands—and rewards—of postliberalization modernity. A similar discourse pertains to the history of medical care, illustrated through the devaluation of general practice and family medicine. This narrative holds that, once upon a time, everyone had a local family doctor who attended to multiple generations of the same family, was considered virtually part of the family, and was invited home to celebrate weddings and festivals.[34] It is a narrative firmly rooted in the urban middle-class experience; some of my interlocutors were keen to stress that the family doctor phenomenon survives in smaller towns, as though defending them against accusation of the ethical erosion of personal relationships under way in the city.

As the last generation of these family doctors dies—the story goes—there is no one to replace them, and patients are left with little choice but to approach venal superspecialists who overcharge for unnecessary tests and are motivated more by money than concern for the patient.[35] This nostalgia is the counternarrative to that of patient demand for superspecialized treatment, and one that, anecdotal though it is, may be the precursor to a revival of family medicine under corporate auspices, as both existing healthcare brands and new ventures recognize the market potential of a more personal approach to medicine.

Family medicine entails its own postgraduate qualification in India and is therefore not the direct equivalent of an MBBS doctor. It is common, however, for an MBBS doctor to undertake a postgraduate course in family medicine alongside her general medical practice. India's 2002 national health policy articulated a need to prioritize family medicine, but the promising policy went the way of so many others, and the 2015 policy did not address the same concern. The more fundamental impediment, however, is that family medicine is not a requirement of the MBBS curriculum as stipulated by the Medical Council of India (MCI). Nor is it taught at AIIMS.[36] The National Board Diploma course produces 200 annual graduates in family medicine and the MD program remains negligible, with—at the time of writing—only two seats offered annually at the Government Medical College in Calicut. The MCI—a body entirely composed of specialists—has been accused of having a vested interest in preventing the establishment of family medicine for fear of it stemming the flow of patients seeking specialist treatment.[37]

Anjali encountered family medicine as a potential career only when she began to explore her options independently. As she put it to me, "Even if we were interested in family medicine, we wouldn't know, because we aren't exposed to it." Even an unusual student such as Hari, who planned to be a general practitioner at home in Calicut—whose college had India's only two MD seats in family medicine—was unaware of this option and maintained that he would need to study for an MD in internal medicine. When I asked her about the likelihood of an AIIMS student pursuing a career in family medicine, Anjali said:

> I've interacted with students from England and everywhere, I've done projects with them and I realized for them family medicine is actually another residency. I mean, you have a residency in family medicine, and then you can stop there. It's actually considered quite good you know, you are not like, "family medicine, pssht." So the thing is for us, at least in AIIMS, no one wants to be the general guy, he wants to be the one who is at the apex of his particular field and the only way to reach there is by superspecializing. I mean, who are you when you are a family medicine guy? You are just another doctor in a small locality. Secondly, everyone looks at finances and everything. No family medicine doctor makes any good amount of money. While when you are doing a superspecialized procedure, you can charge as your fantasy wishes. So yeah, I mean that's something that's going to be . . . that was predictable at the very onset of . . . when you join medicine, or even when you take up biology.

A former AIIMS director I interviewed offered a more succinct appraisal of the situation: "AIIMS killed the GP."

As we saw in chapter 2, following its establishment in 1956, AIIMS was not supported by the primary and secondary care infrastructure necessary for it to function as a tertiary referral institute. As the former director explained:

> [AIIMS] didn't take more than five years to establish itself. . . . And soon the country knew that it was an institution which was different. Now, where did we go wrong is what I would like to tell you. AIIMS, as I said, was created to be a center for teaching. Right? And I can't say AIIMS went wrong, but the government went wrong. They thought, "we have created the All India Institute, we won't do anything else." You see? So the net result was that the state of Delhi, where, as the population grew, you should have created centers of healthcare, of medical education—the government didn't do it. So the net result was that AIIMS, which was a specialized sector, where the emphasis was really on postgraduate education—everyone who had a cough and cold and diarrhea started coming. And we had no means to close our doors. So

you paid for your efficiency. You should have really not have seen the primary care, secondary care, and you should have been looking at tertiary care. That is what you were created for. That is what it was for. But since the government did not create other places of healthcare, where do people go? People said we will lie outside the hospital till we get admission. Because the government did not step in to [provide] healthcare on a national scale.

I asked at what stage patients first began appearing at AIIMS with symptoms requiring primary care:

Day one. It just increased. There was nothing you could do . . . in 1960, the early '60s, they envisaged that we will have 600 patients coming in a day to the OPD. By the 1990s, that is 30 years later, there were 3,000 people coming in, which means five times more, and today there are 10,000 every day, I'm told, coming to the OPD. Of course it was realized that we ought to do mid-course corrections. A committee was set up to look into the working of AIIMS and give mid-course corrections. And we did prepare a report for that and gave it to the government; it must be lying somewhere. We said, separate out primary care, secondary care. We can't close our doors, but we can separate out [levels of care]. But it wasn't done. That still can be done. If the government wants, it can be done.[38]

Dr. S, one of the first AIIMS faculty members, agreed:

When it started it was meant to be a referral center, it was not meant to be a general hospital. And that character could not be kept due to reasons, probably, of population pressures, or patients or whatever. If it had remained as a referral center, it would have been easier for people to work. I feel sorry for those clinicians who are seeing loads and loads of patients, you know. I mean it's not fair to expect them to work under these conditions. Otherwise so far I think it's holding on, it's bursting at the seams, but it's holding on.

The only educational advantage of this situation was squandered, the director said:

Now the only saving grace was . . . the undergraduates learnt primary care also. Otherwise the graduates of AIIMS would learn only tertiary care. But as medicine developed, specialties developed and superspecialties developed, the basic material in AIIMS was so good that they could very easily slip into specialties and superspecialties. Of the 50 students that got in there, I think maybe all 50 of them would do post-graduation. So what did we do? We killed the GP. So these are mistakes that were made. We did not see GP as a specialty; we did not see emergency medicine as a specialty.[39] But we saw all the cardiac, neuro, nephro, what have you, as our own specialties and we created all those. But we killed the GP and we killed emergency medicine.

Madan heard similar criticisms in the 1970s. "The emphasis on specialties and superspecialties produces doctors who are unwilling or unable to deal with the most common disorders and therefore most patients," one faculty member said. Another told him that "right from its inception, the institute has had a highly trained and specialty-oriented faculty. The result is that we have here zealots cultivating their specialties and a sound general education suffers by default. How can you produce good doctors without emphasizing *general* medicine and surgery?"[40]

In the previous chapter I discussed how AIIMS students benefit from exposure to a very large number of patients with diverse conditions. This dimension resurfaces here in relation to the claim by the former director that AIIMS bears responsibility for the demise of the general practitioner, despite the advantages of student exposure to primary care. It feeds into my contention that AIIMS is complicit in the broader landscape of health inequity given that the value patients add to students' education is not converted by the institution into an attribution of value to the medical generalist whose skills may partially alleviate the demand for nontertiary treatment at AIIMS. Too little attention was paid to questions of social accountability at AIIMS, Dr. L told me. The institute took more pride in students' USMLE results than in those who went to work in primary care, she said, and the lack of role models was another impediment to the pursuit of alternative careers.

The fragmented body (3)

A middle-aged woman enters the consultation room alone. She appears malnourished and disorientated. Her speech is vague, sluggish, and difficult to comprehend, although she says very little. Behind her ears linger a few traces of Holi pink, and in my mind her life briefly expands beyond the hospital, becoming bigger than the affliction that has brought her here. Among the papers she gives to Dr. L are an insulin prescription and a note from a cardiologist. Given the communication difficulty, Dr. L is not able to tell whether the woman has had certain tests done, or whether she is taking any medication. She tells me that the woman's visit is an example of "doctor shopping"—another symptom of unstructured care and the conventional wisdom that has become attached to the pursuit of specialized treatment. But nothing about this woman suggests a capacity for such strategic pursuit of multiple opinions, and I wonder what is really going on, and what her story is.[41]

DOCTOR-CITIZENS

All the student voices in this book are representative of an aspirational middle class. But within this broad bracket there was also great variation, illustrated most clearly by the experiential gulf between Anjali, upper-caste and the latest of five generations of city doctors, and Sushil, from a Scheduled Tribe family with minimal literacy and no English. These variations did not have automatic corollaries, however, when it came to students' aspirations.

In her work on the discursive relationships between merit and caste identity at IIT Madras, Ajantha Subramanian describes the ability of upper castes to erase the contribution not just of accumulated social and cultural capital but also the role of the state in their achievements. Writing about the career aspirations of IITians, she notes that while the merit of earlier generations was established by becoming a scientific professional associated with the state, these days "merit has acquired a new valence as the transcendence, not just of politics, but also of the state and the public sector."[42] Subramanian cites a professor who bemoans the fact that an IIT education has become little more than a subsidized ticket to a lucrative private-sector salary, frequently outside India.[43] This lament is also heard at AIIMS, although my conversations with students revealed more ambiguity about the public sector than that heard by Subramanian among

IIT students and alumni. This may be another example of the distinction between engineering and medicine, the latter of which retains an aura of vocation and public service (even if this is not always warranted), despite its frequent coupling with engineering as an interchangeable career option.

Students' experiences of the state differed, and therefore so did its influence over their aspirations for the future. For a student from an affluent background, AIIMS was likely to be her first encounter with the state as a provider of education and of healthcare. For those already acquainted with the state in this guise, however, AIIMS represented continuity and the ongoing accumulation of obligation alongside achievement. Nikhil was very conscious of having accrued a debt to the state for his education at one of the Jawahar Navodaya Vidyalaya schools administered by the central government. He lived at the school from class 6 to 12 and recalled that they provided him with everything, from education and accommodation, the books he needed, down to clothes and a toothbrush. "From class 6 onwards I have been totally government funded," he said. Would this affect his future plans? I wondered. He nodded and confirmed that he would stay and practice medicine in India—although not necessarily in a government facility. *Banta hai itna* (I owe this much), he said.

Azam had not been to a government school, but he also explained his commitment to working in India as a means of repaying a debt he felt he had accrued through his highly subsidized training at AIIMS. At the time, an AIIMS MBBS cost less than 6,000 rupees (£60). Azam said: "So whatever I am getting is the money of the public. Whatever I do is, like, I do with their money. It's their tax, VAT, even if they buy a packet of biscuits they are giving some tax and that is the money behind my studies. So I have some duty and I have to pay them back."

The "clash of perceived obligations" to family, profession, state and patients that Wendland observed among medical students in Malawi and Pentecost and Cousins identified in South Africa was also visible at AIIMS, along with a heightened sense of attachment to home among students intent on remaining in India.[44] However, a commitment to staying at home did not necessarily equate with a sense of obligation toward national welfare or development.

Historically, large numbers of AIIMS graduates have left India to establish careers elsewhere, predominantly in the United States.[45] While considered unremarkable among current students, and treated as a matter of pride by the AIIMS administration according to Dr. L, emigration remains an emotive subject among older doctors who have spent their careers in India. "What did you give back to this institution? To this nation? Nothing," said Dr. E when we discussed this. "How many bricks have they laid here? None." An interlocutor in Madan's study in the late 1970s described the emigration of up to 80% of the early AIIMS batches as "a colossal national waste."[46] This trend has slowed in recent years. Students repeatedly told me that the increasing opportunities for a comfortable life as a doctor in India made going abroad unnecessary. Others chose to stay at home to remain close to families and friends, even if the US still held some allure. Of those intending to go to the United States, several students already had a support network of friends and family in place. A couple of students planned to study and then return to India to practice, although this claim was often met with skepticism by others. Neha and Anjali both challenged the assumption of financial motivations for emigration—their ostensibly conventional plans disguised the pursuit of an independence denied them at home, as I explain toward the end of this chapter.

Vivek was unique among the students I spoke with for having spent part of his childhood in the United States, which had engendered an expectation of, and comfort with, global mobility. Vivek's perspective was that of a nascent global citizen, for whom distance and national borders were no impediment to making a contribution to India:

> Even if I choose to live in the US, I don't think that there is any reason I will not be able to help out India, because it's an era of globalization. People do video conferences, people go here and there. They deliver lectures, they start seminars, they do workshops. I know an emergency physician who is a family friend in the US and he started emergency medicine departments in about four colleges in India. So it doesn't mean that you cannot help out India if you are not living here.

The growth of digital healthcare means that this approach will become more common within India too, as doctors reluctant to leave urban centers are offered more opportunities to contribute to rural medical provision from a distance.

Alongside their expertise, AIIMS doctors attract respect for the material sacrifice that they are believed to make by practicing public-sector medicine. There is an ethical assumption embedded in the admiration of senior faculty members who remain at AIIMS despite the allure of high private-sector salaries, just as there is in the judgement of those who left for the United States several decades ago, never to return. These days there is little reason to assume that a desire to stay in India equates to a desire to work in the public sector, particularly if it is the new opportunities in corporate healthcare that are discouraging graduates from emigrating. That said, oversimplified narratives of a public-private dichotomy have long obscured the regular transit of patients and doctors between sectors in pursuit of treatment and/or employment.[47] Rama Baru has written about retired AIIMS doctors and their views of the private sector and argues for a more nuanced understanding of the processes that have led to the alienation of both patients and clinicians from public healthcare in India. These processes, she suggests, are associated with the changing composition of the Indian middle class and the economic structures in which they are embedded. Echoing an exaggerated the narrative of "the Fall" of the Indian middle classes, from the postindependence Nehruvian era of a frugal lifestyle of national service to a contemporary postliberalization predicament of selfish consumerism,[48] Baru's informants describe a change in the Indian medical profession in recent decades as opportunities to earn large salaries in the private sector have increased.[49] At the other end of the scale, however, small, local private practices have always been a prominent feature of the healthcare landscape.[50]

In our conversations, students often began by articulating a preference for public over private practice, before explaining the various structural and ideological impediments to fulfilling this ideal. Some students did have a tangible commitment to public service. Rahul's desire to work in a public hospital was a direct consequence of the debt he felt he had accrued during his education, coupled with a distaste for profit-making from suffering:

I'm not interested [in the private sector]. Because they charge you, just for a basic consultation, so many hundreds . . . and here we are doing this thing for free. So that would be a wrong thing on my part that I am exploiting my . . . the government is spending . . . I'm studying in 100 dollars and I am still taking so much money from the people who spent taxes on my education! That would be a bad thing. They have invested in me, so I need to pay back also. Obviously the service is not as good and sophisticated as provided by private . . . but when I go to work in a private, I will feel like I'm taking benefit of someone's disease, that he is suffering and I'm taking advantage of it. That is a bad thing to do; that is what I have been taught.

For Balraj, too, working in the public sector was a question of personal ethics that guarded against the corrupting nature, as he saw it, of private medicine:

I want to work in public sector because the kind of patients I want I will get only in these public-sector hospitals. Because in private sector it's a very difficult job, and once you enter private sector you tend . . . I don't know why but your mentality becomes like you have to earn money only, you forget any humanity. So I don't want to carry that ethos in my life. So I want to work . . . if I get a chance I would like to work in AIIMS only. That is the best place.

The exceptional nature of AIIMS New Delhi was reflected by its unique position within students' aspirations. More than one student was inclined to pursue a private career for the sake of material comforts, unless a position at AIIMS arose, offering status and research opportunities in exchange for a lower salary.[51]

Alongside a feeling that he would gain greater satisfaction from treating disadvantaged patients, Krish anticipated less anxiety in public practice:

Because no competition will be there during my practice. People will come, people will go, I will treat. But in private sector, the competition among the doctors is higher. Because to get the patients . . . if the patients are less, [doctors] will have problems with the management of the hospital. But in public sector, nothing like that. If we are sincere, we can do work even though the money we get is less, but satisfaction will be higher, stress level will be less. Happier life.

For Mihir, in contrast, the only advantages of working in a government hospital were that he thought doctors were less threatened by litigious patients, and there was less of an unethical financial nexus between doctors and diagnostic facilities.[52] These supposed advantages posed their own constraints however, and Mihir was not sure he was willing to defend the marriage of medicine and ethics if it meant denying himself more lucrative opportunities: "So if you want to practice ethically . . . government is still better than private. But what I have seen is that it's not that rewarding. You can stick to your ethics for only some time, after that you feel you are missing out on a big part. . . ."

WASTE, ABSENCE, LACK

> These kids have been told that they are the best 36 students
> in the whole country. I mean, what could you tell them
> to persuade to be the local community guy . . . right?
>
> —Anjali

All MBBS students spend seven weeks of their fourth year at the Comprehensive Rural Health Services Project in Ballabhgarh, Haryana. During one of my visits, I accompanied students to a particular *anganwadi* center that acts as an exemplar of the services prescribed under the central government's Integrated Child Development Services program. The walls of the center's small rooms were painted in turquoise distemper, adorned with the weekly menu and posters depicting various government schemes and exhortations to vaccinate children. One poster was a calendar of dates relevant to health policy. Students began to take photos of it on their phones, converting it into a study aid for memorizing the dates that they already knew would appear on the community medicine exam. This seemed to encapsulate the general student reaction to the community medicine posting as a box to be ticked, a list of policy provisions to be remembered, and an interesting glimpse into "village life," with little bearing on their career aspirations.

Anjali summarized the general perception of community medicine among her peers:

It's pretty underwhelming, yeah. You talk to anyone about community medicine and they will be like, there is this book, and you are supposed to read
about sanitation and mosquitoes. Like who wants to know about that and
how to make a toilet? I mean we are going to be people who are going to
cut out appendixes in five minutes! It's seen as a thing that needs to be completed in order to reach the goal of cutting out appendixes.

Susan Bayly writes about the "complex geographies"—the temporal and
spatial dimensions—of achievement.[53] We can also view achievement and
aspiration at AIIMS through a spatial lens, via the demarcation between
the rich prospects of the city and the absences perceived to lie beyond. In
her work on urban doctors moving to rural Rajasthan, Jocelyn Killmer
describes absence as the defining lens through which her interlocutors
understood the rural landscape, including its people.[54] At AIIMS, students
cited notoriously poor medical infrastructure as the main obstruction to
working in the public sector beyond the city.[55] A lack of security, particularly
for women, of a support network and of surrounding infrastructure were
also features that underscored the comparative abundance of the city.[56]

Through its neglect of public healthcare beyond the city, the state appears to collude in the production of value attached to urban, superspecialized, and usually private medical practice. For some students, this situation
emphasized the unique value of an AIIMSonian by illuminating the type
of medicine they could not be expected to practice, as Vipul explained:

The public health system is more . . . the government, I don't know, they expect
too much. As I said, the primary healthcare system, they don't have enough,
they don't have ECGs, X-rays or anything. . . . If they want, if they expect an
MBBS doctor to go over there and practice, so you have to give him enough
opportunities to practice what he has gained all five years. But the government
won't. . . . [T]hat is why most people don't want to go over there. And, like, the
pay is not an issue at all, because in Delhi and Haryana area, the pay is enough.

Sushil agreed that money was not the primary deterrent and argued
that doctors should be willing to improve rural practice if the government
does its part to improve conditions:

Government should make . . . their state primary health centers should be like, their conditions and environment should be like people can work there. Like at primary health centers, there are buildings but they don't even have an X-ray machine. They don't have medicines there, they have limited amount of medicines only. They have no beds . . . no doctor. The doctor is somewhere doing his private practice and he is getting his attendance done somehow and he is practicing outside and he is earning money . . . So somehow on our parts also, we should also think as a doctor. The health system is not a money-making business. Engineering, lawyer, businessman, they are. If you have chosen this profession then you should not be going behind money. You can't compare health in terms of money, someone's life in terms of money. I think it's on both, on our part and the government's part, to change the primary health system. We should also be ready to go there and work.

Pentecost and Cousins note that in South Africa the dominant archetype in "institutional and public imaginations of medicine" is "the doctor who saves lives while advancing medicine and science through technology."[57] Reflecting on Malawi, Claire Wendland suggests that "biomedical technologies may also shape values even when they are absent: that is, they alter the medical imaginary, and in so doing, they alter its economy."[58] At AIIMS, the thought of inadequate technology beyond urban centers informed students' perceptions of political priorities, and by extension the relative legitimacy or value, of particular types of medical careers. I do not suggest here that concerns over a lack of technology are unfounded or that highly technologized medicine should be considered "divorced from affect, nor from 'caring,'" as DelVecchio Good puts it.[59] Indeed, absent technology also implicitly informs perceptions of how the state comprehends and enacts (or neglects) a responsibility for the lives of the predominantly rural poor, whose bioavailability in the city may augment medical training, but who are rarely the recipients of similarly competent care at home.[60]

For some, however, there was a more complex understanding about rural medicine embedded in the frustration about absent technology. There was a feeling that this was not the sort of medicine an AIIMSonian was meant to practice because it was insufficiently complicated. Nikhil spoke of not using himself "as a whole" even if he were to work as a specialist in a district hospital, while Mihir described it as "a waste of effort":

> With the type of training we are given, if you go to a peripheral center, you will be seeing mostly cases which won't utilize all the knowledge you have. We are given so much knowledge in these five years . . . plus maybe three years of postgraduate training—a person with so much knowledge, why would he want to waste all this effort he has put in? He will be able to do nothing, write paracetamol or something for everyone.

Rural practice was often associated with the symptomatic treatment of colds, fevers, and diarrhea; with the prescription of rehydration salts or paracetamol and the bandaging of minor wounds.[61] It was not only a lack of equipment that discouraged students, then; it was also the perception of "rural illnesses" that this absent infrastructure reinforced—a lack of sufficiently complex conditions to do justice to the superiority of an AIIMSonian's training.[62] This recalls a reflection by Subramanian on her discussions with IIT alumni that their sense of exceptionalism was derived in part from a feeling that the IITs were "temporally out of step with the nation"—that the institution were created before the rest of the country was ready to absorb the graduates it produced.[63]

The complex unfolding consequences of achievement and its associated ideas about value and legitimacy become apparent when we place this perception of the insufficient challenge of rural healthcare alongside the testimony of students in the previous chapter who considered themselves unequipped to practice medicine *of any kind* after the MBBS.

In Malawi, Claire Wendland observed a radicalization of some medical students as they encountered the shortcomings of a "pathological" government and a "pathogenic" national economy, which informed both the devastating poverty and disease that brought patients to hospital, and students' own inability to provide effective medicine in the face of resource constraints and a corrupt politics of healthcare.[64] This status quo produced a sense of identification with patients, an alliance within a shared predicament that allowed for what we might think of as the "shared existential moments" that I have argued are uncommon at AIIMS.[65]

Wendland notes the contrast between this student behavior and that reported in the Global North, where research consistently highlights the "cynical talk" about patients by students.[66] In my experience, students at AIIMS hovered somewhere in between these two orientations—as indeed does the hospital infrastructure and the socioeconomic nature of India itself. In this book, we have seen that the power differential between doctors and patients at AIIMS is exacerbated by socioeconomic difference, and that poor patients with little education are considered both an impediment to efficiency and a bioavailable educational resource at a well-funded institution. But we have also seen that students are cognizant of the shortcomings of India's public healthcare system that compel patients' journeys to AIIMS in large numbers, and aware, sometimes acutely, of the conditions in which many of these patients live. The Malawian students, by contrast, training in a resource poor hospital, consider themselves different sorts of victims of the same systemic failures that afflict their patients. Wendland suggests that this empathic relationship is productive of a form of biological citizenship in which doctors can participate alongside patients: "If we understand the notion of biological citizenship as, to some extent, an instance of the traditional 'patient' role writ large (that is, a collective patient identity, based in shared biological vulnerability or pathology, and entitled to make therapeutic claims on the state), then we might also conceive a parallel reconfiguration of the traditional doctor role on the national or transnational stage. Here the doctor's responsibilities for diagnosis and treatment are exercised in relation not (solely) to the patient's body but rather in relation to the collective patient, the body politic."[67] At AIIMS, it was not necessarily a shared current experience of straitened circumstances that produced the possibility of a biological, or medical, citizenship encompassing both doctors and patients. Rather, it seemed to be inspired by preexisting experience and/or an undertaking during the MBBS to seek an extracurricular education in the politics of health, as in the case of Purush:

> Healthcare has been like a luxury for people. So they are the kind of people, the ruling classes, they get good healthcare out of whatever institutions we have. They personally don't want to focus on it because they are not pro-

people governments as such. Because they haven't come out of any movement as such, because their selection of the candidates or whatever, the selection of the government, that is not true democracy. So when there will be a broader movement, which will change the form of democracy, obviously the healthcare and education and everything will change. And even in isolation they keep these small pilot projects and movements which keep changing, some reforms. But I still think these reforms are not enough because anyway people are not interested in changing it, whoever is at the helm. They keep calling people who are doing this good job . . . they keep calling them and put them on advisory board of government, but there is no use of that if you don't have the political will towards working and economically funding it. That poverty and neglect thing we talked about . . . so ultimately even if you focus on the primary healthcare but don't focus on the people's overall standard of living and poverty, then also there is no meaning to that. So a holistic approach towards the thing and political and economic dedication, is needed. And that cannot come out of these kind of systems that we have right now.

Both Purush and Sushil had undergone a form of political education at AIIMS under the influence of former students and particular faculty members. Inspired by projects such as Jan Swasthya Sahyog, a community health service established by AIIMS alumni in rural Chhattisgarh, Purush and Sushil planned to complete their postgraduate training and establish rural healthcare projects of their own, focusing on local needs while remaining fully aware of the unlikeliness of any forthcoming political sea change.

As at the college Wendland studied in Malawi, an AIIMS education places the highest value on curative, individualized medicine at the expense of public health and preventive medicine, despite the periodic efforts of the community health faculty.[68] In South Africa, while students are required to complete a year of community service following graduation, Pentecost and Cousins stress that medical training still privileges "the pursuit of individual career advancement over commitment to patient wellbeing and attention to the ways in which suffering is structurally produced."[69] As I relate in her story later in this chapter, Anjali was initially attracted to a career in public health after her stint in Ballabhgarh made clear to her the failure of the MBBS curriculum to teach students a comprehensive politics of health:[70]

I don't think at any point in the curriculum we are actually given a comprehensive introduction to how everything really works. Yeah, we are taught all the peritoneum folds that cover the rectum and everything, but no one really teaches us where the guidelines are coming from, what's going on at the international level, what kind of pressures are interacting, how policies are being made, who is devising the policy . . . No one really talks about it, because it's kind of . . . I mean I don't know, it's probably our fault and it's probably . . . it's a very multi-factoral kind of problem, it's nobody's specific fault. It's just that we come with this kind of conception that OK, I am going to open up people's brains and that kind of thing, I don't need to know all those kind of things. And the doctors are themselves practicing physicians who are into whatever they do and they only talk about that. So there is no one who is going to tell you about this as a whole. The community medicine faculty tries, but fails. One, because no one really thinks it's very important to know all those kind of things. And secondly, I don't believe the faculty is very good at communicating it either.

By way of contrast, Mihir's candid reflection on his time in Ballabhgarh made clear that it would have little impact on his worldview or his future plans, at least in the medium term:

Generally you feel that when you are in such kind of places like AIIMS and you know what facilities are available and you know what you can do with them, you would want to work in the best possible sense. And we aren't that much socially conscious that we will be moved by all that, you know, poverty, or basic things being absent in those regions. It really doesn't move us that easily. So yeah, our stint in Ballabhgarh it increased our awareness definitely. But I won't say that it convinced me to go into public health, as of now. Maybe if I am say financially secure and totally content at 40 or 45 I'd think of that. But not now.[71]

Students planned different approaches to resolving what they understood as India's problems. Shankar was already pursuing an entrepreneurial route, establishing a health education business with colleagues. He intended to apply to joint MBA-MPH programs in the United States, with Harvard as his top choice. Leaving medicine altogether and pursuing an MBA to enter the financial sector was an option that students mentioned in a generic sense, but no one I spoke with intended to do this. Among those who planned to leave clinical medicine, all but two were doing so to join the Indian Administrative Service (IAS), the most popular of the fiercely competitive civil services.

These students shared a perceptible discomfort with the consequences of poverty and inadequate healthcare provision that they had encountered, whether at AIIMS, at the Ballabhgarh clinic, or, in Tashi's case, at home in Arunachal Pradesh. Unlike the radicalization that Wendland observed among students in Malawi, however, these AIIMSonians did not intend to enact their critique of the state through patient-allied medicine, but by becoming part of the state machinery itself, in the hope of one day obtaining sufficient influence over its operation. Karan had come to this conclusion after spending several months at a community health center in mountainous Uttarakhand following his graduation from AIIMS:

> As a doctor I cannot work for the emancipation of the underprivileged. Because there are many factors, primarily the lack of basic amenities in interior Himalayas. Unless and until they are going to get that, I am doing nothing good for them. Nothing sustainable . . . there will not be a positive sustainability. You know I am there, I am trying to provide them healthcare to my best, but it's not going to be sustainable.

In the context of HIV/AIDS testing, Sheikh and Porter have written that many Indian doctors feel possessed of the "negative power" necessary to resist governmental guidelines and act according to their own judgement, but not of the "positive power" to voice their objections in public as a means to influencing policy making itself.[72] This, they suggest, is a symptom of an unproductive mutual exclusivity between public health discourse and medical practice in India. A perception of this divide seemed to inform the decisions of AIIMS students to leave medicine, although more often for the civil services than for a career in public health, suggesting that their exposure to community medicine at AIIMS had failed to convince them of its potential for influence over health policy and ground realities.

A shared ambition to join the IAS did not translate into a shared strategy for transforming Indian healthcare, however. While Neha spoke of designing new medical curricula, Santosh was intent on promoting behavior change through surveillance and punishment. He intended to suspend poor-performing doctors and teachers. "If I scold them in public, I think that will work," he told me, and I wondered if his experience at AIIMS had done anything to disabuse him of that notion.

Dr. N was one of the faculty members who tried to informally introduce students to the political economy of Indian healthcare. He was sympathetic to students' instincts to leave medicine, but impatient with what he saw as their naïveté. "They shouldn't live in that fools' paradise," he said. "They can't do anything if they join the bureaucracy. They can do more as doctors." But who will convince AIIMS students of that? "We need good role models at this stage," Dr. E had already told me. "Very badly."

PRECLUDED FUTURES

> The ultimate freedom is not the freedom to create or
> accumulate value, but the freedom to decide (collectively
> or individually) what it is that makes life worth living.
> —David Graeber, *Toward an Anthropological Theory of Value*

Students' achievements occur within a web of relationships. On the one hand, this is usefully akin to illuminating the different forms of requisite capital that are obscured by a narrative of individual merit. But on the other hand, it means recognizing the ways in which such a network has the potential to act as a constraint upon individual desires, influencing decisions and leading to unanticipated outcomes. In chapter 4 we saw how Purush and Sushil had to contend with assumptions by upper-caste batchmates about their right and ability to practice medicine befitting an AIIMSonian given their reserved seats at the college. Here I relate two cases of general category female students whose ambitions were constrained by other types of social norms.

Neha
On the right-hand door of the metal wardrobe in the corner of her small hostel room, Neha had taped a list. The list was composed of A4 sheets

of paper covered in tiny writing. The writing detailed the syllabus Neha needed to study for the notoriously challenging civil services entrance exam. "I put it here to motivate me to study," she said, laughing as I shuddered at the scale of the task she had set herself alongside completing the fourth year of her MBBS. I asked her why she planned to leave medicine. She replied that her Ballabhgarh posting had introduced her to the healthcare needs of rural India, which she felt she would not be able to sufficiently redress as a doctor:

> So, then I changed my mind. And now I'm looking at Indian Administrative Services, to bring in some change at the ground level. So that I can impact more people. If I become a doctor, I'll probably touch a few handfuls of lives, save them. But if I become an IAS officer, then I'll be able to change some policies. So that they can be helped.

One of her plans was to reform the medical curriculum:

> I think I can help make a new curriculum, which is shorter than MBBS duration. Like we have a five-and-a-half year course—I think it is too prolonged. You can teach . . . like this entrance to the MBBS program is also very tough and there are many students who are from poor background and cannot afford coaching. Coaching is a must for getting through this exam, I also took coaching, everyone takes coaching to get into colleges. So I can make some other program, which is of shorter duration so that they can tackle the basic healthcare problems. And that the entrance should be easier, so that a lot of people can enter into that field.

Several weeks later, I met Anjali at the campus coffee shop. We chatted for a while about Anjali's own evolving plans, but when I asked about Neha's exam preparation, Anjali shook her head. Neha had abandoned her IAS plan to focus on the USMLE. Her family had begun mentioning marriage, and while her AIIMS credentials would be deployed in the matchmaking process, Neha feared that she would be married into a family that would exercise control over her career and might not even permit her to work outside the home.

Neha didn't respond to my request to meet before I left Delhi, but I bumped into her outside the girls' hostel during one of my brief return visits. I said I'd heard from Anjali that her plans had changed. She looked at me searchingly, as though unconvinced by her motives, and asked, "What do you think?" I hesitated, conscious of the trust implied by the question. I told her that I could see how complex the decision was and that I understood that she might feel she would have greater freedom in the United States. "Yes," she said, nodding and looking relieved. "That's what."

Anjali

Anjali was the latest of five generations of doctors in her family, and she found herself at AIIMS more by default than design, fully aware of the myriad ways the path to entry had been smoothed by inherited privilege. When we first met, she was unsure of her future plans:

> Just being a doctor is not what I want to be. Because if you are like a surgeon . . . or if you are a doctor at a very high level, you are just a doctor right? Not doing much beyond that in your life. I don't think I like it that much, for it to be the whole of my life. I decided 2015 was going to be about knowing myself. And realizing what I want do.

Anjali, like Neha, had been inspired by the Ballabhgarh posting, to the extent that she had begun to explore the idea of pursuing a master of public health degree (MPH) after her MBBS:

> I was like, this is what I want to do, this is so amazing! I mean we have all the techniques and who is receiving them? Just like 1 or 2% of the population. And I was, like, sure that this is what I want to do. Then obviously some sense was drilled into my head by my parents and everyone.

Anjali was visibly excited at the prospect of studying public health. Like Neha's view of the civil services, she saw it as a means to instigate change, and explained her motivation to tackle health inequalities as follows: "There are a lot of people in the army, but the strategy making and pretty much the outcome of the war would be decided by the general. I mean, who wants to be in the army when you can be the general?"

The efforts by her "parents and everyone" to "drill some sense" into Anjali's head seemed to be running in parallel to her own explorations of what might be possible. "At this point of time," she told me, "my aim is to talk to as many people as possible so I know what I can do with my life." Before the revelation about her MPH ambitions, Anjali had told me that she planned to apply for an MBA. This, she later explained, was strategic: "My parents don't think very highly of MPH, no one does. So I figured if I could at least get out of the country and do an MBA there I might end up in a more public health kind of set-up." That her parents didn't think very highly of the MPH turned out to be an understatement. In a conversation a few months later, Anjali told me that her mother had declared that an MPH was a "useless degree" and that anyone she had ever met with an MPH "was an idiot."

From her liminal position, Anjali's future was inflected with multiple possibilities, but this liminality, or "freedom," was also threatened by the ultimate authority of her parents. Despite her public health commitment, she had not abandoned the prospect of clinical practice; when I asked which branch of medicine she might hypothetically pursue, it turned out she had already taken the first stage of the USMLE exam. Bets were being hedged and relationships managed. "I just might end up doing it, because if my mom calls me [and says]: "Anjali! I think you should be a surgeon! Start preparing!" then I would do that. That's how I have been programmed . . . to obey my parents." Choices here, too, had their complications. A while later, Anjali went to discuss her options with an uncle who was a former head of a surgical department. He told her that "there are things girls can never do—such as surgery—because they have to raise kids." She gave a slightly confused laugh and said, "Which doesn't really seem right." Value hierarchies, within and without medicine, intersected with social norms and family expectations until the path ahead appeared ever more opaque; imagined futures ever more precluded.

A while after our initial conversation, I bumped into Anjali at the campus coffee shop. Her new plan was to complete the USMLE and pursue her residency in the United States, then to explore the public health option if possible. But she had also been warned that she was unlikely to stop at residency, given the "Indian system of competition" and a "constant striving for progression," and she acknowledged the potential truth of this. Her family wanted her to "follow a conventional path first," she said. Since a recent family wedding, Anjali's own engagement was on her parents' agenda; two female students in her batch had recently become engaged. "I just mute the phone when the subject comes up," she said. She could envisage her Indian future, could see herself being propelled straight into her parents' private medical practice, into marriage. "Trapped," she said. "I can't do that." As for Neha, emigration became a means of escaping suffocating expectations, but at the expense of an aspiration to work in the interests of those most marginalized by India's politics of health.

A few months later, Anjali had accepted that she would settle in the United States. "Even if I say I'll come back . . . no one comes back." At least not until they are in their 50s, with the stature of Naresh Trehan, she added.[73] Anjali maintained that life in the United States would allow her greater independence, and a more flexible training system would let her explore wider interests. And she wouldn't be leaving for another couple of years. Her parents were "fine" with it, she said, "as long as I get married," and to that end they were determinedly groom hunting (having overcome their disappointment that Anjali was no longer dating last year's PG topper). Anjali said she saw their point—"no one has gone there alone," she said of her seniors—and she didn't mention muting the phone when the subject came up.

On paper, Neha and Anjali are just another two AIIMS graduates who will leave for the United States, earning the approbation of some and the respect of others in the process. In the telling, their early aspirations to instigate policy change in the interests of India's rural poor will be obscured by a narrative of ever-greater achievement befitting an AIIMSonian, in combination with gendered expectations of their futures as married women. And the courage of their pursuit of independence—which we might interpret as an effort to adhere to their personal definitions of value, enabled by privilege—will be reinterpreted as the embodiment of appropriate ambition.

In Anjali's hostel room, beside her bed, she had written quotations on the wall. One was a line from Tennyson's "Ulysses": "How dull it is to pause, to make an end; to rust unburnish'd, not to shine in use!" Another was from Anna Karenina: "There was no solution, save that universal solution which life gives to all questions, even the most complex and unsolveable: one must live in the needs of the day, that is, forget oneself."

"It is value, then, that brings universes into being," David Graeber suggests.[74] The politics of medicine, and its associated values, is in some ways a microcosm of India's postcolonial tussle with competing instincts about what the modern nation should be. The idea of what a doctor is and should be is the repository of a dissonance that allows the coexistence of the private-sector doctor celebrated for his or her success while suspected of corruption, the benevolent rural doctor who is both heroized and assumed to be incapable of complex practice, the neglect of public healthcare by the state, and the expectation that an AIIMS student will embody the pinnacle of medical modernity through superspecialized urban practice. This dissonance was made explicit during Prime Minister Narendra Modi's speech to graduating students at the AIIMS convocation ceremony in October 2014. As reported in the press, Modi implored graduates to remember the debt to the nation they had incurred during their training, and he concluded by saying, "I leave you in hope that as children of mother India who have been lucky enough to study here, you will give back to society which has given you so much love."[75] Shortly after this moment, the Modi government cut the national health budget by almost 20%.[76]

AIIMS was established as a definitive postcolonial institution in the Indian landscape, propelled as much by a Nehruvian techno-scientific vision of development as by the need for comprehensive healthcare. Social scientists have explored how narratives of development and modernity offer frameworks within which different people attempt to (re)craft themselves using technologies of the self; whether through concepts of "hard work," making oneself bioavailable to the new medical technologies of the state, becoming a self-regulating consumer of proliferating healthcare goods and services, or being the "best" sort of doctor.[77] Students at AIIMS are therefore distinguished not only by the social achievement of having passed the entrance exam but also by their position at the vanguard of Indian medical modernity, an understanding of which implicates notions of value and legitimacy, which in turn influence students' imagining of their future selves.

Ultimately, we might understand the achievement of gaining a seat at AIIMS as a form of both value production and confirmation. This is augmented by the circumstances of medical training, before going on to inform not only what particular students desire to do afterward but what they consider they *ought* to do, given the matrix of relations in which their prior achievement has placed them. Consequently, for a graduate to choose an alternative future to that which is expected might be understood as a decision not only to question the pursuit of a particular career path but to challenge the legitimacy—the value—of the new conventional wisdom itself.

MBBS students are 18 years old, or occasionally 17 years old, when they enter AIIMS. They have often committed years of their lives to winning entrance to an elite club without knowing, or being asked, if and why they want to study medicine. It is easy to forget how young they are, just as it is easy to forget that part of the All India Institute's founding purpose was to train teaching doctors who would work across the country in response to the needs of the country's poor. These details get obscured at an institution overwhelmed by demand and primarily concerned with upholding a reputation for excellence defined as ever-greater medical specialization. In the process, opportunities are lost to promote undergraduate medical education as an endeavor concerned as much with citizenship and individual potential as with the pursuit of predetermined, socially sanctioned ambition.

CHAPTER 7

CONFRONTING INEQUALITY
The Potential of Medical Education for India

Medicine is a social science, and politics
nothing but medicine at a larger scale.

—Rudolf Virchow

IN MARCH 2016, I gave a talk at the Public Health Foundation of India
(PHFI) with the title "AIIMS killed the GP," alluding to the comment by a
former AIIMS director that I discussed in chapter 6. On arrival I was told
that my title had caused "some consternation" and that the presentation
would be followed by a debate in which members of the audience could
rebut my proposition.[1] Ultimately, the seminar convenor deemed a debate
unwarranted, given what was a less inflammatory presentation than perhaps anticipated. In an effort to diffuse any lingering tension, the convenor
suggested in his closing summary that rather than being solely responsible
for the death of the GP, AIIMS might be understood as representing a
general trend under way throughout India. What this tactical response
avoided was the question of how AIIMS itself acts as an establisher of
norms by virtue of its founding mandate and its enduring reputation as
the country's preeminent medical college. And what it confirmed was the
role of AIIMS as an emblem of a type of medical education and practice
that retains a unique status in the Indian landscape. It also recalls Sarah
Pinto's description of "institutional authority as a site of imagination and
practice" and asks us to consider the potential this holds for a transformative approach to the training of young doctors that works to challenge,
rather than reproduce, social—and therefore health—inequalities.[2]

AIIMS was conceived in the final years of the British colonial regime but brought to fruition by the government of newly independent India. The mandate for the institute was ambitious and reflective of a moment in which a postcolonial ethos of scientific development was not supported by attention to grassroots health infrastructure. AIIMS was tasked with becoming India's premier medical institution, combining the finest research and medical facilities with high-quality training of new generations of Indian doctors. It was intended to set a new standard—it was created to be the best. It was also intended to apply social medicine to the nation's myriad health challenges, many of which were, and continue to be, entangled with poverty and social exclusion. This complex mission ensured that AIIMS was immediately implicated in tensions between the techno-scientific emphases of development and the wider social determinants of health, while having to manage the consequences of a lackluster policy approach to public healthcare beyond urban hospitals, and the conflict inherent in tasking a consciously elite institution with playing a part in remedying inequality. As this book has shown, these complexities endure and are made visible through the experiences of MBBS students and in the image of the doctor that students are trained to become.

In the conclusion to his study of AIIMS doctors in the 1970s, T. N. Madan suggests that "an institution must grow, not stagnate, and those who set it up may not be able to foresee the requirements of a future generation."[3] In a literal sense, AIIMS has grown exponentially since its creation according to every numerical indicator: budget, buildings, departments, patients, faculty, aspiring students (hugely), and actual students (modestly). Most dramatically, AIIMS as a model has multiplied, with fourteen new institutions established since 2012 and several more at various stages on the drawing board. All are intended to replicate the original institute in Delhi, including its approach to education: anecdotal evidence suggests that attempts to shift toward a more community-oriented MBBS curriculum will not be welcomed by those with the power and resources to stipulate the terms on which the new institutions will operate.

AIIMS New Delhi continues to compensate for the paucity of competent and affordable healthcare in North India, and its reputation for providing the country's best medical education endures. The AIIMS brand is sustained not only by the visibility of alumni in high-status positions but also by a market mechanism that ensures that the vast majority of candidates who take the entrance examination do not succeed. As we've seen throughout this book, not all students were impressed by the reality of the MBBS experience at AIIMS. That said, even those among my interlocutors who were disappointed noted the superiority of AIIMS over other colleges in terms of infrastructure, financial resources, class size, quality of teaching by particular faculty members, and opportunities for research and conference participation, alongside the social freedoms that many (but not all) enjoyed. Faculty members who excoriated the institute for its persistent caste discrimination acknowledged that AIIMS remained a far better place to work than other colleges, particularly in North India. And a large majority of patients were unequivocal about their expectation, and experience, of superior treatment at AIIMS compared with other hospitals.

Whether AIIMS has grown in a figurative sense is far more debatable, particularly when it comes to how the institute practices its mandate to set national standards for undergraduate education and the model it promotes of what an excellent doctor looks like in contemporary India. Over the course of this book I have offered a variety of lenses through which to see more clearly the future possibilities and current limitations of AIIMS as a site of transformation. This has meant paying attention to how a combination of social and cultural capital, financial resources, and luck are at the heart of the MBBS admissions process, to the exclusion of any demonstration of motivation for becoming a doctor; discussing how discourses of merit and medical excellence are refracted through exam rank and narratives around affirmative action; illustrating how social inequality in the clinic is compounded rather than confronted as part of students' learning; and describing how the institution thrives on the reputation of AIIMSonians who go on to become superspecialists at the expense of self-reflection and the pursuit of meaning in medicine among the institute's youngest trainees.

In the process, we have seen that AIIMS is an institution neither insulated from the fissures of social difference nor convulsed by the overt violence of discrimination, but rather it is a place in which the dynamics of inequality slip in and out of sight—of students, of faculty, and of a researcher analyzing her field notes. It was during conversation with Purush that I was prompted to consider whether it is the elitist nature of AIIMS that both discourages a more committed orientation to health inequalities and impedes the kind of institutional reimagining that we might imagine a string of student suicides should provoke at a medical college. Such a reimagining would begin with a challenge to the comfortable assumption that interrogating social inequality is not the responsibility of a medical college or of the trainee doctors who upon graduating will swear an oath to do no harm. It would mean expecting public institutions of higher education to complement the provision of technical skills with the training of students to deploy a combination of critical thinking and self-reflection within which lies the truly humane and transformative potential of medicine for society.

MEDICAL EDUCATION IN A TIME OF PANDEMIC
It has taken a while for this book to appear in the world. In the intervening years since my research at AIIMS, some things have inevitably changed. A modernization project contracted to Tata Consultancy Services has resulted in upgraded branding and clearer signage around the hospital, the expansion of sheltered waiting areas, and the introduction of a digital appointment system. The current prime minister has increased the visibility of public healthcare on the political agenda through a combination of insurance schemes and infrastructure development—including the rapid expansion of the AIIMS network—albeit of a largely tertiary specialized type. There are plans afoot at AIIMS to revisit the MBBS curriculum, and in the wake of a revealing new annual survey of patients, the AIIMS administration has said that it intends to pay more attention to inculcating communication and—in a telling phrase—"soft skills" in its doctors.[4]

At a national scale there are examples of things having taken a darker turn, with the exploitation and violent exacerbation of social inequalities.[5] As I write the final words of this book, these divisions are being both illuminated and entrenched by a pandemic that has overwhelmed the world. The COVID-19 outbreak is shedding an unavoidable light on how everyday structural oppression determines who suffers the most during a health emergency. For India, this demands an overdue reckoning with the real meaning of public health and a legacy of political neglect. This does not stop at a diagnosis of inadequate infrastructure that cannot cope with the complexity of a pandemic. Rather, it asks for a confrontation with the reality that inequality in India is sustained in part by the absence of an association of "public" with a sense of interdependent citizenship. Instead, in a context in which the state is "a high stakes or competitive game in which individuals or groups seek advantages on particularistic lines,"[6] to return to Pratap Bhanu Mehta's words, "public" connotes dependence on precarious state services by those who cannot afford a privatized existence within the social boundaries of a specific community.

The novel coronavirus has demanded recognition of a biological interdependence of Indian bodies that affluent social groups cannot easily consume their way out of. As yet, there is no device to filter viral threats from household air as there is to cleanse it of polluting particulate matter. The pandemic is not a social leveler of risk and vulnerability, however; rather, it is confirming what we already knew, namely that health emergencies exacerbate existing inequality.[7] In India, the deaths of migrant workers trying to get home from cities where they had been left unemployed by lockdown are a stark illustration of how tenuous a hold on life many marginalized citizens have.[8] This is a quality of existential precarity that privileged Indians do not experience. But it remains the case that in this unprecedented moment in the life of modern India, the privileged can no longer choose to believe that the health of the poor has little to do with them. In a time of pandemic, rich households cannot stay healthy if poor households cannot stay healthy, and vice versa. Marginalized communities have little chance of remaining healthy, or recovering their health, when they are denied sanitary living environments and affordable treatment.[9] Political leaders can no longer hide from the extent to which India's myriad social inequalities impact the health of its entire population.[10]

This reckoning with the implications *for* public health *of* public health comes as the weave of any remaining shared social fabric is being concertedly unpicked. Before the pandemic was even a rumor, some of India's most marginalized communities were already reeling from a surge in targeted violence.[11] The epidemic of suicides among indebted farmers in drought-stricken areas of the country has been in and out of the news for years.[12] And violence against women and girls of all castes and classes has become ever more visible.[13] India exists in a permanent state of public health emergency: the pandemic has simply brought it to the attention of people who have previously had little incentive to notice.

Reconfiguring excellence

What does such a moment ask for from medical education in general and from an institution mandated to set national standards in particular? Not least, I suggest, an interrogation of prevailing conceptions of excellence and the role of the doctor in society that is imparted to students through both implicit suggestion and explicit example. "Excellence," Satish Deshpande writes, "is a powerful idea with deep roots in both traditional and modern ideologies" and has a critical role to play "in shaping the social structures of legitimation."[14] The power of this idea, he continues, derives in part from its deployment "in translating the waning forms of past entitlement into the newly ascendant forms of the present."[15] Here Deshpande is discussing excellence as synonymous with the concept of merit that upper castes use to defend unspoken historical privilege, as we saw in chapter 4. If excellence in medicine is, at its heart, a gatekeeping tool used to protect the interests of the elite, then it seems foolhardy to anticipate redefinition in response to inequality. But perhaps there is a glimmer of opportunity when an indiscriminate national health emergency overlaps with the liminal moment in which MBBS students could be exposed to more expansive ideas of medicine in the public interest.

It is a founding objective of AIIMS to demonstrate the highest standards of medical education to other institutions around the country. These standards cannot be static, as Madan alluded to above; they must be responsive to the needs of the country in a given period. As long as social inequalities are naturalized rather than interrogated, they will continue to be reproduced as part of medical education. In India, what is being revealed by the pandemic is that the nation has long needed a model of medical education that foregrounds inequality and equips young doctors to apprehend the social determinants of health as they have an impact on everyone, physicians included.

During his Nehru Memorial Lecture in 1975, then director of AIIMS V. Ramalingaswami lamented: "Physicians in developing countries become estranged from their own people in the course of their training. The ablest men and women are not tackling the most acute and difficult problems."[16] This reflects an important aspect of how excellence is defined and in whose interest, namely how "difficulty" is understood in medical education and practice. We saw in chapter 6 that the pressure to uphold the AIIMS brand of excellence by pursuing highly specialized medicine produced an outcome in which some students claimed that rural medicine was beneath them; at the same time they felt unprepared to practice any kind of clinical medicine given their inexperience. As Anjali told me, AIIMS MBBS students expect to be "people who are going to cut out appendixes in five minutes." Mugging up some information about mosquitoes and sanitation is an obligatory curriculum requirement on the way to the operating table, which in the eyes of students is where the real challenge lies. The ways that social and environmental inequalities influence and complicate the illness experience of patients and the response of doctors are not themes that AIIMS students are conditioned to think of as difficult. The MBBS admissions process demands single-minded preparation for an exam in biology, chemistry, and physics to the exclusion of all else (in the wake of school exams that valorize excellence in exactly the same way), and at no point asks why applicants want to study medicine. Precisely by virtue of the route that must be strictly followed to pass through the AIIMS gates as an MBBS student, most of these young people have not been encouraged to think about inequality or the social role of doctors at all.

But as we have seen throughout this book, many students are curious, thoughtful, and sometimes opinionated about the life of medicine beyond the MBBS curriculum. Purush spoke of his expectation that becoming a doctor and viewing everyone as a potential patient would act as an equalizer by subsuming preexisting personal identities. Mihir indirectly countered this by casting some of his peers as a threat to the life of patients and the reputation of elite medicine by virtue of how affirmative action enabled their presence at AIIMS. On the wall of her hostel room, Anjali had written quotes from literature about the nature of a purposeful life. The need for MBBS education to engage and challenge neophyte doctors in more comprehensive ways is made plain by students themselves—as is their capacity to respond. It is critical that this opportunity is taken while they are still at the most formative stage of their journey toward becoming doctors, before they are shepherded onto ever-narrower paths to prestige.

Taylor and Wendland remind us of the potential for change within models of education: "Institutions of education systematically teach people to *unsee* their social world in ways that contribute to the maintenance of existing relations of class and power—but education *could* teach people to *see* their world clearly, and support their capacity to transform it."[17] Given that most faculty members are the product of the same system that MBBS students are created by, it makes little sense to expect that they should conceive of or implement a different way of training new generations of doctors without being exposed themselves to other possibilities. At AIIMS, this process might begin with a return to clause 14(c) in the original AIIMS Act, which records among the intended functions of the new institute "the teaching of humanities in the undergraduate courses."[18] Liberating the social determinants of health from the confines of the unfashionable community medicine module and repositioning them within a health humanities course encompassing anthropology, philosophy, history, art, film, and literature would invite students to approach not just illness experience and inequality from a variety of perspectives but also conceptions of excellence and the role of the doctor in society.[19] As Arthur Kleinman puts it: "The pedagogy for engaging hidden values and divided selves is the moral building of the clinician as a fully developed human being. Such pedagogy uses the humanities not to educate students to be social scientists, humanists, or ethicists, but instead to cultivate and develop a deeper, richer, and more receptive sensibility: critical, aesthetically alert, and morally responsive."[20] Integrating the humanities into medical curricula as a means of confronting social inequality is not about tasking young doctors with finding a remedy; it is about opening spaces for new and different ways of paying attention. For Rudolf Virchow, the founder of pathology, whom I quote at the opening of this chapter, medicine *is* a social science, but that doesn't mean, he notes, that doctors have the responsibility to solve social problems. What they *are* obliged to do is to "point out problems and to attempt their theoretical solution."[21] This cannot be done without creating structures within which medical students can reflect on how becoming and being a doctor with one's own sense of ethics is, as Pentecost and Cousins phrase it, "shaped by social, cultural, political or economic processes, and subject to local moral worlds."[22]

A single institution cannot be expected to change the medical culture of an entire country, even an institution mandated to do just that. But it can use its privileged position to show the way. At present, the production and reaffirmation of narrow norms and conceptions of excellence at AIIMS acts to stifle the potential of the MBBS program and its students, and with it the transformative impact they could eventually have on Indian health and medicine. A reenvisioning of the purpose of undergraduate education at AIIMS has the potential to make graduating from the country's most prestigious medical college more meaningful for all concerned. In the process, it could also make for an institution as exceptional in practice as it is in the imagination.

Speaking to what ethnography can reveal about medical training, Vinceanne Adams and Sharon Kaufmann write: "Efforts toward social justice and health advocacy start . . . with individual ethical reflection on the nature of one's work, one's place in the world, and one's personal sense of effectiveness as a health professional, but such personal commitments can have effects far beyond one's expectations."[23] This, it seems to me, is as applicable to social scientists as to health professionals. If nothing else, this particular moment in the history of human health exhorts all of us to work harder to illuminate and address how inequality determines the different life chances of people with whom we share the planet. Although this book has been a study of a specific institution, I also offer it as a broader argument for paying more attention to medical education as part of health systems. If we are to deepen our understanding of how health inequalities are produced and sustained, we must deepen our understanding of how dominant models of medicine and doctoring generate and reproduce structural inequality through education and the implications for both trainee doctors and their future patients. We must all—health professionals included—be students of the formation and reproduction of power as well as the consequences of its uses. And elite institutions themselves must commit to look within, to confront unflinchingly the ways that they inculcate and reproduce social and health inequalities, and then find the will to transform in the interests of everyone.

ACKNOWLEDGMENTS

This book has been a labour of love and patience over several years. Reaching this point has been far from a solo effort, and I'm glad to have the opportunity to share my gratitude in print.

First and foremost, thank you to the faculty, administrators, students, and patients at AIIMS New Delhi who entertained the curiosity of a stranger and made this work possible. Above all, thank you to Dr. B, who opened the door and chose to trust me.

To my parents, Terry and Ben Ruddock: a book, at last! Thank you for your unstinting support of this and all my endeavors. And for the care and sustenance that made this book, possible (this one's for Grandpa, too).

To my brother, John, thank you for cheering me on via the medium of bemusement at my perseverance. Thank you to Siriol for encouragement, and to Olwen for turning up in the world three years ago and throwing life into a sweet new perspective.

For support gaining research access to AIIMS, particular thanks to Sunil Khilnani, Virander Paul, and Keshav Desiraju.

Thank you to my RA, Preeti Gulati, for making my fieldwork possible. She was an indispensable sidekick who managed to keep her dislike of hospitals entirely concealed (almost).

For encouragement, conversation, opportunities to share work, and friendship through the course of this project, thank you to Nayantara Appleton, Rama Baru, Debanjali Biswas, Daniel Kent Carrasco, Pratik Chakrabarti, Liz Chatterjee, Susannah Deane, Vipul Dutta, Surekha Garimella, James Hannah, Venkatesh HR, Kriti Kapila, Raphaëlle Khan, Aasim Khan, Jocelyn Killmer, Rachel Lloyd, Siddharth Mallavarapu, Jean-Thomas Martelli, Keerty Nakray, Devaki Nambiar, Avinash Paliwal, Bron Parry, Ale Pereira, Sankalp Pratap, Krishna Dipankar Rao, Kabir Sheikh, Ann Snow, Veena Sriram, Claire Wendland, and Saskia Wilven.

For encouraging and supporting the evolution of this work into book manuscript, thank you to Marcela Maxfield, Thomas Blom Hansen, and the team at Stanford University Press; two anonymous reviewers, whose comments elevated the manuscript; and Satish Deshpande, Stefan Ecks, and Karina Kielmann.

To the Misra family—Suhas, Abha, SN, Nidhi, Rohit, Shreya, and of course Aadya—who welcomed me into their family over several years, thank you, for your warmth and your kindness. Thank you to Suhas for our adventures together, and for all the conversation and analysis that informed and improved this book.

I completed this book while riding out the COVID-19 pandemic at home with Anna Gkiouleka. Thank you for the soothing and the celebrating; for reading my words; and for helping me to be brave: in this and all things.

APPENDIX
On Methodology

"ARE YOU A SPY?"

> In things of that kind the Castle moves slowly, and the worst of
> it is that one never knows what this slowness means; it can mean
> that the matter's being considered, but it can also mean that it
> hasn't yet been taken up . . . and in the long run it can also mean
> that the whole thing has been settled, that for some reason or
> other the promise has been cancelled. . . . One can never find
> out exactly what is happening, or only a long time afterwards.
> —Franz Kafka, *The Castle*

In April 2014, having listened patiently to the wry and occasionally de-
spairing account of my effort to gain research access to AIIMS, a friend
gave me a copy of Kafka's *The Castle*. In the novel, K. arrives in a village
believing he has been appointed as a land surveyor by the authorities that
inhabit The Castle, which sits on a hill and pervades the life of the village.
The story revolves in increasingly dizzying circles around K's efforts to have
his position recognized by The Castle in order that he may begin work.

I arrived in Delhi in January 2014 believing that arrangements were in
place to begin my research at AIIMS, following nine months of preparatory
work. This began with an exploratory trip to Delhi in April 2013, during
which time I met senior doctors and administrative staff. One particular
member of the administration informed me with a blank smile that my
research was out of the question and that if I "applied my brain" to reading
the guidelines he had thrust at me, I would see the truth of the matter.
Through the same contact in London who had connected me to AIIMS,
I was able to appeal to the Indian Ministry of Health and Family Welfare,
and I did so, though not without a degree of discomfort about the role
of elite networks in the facilitation of my research. Was my credibility as

an independent actor already compromised by my willingness to utilize such contacts, I wondered. And what grandiosity of intent was implied by my willingness to badger senior civil servants into letting me conduct my research?

At the ministry, I was escorted to a desktop computer in an assistant's office and told to write a letter to the secretary of health explaining the situation. I duly did so. From there I was ushered in front of the secretary himself and told to present him with the letter I had typed in an adjacent room a few minutes earlier. An early confirmation of the unassailable power of words on paper in South Asian bureaucracies.[1]

The secretary read the letter and muttered a few things about AIIMS leveraging and resigning its institutional autonomy as it suited the circumstances. He looked up at me: "So: are you a spy?"

ACCESSING THE INSTITUTE

The challenge of securing research access to AIIMS was inflected with moments of comedy, suspicion, despair, and triumph.[2] The variety of strategies and personalities involved speaks to the specific characteristics of seeking permission to conduct research within a prestigious government institution. Not that my experience can necessarily be considered typical, particularly outside India. While Phillip Abrams has written about the paradox wherein public institutions are more challenging to access than private organizations,[3] Marcia Inhorn found gaining research access to public hospitals in Egypt and Lebanon more straightforward than seeking the same permission to study private clinics.[4] In Papua New Guinea, Alice Street describes how she was welcomed by the hospital staff as a witness to the challenging circumstances in which they worked.[5]

In my case, while everything hinged on the crucial letter of official permission that was eventually written by the dean of research, personalities and the establishment of rapport—those traditional hallmarks of anthropological fieldwork[6]—were central to the negotiation of the institutional labyrinth. From the outset, I was extremely fortunate to have the support of a senior doctor at the hospital—Dr. B—whose calm, good-humored kindness and generosity continued throughout my fieldwork. From the outset Dr. B made it clear that he was helping me because his batchmate in London—my original AIIMS contact—had asked him to. He did express a genuine interest in my work and encouraged me to pursue it, but his initial motivation spoke to the network of relationships that enabled that pursuit. Although personal perseverance was crucial, gaining research access was by no means a solo effort—I remain convinced that I would not have been granted research access without the support of Dr. B.

My greatest challenge during the permissions process was posed by the senior member of the administration mentioned above who had no intention of allowing my research to proceed.[7] During a meeting, another administrator, who was very supportive and on the brink of granting me permission, decided to consult this particular colleague, who went on to explain that "the problem" was that I might publish my research and that no one wanted to be responsible for setting in motion a chain of events potentially damaging to AIIMS. For all his efforts to block my access to the institute, I felt a certain respect for this explicit articulation of what he feared may ensue. It was not surprising, but it had hitherto remained implicit. In this light, the administrator perhaps proved the person most conscious of the potential power of ethnography as a method, which, as Fassin notes, may be perceived as warranting "avoidance, suspicion or prohibition" precisely "because it allows witnessing where those in power do not want evidence of what is ongoing to be seen."[8]

That said, once I had official permission to conduct my research not everyone found my methods either threatening or alien. The research culture of AIIMS, while strained by the demands of clinical care, is an important facet of the institution's identity, and I suspect this inclination informed the encouragement of my work by certain faculty members, even if it was in a very different vein to their own.[9] To my relief, the particular meeting I described above concluded with the agreement I would need a senior faculty member to vouch for me with the director.[10] True to form, Dr. B was generous enough to agree to take responsibility for me. Initially, I felt my critical capacities smothered by sheer joy and gratitude at being a legitimate presence within the institution, and I feared it might have remained that way. In time I regained perspective, and the distance enforced by the writing process in particular allowed for the coexistence of a critical analysis of MBBS student experiences at AIIMS with explicit gratitude toward the actors implicated in both the life of the institute and the facilitation of my research.

I began fieldwork proper in early May 2014, and I left Delhi one year later. The promised formalization of my position under the auspices of the Research Department never occurred, but the letter of permission acted as my passport into the institution and continued to serve its purpose throughout my fieldwork. The envelope had fallen apart by the time I left Delhi; the letter itself, also beginning to disintegrate, remains a symbol both of perseverance and of the willingness of certain individuals to open their institution to scrutiny by a stranger.

METHODOLOGY

During my 12 months of fieldwork, I conducted a range of interviews and I also spent structured periods of observation in specific clinics and on Dr. B's wards. These coexisted with the less structured time I spent on campus, whether conducting interviews with students at the coffee shop and patients around the hospital, spending time at the Pulse festival, or generally milling around between appointments.

On hospital ethnography in particular

Although community-based studies of illness experience and health-seeking are well established in India, hospital ethnography remains a nascent subfield with its own methodological and ethical dilemmas. Gitte Wind describes her position in the Dutch rheumatism clinic that she studied as dependent on "a daily on-going negotiation," which went better on some days than others. Some staff members were delighted by her presence and interest in their work. Others were puzzled, anxious, or suspicious that they were under surveillance.[11] Similarly, Zaman's research participants in a Bangladeshi hospital sought an explanation of the practical utility of his work, and Nichter faced the same demand from a policy maker in India.[12] At AIIMS, once I had the talismanic permission letter in my hand, I was generally made welcome; doctors would make comments to me during an OPD, explaining processes, and encouraging questions despite working under significant pressure, while I sat on an extra chair that an assistant had squeezed into an already-cramped consultation room.

This book is based on research I undertook for my PhD at King's College London, which granted ethical approval for the study. Accordingly, I sought informed consent from everyone I directly interacted with. All the students and faculty members I interviewed provided written consent. When conducting short interviews with patients with my research assistant Preeti, we accepted verbal consent following an explanation of my role and the nature of the study, as the crowded conditions and minimal literacy of many patients made written consent impractical. The uncomfortable environment and lack of privacy meant that we kept these interactions deliberately brief unless guided otherwise by the patients themselves. Those who were keen to share their stories in more depth are among the voices featured in chapter 5. The extremely crowded environment and rapid turn-around during the outpatient clinics that I observed meant that I was not able to seek informed consent from the patients who attended during my visits. I accepted the consent of the doctor holding the clinic to observe their interactions, and in doing so I am conscious that I was operating as part of the hierarchy I was there to study.[13]

I have anonymized everyone who appears in this book. I have also anonymized the clinics I observed, from which the vignettes in chapter 5 are taken. One could argue that I could have guaranteed the anonymity of individuals only by anonymizing AIIMS itself. This is feasible in studies of phenomena that are not germane to a particular institution, but in a case such as this, where the focus of the research is a very particular high-profile institution, anonymization would have emptied the work of its intended substance.

Identifying the institution, however, does make the anonymization of particular actors more challenging.[14] While I have not specified the names of the departments in which I observed outpatient clinics, it may be possible to deduce their identities through my descriptions if a reader were so inclined. Identification of individuals is also made more possible through gender pronouns, which I have not disguised. Similarly, while I have anonymized names, the excerpts from interviews with retired faculty include details that may aid identification, but I include them with consent.

I recruited my research assistant, Preeti, from Jawaharlal Nehru University, where she was studying for an MPhil in history. Preeti assisted me in conducting short interviews with patients around the hospital, and she transcribed and translated these into English—I retained the Hindi originals for clarification purposes. Preeti also helped arrange interviews with some senior residents at AIIMS, which I conducted alone in English, and she also did some archival work at the Central Secretariat Library. I describe Preeti's role not only to act against the "silencing" of assistants that some researchers are guilty of but also to shed light on my experience of conducting fieldwork with a chronic illness, which I expand on below.[15]

THE STUDENTS

The majority of the students that populate this book were, at the time of my fieldwork, in the fourth or fifth year of the MBBS course at AIIMS. I also spoke with junior and senior residents and recent graduates, but in fewer numbers (see table 2). The fourth-years were in their final two semesters of the taught curriculum, while the fifth-years had completed their final exams and were accumulating clinical experience as interns rotating through departments, at least in theory.[16] I first encountered the fourth-years during my visits to the Comprehensive Rural Health Services Project at Ballabhgarh. A group of 15 students had just begun their seven-week posting, and I accompanied them on their outreach and learning activities in local villages. I conducted semistructured interviews with several of these students and reached others through snowballing and the contact list given to me by the class president. I met the interns at the AIIMSonians picnic in February 2015 and conducted interviews with students in the months that followed. I chose not to seek permission to observe students during classes. Aside from the challenge of seeking further necessary permissions, I decided to remain focused on life outside the classroom, as my interest was less in how students were explicitly taught medicine at AIIMS and more in the less tangible influences on their formation as doctors.

The group I met at Ballabhgarh had just begun their fourth year of study and brought to our interviews sufficient experience to be able to reflect on their time at AIIMS and to consider the increasingly imminent post-MBBS future. The perspective of the interns I encountered a few months later was similarly informed, but with the notable difference that the post-MBBS future was now very real, with a consequent undoing, for some, of the certainty they had felt about their career aspirations a year earlier. These two groups of students therefore brought reflections both on what was behind them and what was to come. Given these advantages, and also a finite amount of time, I chose to focus on developing relationships with, and an understanding of, these cohorts. The obvious consequence of this approach is that students in their early years at AIIMS are not sufficiently represented in this book to offer a more longitudinal perspective on the MBBS experience.

I interviewed all the students cited in this book in-depth and in a semistructured format; interview lengths were largely determined by responses and ranged from 25 to 70 minutes. I engaged with several of these students on more than one occasion following the initial interviews and during my short follow-up visits to AIIMS in September 2015 and March 2016. Most interviews with students took place at the outdoor campus coffee shop, which had the advantage of being easily accessible for students while allowing me greater immersion into campus life and also, in time, facilitating chance meetings with students I had come to know. These casual encounters and unstructured conversations are integral to my broader ethnographic material—whether they took place at the coffee shop, around the hostels, or on the bus to Ballabhgarh.

Securing interview appointments could be challenging. Faculty members had extremely busy and often unpredictable schedules; students had to balance the demands of academic and social lives (and sleep), and while many were generous with their time, others were harder to pin down. There were the inevitable last-minute cancellations, and silences in response to my attempts to set an interview date with students who had previously agreed to meet quite enthusiastically. Frustratingly, several of these cases were of female students whom I was particularly keen to speak with given the significant male skew among MBBS students. The lack of gendered analysis is a shortcoming of this book that I acknowledge and regret.

The voices throughout this book belong to students with opinions and experiences that they were willing, and sometimes extremely keen, to share with me. I cannot know how the experiences of students unwilling or unable to speak with me might contradict or complement these narratives and potentially alter my analysis. Had I spent more time socializing in the student hostels I would likely have accrued a greater number of casual informants. As things stand, however, I am content to acknowledge the partial truth of any ethnographic endeavor.[17] And when thinking about interview-rich research, I follow Claire Wendland's reflection that "I have to assume both that students were the best source of evidence about their own process of becoming doctors and that some evidence was missing or misleading."[18]

In addition to students, I also conducted in-depth semistructured interviews with current and retired faculty, with two members of the first AIIMS MBBS class, and with external actors. The complete set of people with whom I conducted in-depth semistructured interviews is enumerated in table 2. This doesn't account for multiple interviews with particular students.

FIELDWORK IN CRIP TIME

Reflexivity, or the influence of the anthropologist's positionality on her field of study, both in the doing of fieldwork and in the writing about it, has been a preoccupation of the discipline since the 1980s.[19] More recently, there have been efforts to decenter the discipline to make room for different types of anthropologist—not in terms of subdiscipline but in terms of personal identity. Doing so has facilitated valuable discussion about the influence of gender, sexuality, and race on ethnographic practice and writing.[20] Here I want to expand this conversation to make space for discussion of practicing anthropology with a disability and to call out the ableism of the traditional association of fieldwork with a normative, non-disabled body.[21] Since adolescence I have lived with a neurological disease called myalgic encephalomyelitis (ME). ME is a complex, chronic and

TABLE 2 Breakdown of interviewees by category and gender.

CATEGORY	INTERVIEWEES	RATIO: MALE TO FEMALE
Third-year MBBS	1	1:0
Fourth-year MBBS	15	13:2
Fifth-year MBBS (intern)	11	8:3
Graduate (class of 2009)	2	2:0
Junior resident	2	1:1
Senior resident	4	4:0
PhD Student	1	1:0
Current faculty	10	9:1
Retired faculty	3	1:2
Class of 1956 graduates	2	2:0
AIIMS Raipur Faculty	2	1:1
Max Healthcare directors	2	2:0
	Total: 55	45:10

dynamic condition defined by severe energy limitation, pain, and cognitive symptoms among others.[22]

Before beginning fieldwork, I had encountered no literature that spoke to the experience of being a disabled anthropologist or how alienating a discipline it can be for a disabled person, with its deep-rooted attachment to endurance as the great virtue of the ethnographer. Methods books in my experience were written by and for non-disabled people with bodies assumed to be compliant research tools. There were several classic processes that played out during my fieldwork. Just as I felt fully immersed, it was time to leave; I ended up with more material than I could use; and I was nevertheless paranoid that I could have done more, seen more, talked to more people, taken more notes. This paranoia is familiar to most anthropologists, particularly graduate students; it is laughed about, but rarely is it interrogated for the ableism that informs an implicit message of "do more; push harder."

Doing fieldwork at AIIMS was a privilege. It was fascinating, exhilarating, and utterly exhausting. I look back and wonder how I managed, until I recall that I did it on my own terms, within the realm of "crip time" that I inhabit.[23] I did not spend full days at AIIMS—I worked in shifts. I did not attend many early morning meetings that I had access to, nor did I socialize with students at night. Even while working within my limits, I spent an average of one day a week too sick to leave the house, and I had to cancel sought-after interviews and clinic observations on more than one occasion. Anxious that I was not "doing enough," I also knew that persistent overexertion would leave me unable to work at all, jeopardizing the whole endeavor. The post-fieldwork exhaustion that some fledgling anthropologists boast of as a rite of passage is not a state of being that everyone can risk. I quickly realized I would need support, and I recruited Preeti as a research assistant to transcribe interviews and assist with unearthing archival and library resources, in addition to her role as interpreter during patient interviews. Without Preeti and without respecting my constraints at the expense of "doing more," I would not have completed this project.

My illness was inextricable from my fieldwork experience. It is also integral to my enduring interest in the formation of professional medical power and its consequences for inequality. I do not want to exaggerate the influence of my disability on my view of the field, however, and I have deliberately not incorporated any such reflection into the book.[24] For now, I offer these brief remarks as a contribution toward making the world safer for difference among anthropology's practitioners as well as its subjects.

NOTES

CHAPTER 1

1. The Indian Institutes of Technology (IITs), India's most prestigious engineering colleges, were established at the same moment with a mandate to integrate the highest standards of science and engineering into the development of the newly independent nation. There are many parallels between the IITs and AIIMS, their place in the national imagination, and the manner in which they reproduce social hierarchies, as I discuss throughout this book. In doing so, I draw on Ajantha Subramanian's work on IIT Madras, *The Caste of Merit: Engineering Education in India* (Cambridge, MA: Harvard University Press, 2019).

2. Government of India, "The All India Institute of Medical Sciences Act, 1956" (1956), 5–6, https://www.aiims.edu/images/pdf/aiimsact.pdf.

3. As an indication of the institution's growth, in his study of AIIMS in the 1970s, T. N. Madan cites the following figures for 1974–1975: 450,291 outpatients, 19,782 admissions, and 33,949 surgical procedures. T. N. Madan, ed., *Doctors and Society: Three Asian Case Studies: India, Malaysia, Sri Lanka* (Ghaziabad: Vikas, 1980), 45. In 2016, a long-planned expansion was sanctioned, which includes the creation of an additional 1,800 beds across seven departments on a new 15-acre site. Press Information Bureau, Government of India, "Health Minister gives go ahead for the expansion of AIIMS Trauma Centre," February 22, 2016, http://www.aiims.edu/images/press-release/HFW-AIIMS%20Trauma%20Centre-22%20Feb2016.pdf.

4. As an illustration of its media profile: a Google search for news stories related to Safdarjung Hospital—an older government institution directly opposite AIIMS—returned 12,700 results while the equivalent search for AIIMS New Delhi produced 468,000 results. News articles and opinion pieces about AIIMS are often critical, alleging corruption (M. Rajshekhar, "High Patient Inflow, Corruption, Nepotism and Talent Exodus: The Problems That Have Plagued AIIMS," *Economic Times*, March 12,

2015), dysfunction (D. Gupta, "Tidy up Delhi's AIIMS before Building Many More across India," *Times of India*, July 21, 2014), and neglect or malpractice (V. Unnikrishnan, "AIIMS Director Mishra in Trouble: RS MPs Seek Privilege Motion," *Catch News*, August 3, 2016). Stories also emphasize the unparalleled expertise of AIIMS doctors in performing complex surgery on patients with rare conditions: "17 Kg Tumour Removed from Woman's Abdomen," *India Today*, March 4, 2015; N. Chandra, "Eight Hours, 30 Doctors and a New Lease of Life: Conjoined Twins with Fused Chest, Abdomen Separated Successfully at AIIMS," *India Today*, July 22, 2013, 10. During the violence in the Kashmir Valley in the summer of 2016, a team of AIIMS eye surgeons flew to the state to examine victims of the pellet guns used by the army to subdue protesting citizens, several of whom were airlifted to AIIMS for surgery (N. Iqbal, "Kashmir Pellet Gun Victims Pin Their Hopes on Doctors at AIIMS," *Indian Express*, July 27, 2016). Young victims of horrific crimes in and around Delhi, most notably child rape, are also usually taken to AIIMS (D. Pandey, "Child Rape Victim Shifted to AIIMS as Outrage Spreads," *The Hindu*, April 20, 2013).

5. At the time of writing there were 14 All India Institutes in addition to the New Delhi original, with another 8 on the drawing board. The shortcomings of several of the new institutes are regularly highlighted in the media, including recruitment challenges and inadequate infrastructure. AIIMS New Delhi remains in a class of its own. Although some faculty have been involved in supporting the development of the other institutes, a general disquiet persists about their impact on "brand AIIMS." Aside from occasional references, this book focuses on AIIMS New Delhi, which I refer to simply as AIIMS.

6. J. Livingston, *Improvising Medicine: An African Oncology Ward in an Emerging Cancer Epidemic* (Durham NC: Duke University Press: 2012). A. Street, *Biomedicine in an Unstable Place: Infrastructure and Personhood in a Papua New Guinean Hospital* (Durham, NC: Duke University Press, 2014); C. L. Wendland, *A Heart for the Work: Journeys through an African Medical School* (Chicago: University of Chicago Press, 2010); S. Zaman, *Broken Limbs, Broken Lives: Ethnography of a Hospital Ward in Bangladesh* (Amsterdam: Het Spinhuis, 2005).

7. V. Patel, R. Parikh, S. Nandraj, P. Balasubramaniam, K. Narayan, V. K. Paul, A. K. S. Kumar, M. Chatterjee, and K. S. Reddy, "Assuring Health Coverage for All in India," *Lancet* 386 (2015): 2422–35.

8. Since my research at AIIMS, a hospital modernization program contracted to Tata Consultancy Services has begun to manifest through a new waiting area and updated signage, as well as the early stages of a digital appointment system.

9. In recent years, there have been two particularly visible instances of political interference in the administration of AIIMS. Following the agitation in 2006 against increased quotas of reserved places for students and faculty from Other Backward Classes, which was headquartered at AIIMS with the alleged support of the director (V. Venkatesan, "The Dynamics of Medicos' Anti-Reservation Protests of 2006," in *Health Providers in India: On the Frontlines of Change*, ed. K. Sheikh and A. George [New Delhi: Routledge, 2010]: 142–57), the Congress government's health minister was accused of persistent interference, culminating in the removal of the AIIMS director (T. Rashid, "Dr. Ramadoss

Plays the Boss, Pushes AIIMS Chief to Brink," *Indian Express*, June 15, 2006). More recently, the civil servant Sanjiv Chaturvedi was removed from the post of chief vigilance officer at AIIMS following his investigations into 165 cases of alleged corruption over two-and-a-half years—a move widely alleged to have been a politically motivated calculation to protect the interests of senior figures in government and the AIIMS administration implicated by Chaturvedi's work. *Business Standard*, "Sanjiv Chaturvedi: The Man Who Uncovered AIIMS Corruption," 29 July, 2015; N. Sethi, "Parliamentary Standing Committee Report on Corruption in the Hospital Has No Foundation: AIIMS," *Business Standard*, June 3, 2016.

10. Several members of the current government have been treated at AIIMS, as were External Affairs Minister Sushma Swaraj and Finance Minister Arun Jaitley before their deaths in 2019. An AIIMS medical board was involved in the investigation into the poisoning of Sunanda Pushkar, wife of MP Shashi Tharoor, which garnered a huge amount of media attention. And in October 2016, a team of specialists from AIIMS flew to Chennai to consult with doctors at the private Apollo Hospital about the treatment of Tamil Nadu Chief Minister J. Jayalaalitha. Following the death of former prime minister Atal Bihari Vajpayee at AIIMS in August 2018, a journalist described him as "a patient AIIMS will remember forever," given the medical attention he received from the institute's doctors over several decades. D. N. Jha, "Humble till the End: A Patient AIIMS Will Remember Forever," *Times of India*, August 27, 2018. Of course, those politicians admitted to AIIMS are treated in one of its private rooms. Of the 2,300 beds at AIIMS, 265 are private.

11. T. N. Madan, *Doctors and Society*, 90.

12. D. Haller and C. Shore, eds., *Corruption: Anthropological Perspectives* (London: Pluto, 2005), 6; S. Nundy, K. Desiraju, and S. Nagral, eds., *Healers or Predators? Healthcare Corruption in India* (New Delhi: Oxford University Press, 2018).

13. V. Das, *Affliction: Health, Disease, Poverty* (New Delhi: Orient Blackswan, 2015), 159–80.

14. For the NIRF results and an explanation of the parameters used, see National Institutional Ranking Framework, Ministry of Human Resource Development, Government of India, https://www.nirfindia.org/2018/MEDICALRanking.html

15. D. Fassin, "Why Ethnography Matters: On Anthropology and Its Publics," *Cultural Anthropology* 28, no. 4 (2013): 621–46.

16. Ibid., 629.

17. T. N. Madan's survey of doctors at AIIMS in the 1970s remains the only substantial enquiry into the institution from a social science perspective. His study is based on questionnaires, interviews, and secondary sources for piecing together the institution's history. While Madan's work is neither ethnographic nor focused on students at AIIMS, it remains an invaluable reference point for how attitudes and orientations within the institute have changed or endured since the 1970s, and I make use of his data throughout this book. T. N. Madan, ed., *Doctors and Society: Three Asian Case Studies: India, Malaysia, Sri Lanka* (Ghaziabad: Vikas, 1980). Historians of medicine and public health occasionally mention the establishment of AIIMS if their focus extends beyond 1947 (R. Jeffery, *The Politics of Health in India* [Berkeley: University of California Press, 1988]), while C.

G. Pandit's memoir of his involvement with the early planning for AIIMS offers insight into the institute's foundation. C. G. Pandit, *My World of Preventive Medicine* (New Delhi: Leipzig Press, 1982).

18. V. Das, *Affliction*.

19. I suggest that social scientists with an interest in Indian health and medicine have largely ignored AIIMS for two reasons. First, those with an eye to health inequalities and social justice are more inclined toward community-based studies that provide insight into local ecosystems of illness and treatment-seeking. V. Das, *Affliction*, 2015; S. Pinto, *Where There Is No Midwife: Birth and Loss in Rural India* (Oxford: Berghahn, 2008); C. Van Hollen, *Birth on the Threshold: Childbirth and Modernity in South India* (Berkeley: University of California Press, 2003). Second, the challenge of gaining research access to large public institutions is formidable and demands a quantity of time that not all researchers can afford—see appendix for my account of seeking access to AIIMS.

20. For a discussion of methodology, and the challenge of gaining research access to an elite government institution, see the appendix.

21. "India's health system defies a uniform definition and is the outcome of strategies that seem to be working at cross purposes: a partially functioning primary care system, heavily overstretched public hospitals competing in the same space with well-funded private hospitals, varied insurance schemes with no single coordinating authority, and a remarkable absence of a sound regulatory environment to control the wild growth of the private sector. In addition, there is rampant corruption and low capacity to supervise, measure, and monitor health gains." S. K. Rao, *Do We Care? India's Health System* (New Delhi: Oxford University Press, 2017), 27.

22. S. Acharya, "Health Equity in India: An Examination through the Lens of Social Exclusion," *Journal of Social Inclusion Studies* 4, no. 1 (2018): 104–30.

23. Data on health disparities in these paragraphs comes from V. Patel, R. Parikh, S. Nandraj, P. Balasubramaniam, K. Narayan, V. K. Paul, A. K. S. Kumar, M. Chatterjee, and K. S. Reddy, "Assuring Health Coverage for All in India," *Lancet* 386 (2015): 2422–35.

24. V. Das, *Affliction*; J. Drèze and A. Sen, *An Uncertain Glory: India and Its Contradictions* (London: Allen Lane, 2013); S. K. Rao, *Do We Care?*

25. The National Rural Health Mission began in 2005 and was subsequently merged in 2014 with the nascent National Urban Health Mission into a common National Health Mission. See S. K. Rao, *Do We Care?*, for an overview of this period from her perspective as health secretary at the time.

26. By the end of March 2015, only 21% of primary health centers and 26% of community health centers were functioning as per Indian Public Health Standards (IPHS) set by the Ministry of Health and Family Welfare. Factors commonly cited as limiting the efficacy of government-run primary care facilities include distant locations, patients' wage losses due to inconvenient opening times, high health worker absenteeism and insensitive attitudes. Patel et al., "Assuring Health Coverage for All in India," 2425.

27. K. D. Rao and A. Sheffel, "Quality of Clinical Care and Bypassing of Primary Health Centers in India," *Social Science & Medicine* 207 (2018): 80–88.

28. Patel et al., "Assuring Health Coverage for All in India," 2427.

29. Government of India, "National Health Policy 2015 Draft," http://mohfw.nic.in/WriteReadData/l892s/18048892912105179110National%20Health%20policy-2002.pdf; J. Drèze and A. Sen, *An Uncertain Glory*, 143–48.

30. See World Bank, http://data.worldbank.org/indicator/SH.XPD.PUBL.ZS. Within several months of Narendra Modi's election as prime minister at the head of a majority BJP government in May 2014, his government cut the healthcare budget by almost 20%, with the blame placed on "fiscal strain." More recently, a parliamentary panel reported that the budget allocation for health in the five years to March 2017 was less than half of that outlined in the Twelfth Five-Year Plan for India's growth and development. In December 2018, Modi committed his government (subsequently reelected with an increased majority in May 2019) to increasing expenditure on public healthcare to a widely advocated 2.5% by 2025. A current slowdown in the country's economic growth together with questionable political commitment suggests this target is unlikely to be met. A. Kalra, "India Slashes Health Budget, Already One of the World's Lowest," *Reuters*, December 23, 2014; J. Singh, "Budget Allocation for Health Less than Half of 12th Plan Promises," *Live Mint*, April 28, 2016.

31. P. Bala, *Medicine and Medical Policies in India: Social and Historical Perspectives* (Lanham, MD: Lexington Books, 2007); I. Qadeer, K. Sen, and R. Nayar. *Public Health and the Poverty of Reforms: The South Asian Predicament* (New Delhi: Sage, 2001).

32. D. Arnold, *Colonizing the Body: State Medicine and Epidemic Disease in Nineteenth-Century India* (Berkeley: University of California Press, 1993); M. Harrison, *Public Health in British India: Anglo-Indian Preventive Medicine 1859–1914* (Cambridge: Cambridge University Press, 1994); P. Bala, *Medicine and Medical Policies in India*, 2007; S. K. Rao, *Do We Care?*.

33. The notable exceptions are Tamil Nadu and Kerala, whose successes in state healthcare provision stand in stark comparison to North India in particular, demonstrating the challenge of tackling a subject that is devolved within a federal system. In Tamil Nadu 80% of children are fully immunized, as compared to an Indian average of 43.5%, and Kerala and Tamil Nadu have infant mortality rates of 12 and 22 per 1,000 respectively, as compared to an Indian average of 44. These successes are widely lauded, but explanations are in shorter supply. Suggestions include a history of political activism around social issues in the south. J. Drèze and A. Sen, *An Uncertain Glory*, 168–77.

34. S. Amrith, *Decolonizing International Health: India and Southeast Asia, 1930–65.* (Basingstoke, UK: Palgrave Macmillan, 2006); P. B. Mehta, *The Burden of Democracy* (Delhi: Penguin, 2003).

35. N. G. Jayal, *Citizenship and Its Discontents: An Indian History* (Cambridge, MA: Harvard University Press, 2013): 22. For a discussion of how campaigners for a right to health articulate this as a dimension of Article 21, see M. Khosla, *The Indian Constitution* (Oxford: Oxford University Press, 2012).

36. J. Drèze and A. Sen, *An Uncertain Glory*, 143–48; P. B. Mehta, *The Burden of Democracy*, 135; M. Banerjee, *Why India Votes?* (Abingdon, UK: Routledge, 2014).

37. L. Saez and A. Sinha, "Political Cycles, Political Institutions and Public Expenditure in India, 1980–2000," *British Journal of Political Science* 40, no. 1 (2010): 91–113.

38. P. B. Mehta, *The Burden of Democracy*, 120.

39. "Superspecialization" is an unpopular term with some doctors, who consider it a corruption of the more accurate "subspecialization" by the marketing departments of corporate hospitals. The term is firmly established in India's sociomedical discourse, however, including among medical students, and I use it in the book for this reason.

40. Land allocation usually involves an obligation by private hospitals to allocate a certain number of beds for the free treatment of patients from Economically Weaker Sections of society. The regular failure to fulfill this requirement has begun to attract media attention. K. K. Sruthijith, "Delhi's Upscale Hospitals Are Turning Away the Poor in Whose Name They Got Land, Subsidies," *Huffington Post* (blog), September 20, 2015. http://www.huffingtonpost.in/2015/09/13/delhi-dengue-hospitals_n_8128704. html; B. Lefebvre, "The Indian Corporate Hospitals: Touching Middle Class Lives," in *Patterns of Middle Class Consumption in India and China*, ed. C. Jaffrelot and P. van der Veer (New Delhi: Sage, 2008): 88–109; V. Patel et al., "Assuring Health Coverage for All in India," 2428.

41. Patel et al., "Assuring Health Coverage for All in India," 2428.

42. A. Phadke, "Regulation of Doctors and Private Hospitals in India." *Economic and Political Weekly* 41, no. 6 (2016): 46–55.

43. V. Das, *Affliction*.

44. J. Baudrillard, *The Consumer Society: Myths and Structures* (London: Sage, 1998): 218; L. Fernandes, *India's New Middle Class: Democratic Politics in an Era of Economic Reform* (Minneapolis: University of Minnesota Press: 2006): 131–36; S. K. Rao, *Do We Care?*, xviii.

45. T. Sundararaman, I. Mukhopadhyay, and V. R. Muraleedharan, "No Respite for Public Health," *Economic and Political Weekly* 51, no. 16 (2016): 39–42. In an effort to address some of these failings, in February 2018 the government announced the Ayushman Bharat, or National Health Protection Scheme. The ambitious scheme confirms India's embrace of the health insurance model and aims to provide 5 lakh rupees (US$7,000) coverage to approximately 100 million families for secondary and tertiary care at approved hospitals. The scheme will entail an 11% increase in the health budget—implementation is expected to cost 12,000 crore rupees (approximately $1.6 billion), to be shared 60%–40% between the central and state governments. The implementation plans for such a complex scheme have yet to be determined. While the scheme may enable some patients to access particular interventions at certain hospitals on a more affordable basis, it is not designed to remedy the systemic failures of Indian healthcare. It will not ensure the integration of tiered levels of care, nor will it address the education, training, and distribution of human resources for health. J. P. Narain, "Is Ayushman Bharat a Game Changer?" *Indian Express*, 7 February, 2018; K. S. Rao, "Deconstructing Ayushman Bharat and Infusing Institutional Reform," Hindu Centre for Politics and Public Policy, November 20, 2018, https://www. thehinducentre.com/the-arena/current-issues/article25545260.ece.

46. V. Das, *Affliction*, 17.

47. C. Lahariya, "Mohalla Clinics of Delhi, India: Could These Become Platform to Strengthen Primary Healthcare?" *Journal of Family Medicine and Primary Care* 6, no. 1 (2017): 1–10.

48. M. Pentecost and T. Cousins, "'The Good Doctor': The Making and Unmaking of the Physician Self in Contemporary South Africa," *Journal of Medical Humanities*, August 23, 2019, 7–8.

49. Among the students with whom I interacted during my research, the number of candidates was variously cited as between 50,000 and 200,000, reflecting the slightly mythical quality that attaches to the ferocious level of competition for seats. The AIIMS annual report states that in 2016, 245,865 candidates registered and 189,357 of those sat the MBBS entrance exam for 672 seats across the seven All India Institutes then in operation. The allocation of seats at the various branches according to a student's entrance exam rank reflects an emerging hierarchy of preference (with New Delhi firmly at the apex), but this had not yet entered the discourse of the students I spoke with in Delhi. Students from AIIMS Bhopal who I spoke with when they visited for Pulse, the annual AIIMS student festival, readily acknowledged their institute's shortcomings in comparison with the Delhi original, however. While I focus on AIIMS New Delhi in this book, there will be great value in future studies of the new branches as they develop identities both independent of and in relation to the original All India Institute.

50. See World Bank, http://data.worldbank.org/indicator/SH.MED.PHYS.ZS.

51. S. Anand and V. Fan, The Health Workforce in India, Human Resources for Health Observer Series 16 (2016), World Health Organization, Geneva.

52. M. G. Deo, "Doctor Population Ratio for India—The Reality," *Indian Journal of Medical Research* 137, no. 4 (2014): 632–35; D. C. Sharma, "India Still Struggles with Rural Doctor Shortages," *The Lancet* 386 (10011), 2015: 2381–82.

53. V. Patel et al., "Assuring Health Coverage for All in India," 2427.

54. Ibid.

55. A. Ruddock, "Incorrect Dosage," *Caravan*, October 27, 2015; D. Shetty, "Fixing Healthcare," *Seminar*, September 2015; M. K. Unnikrishnan and A. Sharma, "Misplaced Reverence for Super-Specialists Has Led to Lopsided Public Health Priorities in India," *Economic and Political Weekly* 53, no. 44 (November 3, 2018), https://www.epw.in/engage/article/misplaced-reverence-for-super-specialists-has-led-to-lop-sided-public-health-priorities-in-india.

56. There are also increasing calls for the implementation of a common exit exam to tackle the variable standards in medical education. S. Rao and S. Naik, "Supreme Court Directive on Making NEET Compulsory Is Move in the Right Direction," *Indian Express*, May 10, 2016. "Govt Plans Exit Exam for All MBBS Students," Economic Times, July 27, 2016.

57. A. Ruddock, "Incorrect Dosage," *Caravan*, October 27, 2015; D. Shetty, "Fixing Healthcare," *Seminar*, September 2015; M. K. Unnikrishnan and A. Sharma, "Misplaced Reverence for Super-Specialists Has Led to Lopsided Public Health Priorities in India," *Economic and Political Weekly* 53, no. 44 (November 3, 2018), https://www.epw.in/engage/article/misplaced-reverence-for-super-specialists-has-led-to-lop-sided-public-health-priorities-in-india.

58. Personal communication, March 9, 2016.

59. In 2015, under direction of the Supreme Court, a three-judge panel was charged

with overseeing the MCI because of long-standing allegations of misconduct. In July 2016, it was reported that a government committee would propose replacing the MCI with a new National Medical Commission. In Sujatha Rao's assessment: "Over the years, the MCI has failed to establish transparent processes of granting recognition to medical colleges, update curricula, curb high capitation fees, or ensure quality and credibility of the products emerging out of the institutions. Such failures have adversely affected our national reputation and the quality of patient care. This aspect is not captured as there are no quality standards to measure outcomes." S. K. Rao, *Do We Care?*, 412.

60. V. Patel et al., "Assuring Health Coverage for All in India," 2428. T. Manuel, "India Produces 50,000 Doctors a Year: If Only Medical Education Were Better Regulated," *The Wire*, August 28, 2015; A. Sethi, "The Mystery of India's Deadly Exam Scam," *The Guardian*, December 17, 2015.

61. For a brilliantly bombastic illustration of corruption in private medical colleges, see the 2007 film *Sivaji* with the Tamil superstar Rajnikanth, directed by S. Shankar.

62. A. Macaskill, S. Stecklow, and S. Miglani, "Rampant Fraud at Medical Schools Leaves Indian Healthcare in Crisis," *Reuters*, June 16, 2015. J. D'Silva, "India's Private Medical Colleges and Capitation Fees," *BMJ*, no. 350, January 21, 2015, https://www.bmj.com/content/350/bmj.h106.full.print; V. Krishnan, "Most Medical Colleges Show Little Interest in Research: Study," *The Hindu*, April 21, 2016.

63. V. Patel et al., "Assuring Health Coverage for All in India," 2427.

64. Rachel Prentice, *Bodies in Formation: An Ethnography of Anatomy and Surgery Education* (Durham, NC: Duke University Press, 2013).

65. J. L. Chua, *In Pursuit of the Good Life: Aspiration and Suicide in Globalizing South India* (Berkeley: University of California Press, 2014); C. Jeffrey, *Timepass: Youth, Class, and the Politics of Waiting in India* (Stanford, CA: Stanford University Press, 2010); R. Lukose, *Liberalization's Children: Gender, Youth, and Consumer Citizenship in Globalizing India* (Durham, NC: Duke University Press, 2009); S. Poonam, *Dreamers: How Young Indians Are Changing Their World* (Delhi: Penguin Random House, 2018).

66. UNFPA, "State of World Population 2017," https://www.unfpa.org/swop.

67. S. Deshpande, "Exclusive Inequalities: Merit, Caste and Discrimination in Indian Higher Education Today," *Economic and Political Weekly* 41, no. 24 (2006): 2438–44; S. Deshpande, "Caste and Castelessness: Towards a Biography of the 'General Category,'" *Economic and Political Weekly* 47, no. 15 (2013): 32–39; A. Subramanian, *The Caste of Merit*.

68. V. Venkatesan, "The Dynamics of Medicos' Anti-Reservation Protests of 2006."

69. A. Subramanian, *The Caste of Merit*, 153–257.

70. C. Jeffrey, *Timepass*; S. Poonam, *Dreamers*.

71. B. Arnoldy, "In India, the Challenge of Building 50,000 Colleges," *Christian Science Monitor*, January 16, 2012.

72. C. Jeffrey, *Timepass*; S. Poonam, *Dreamers*.

73. Thus far, AIIMS has escaped any political interference in its curricula, notwithstanding Narendra Modi's now-infamous comment inferring the ancient Indian origins of plastic surgery from the Hindu myth of the elephant-headed god Ganesh. On rewarding private donors, see A. Kohli, *Poverty Amid Plenty in the New India* (Cambridge: Cam-

bridge University Press, 2006); N. Sundar, "India's Higher Education Troubles," *New York Times*, August 5, 2018.

74. P. Bourdieu, "The Forms of Capital," in *Handbook of Theory and Research for the Sociology of Education*, ed. J. Richardson (New York: Greenwood Books, 1986), 83–95.

75. J. L. Chua, *In Pursuit of the Good Life*, 5–6.

76. V. Turner, *The Forest of Symbols: Aspects of Ndembu Ritual* (Ithaca, NY: Cornell University Press, 1967).

77. S. Pinto, "Development without Institutions: Ersatz Medicine and the Politics of Everyday Life in North India." *Cultural Anthropology* 19, no. 3 (2004): 337–64.

78. F. W. Hafferty and R. Franks, "The Hidden Curriculum, Ethics Teaching, and the Structure of Medical Education," *Academic Medicine* 69, no. 11 (2004): 861–71; J. S. Taylor and C. Wendland, "The Hidden Curriculum in Medicine's 'Culture of No Culture,'" in *The Hidden Curriculum in Health Professional Education*, ed. F. W. Hafferty and J. F. O'Donnell (Lebanon, NH: Dartmouth College Press, 2014), 53–62; K. Ram, "Class and the Clinic: The Subject of Medical Pluralism and the Transmission of Inequality," *South Asian History and Culture* 1, no. 2 (2010): 199–212.

79. S. Bayly, "For Family, State and Nation: Achieving Cosmopolitan Modernity in Late-Socialist Vietnam," in *The Social Life of Achievement*, ed. N. J. Long and H. L. Moore (Oxford: Berghahn, 2013), 158–81; N. J. Long and H. L. Moore, eds., *The Social Life of Achievement* (Oxford: Berghahn, 2013).

80. S. Pinto, "Development without Institutions."

CHAPTER 2

Parts of this chapter appear in "The 'Indian Predicament': Medical Education and the Nation in India, 1880–1956" by A. Ruddock and P. Chakrabarti in *Medical Education: Historical Case Studies of Teaching, Learning, and Belonging in Honour of Jacalyn Duffin*, edited by S. Lamb and D. Gavrus (Montreal: MQUP, 2022).

1. R. Jeffery, *The Politics of Health in India*.

2. I use the description "Western medicine," rather than the more contemporary "biomedicine," in adherence to the terminology used during the period in question. The term became more contested after 1947. India's first prime minister, Jawaharlal Nehru, preferred "modern medicine" as a means of signifying scientific knowledge that developed as a result of efforts in both "West" and "East." J. Nehru, *Jawaharlal Nehru's Speeches*, vol. 2, 1949–1953 (Delhi: Publications Division, 1958), 550. Of course, the longer history of medicine and healing in India begins with the region's earliest populations; P. Bala, *Medicine and Medical Policies in India*.

3. R. Jeffery, "Recognizing India's Doctors: The Institutionalization of Medical Dependency, 1918–39," *Modern Asian Studies* 13, no. 2 (1979): 302–3.

4. P. Bala, *Medicine and Medical Policies*, 72–74; K. Kumar, *Political Agenda of Education: A Study of Colonialist and Nationalist Ideas* (New Delhi: Sage, 2005), 52–54.

5. D. G. Crawford, *A History of the Indian Medical Service*, 2:436, cited in R. Jeffery, *The Politics of Health in India*, 78. Vernacular education was reintroduced at certain institutions (though not the teaching of indigenous medicine) but was steadily transferred from the

major medical colleges to peripheral schools in order to ensure good favor with the medical authorities in Britain. K. Kumar, *Political Agenda of Education*, 133–36.

6. R. Jeffery, *The Politics of Health in India*, 76.

7. R. Jeffery, "Doctors and Congress." The GMC made it clear that Indian medical degrees would receive international recognition only if there was a clear distinction between those trained in Western medicine and those who had studied indigenous systems. Initial support within the All India Medical Association (later renamed the Indian Medical Association) for the inclusion of Indigenous practitioners was withdrawn, and a separate register for indigenous doctors was established in Bombay Presidency in 1938. R. Jeffery, *The Politics of Health in India*, 53–55. In later years Nehru seemed more concerned to recognize the achievements of India's own medical traditions, and he suggested in his convocation address to AIIMS graduates in 1964 that the institute work to "bridge the gap" between the two traditions. B. Singh, *Jawaharlal Nehru on Science and Society*, 264–66.

8. The IMS originated with the "surgeons" placed on the ships of the East India Company—a service organized by the company's own surgeon general as early as 1614. By the 1670s, these surgeons were recruited specifically to serve the company's civil employees in India, and by the time recruitment began for its standing army in 1749, it recorded 30 "medical men" in its Indian employ. Between the newly established Medical Services of Calcutta, Bombay, and Madras, the numbers of medical employees grew significantly from 1763 onward: by 1823, there were 630 commissioned officers in the medical departments of the three presidencies. R. Jeffery, *The Politics of Health in India*, 60–61.

9. Reliable data on the precise demographics of medical students is scarce, but we know that there was a broad dominance of high-caste Hindus, although fewer Brahmins than in other sectors of higher education (see P. Bala, *Medicine and Medical Policies in India*, 30, on the historical association of medicine with impure practice unbefitting Brahmins), and that Christians (initially European and later Eurasian or Anglo-Indian) were disproportionately represented, along with Parsis in Bombay. Muslims began to be proportionately represented only as a consequence of the introduction of reserved seats in the 1920s and 1930. R. Jeffery, *The Politics of Health in India*, 84.

10. Ibid.

11. A. Phadke, "Regulation of Doctors."

12. Bengal Administration Report, 1885, 306–7, cited in R. Jeffery, *The Politics of Health in India*, 83.

13. R. Jeffery, *The Politics of Health in India*, 33.

14. Ibid.

15. M. Harrison, *Public Health in British India*, 20–21.

16. R. Jeffery, "Recognizing India's Doctors," 311. Following the introduction of a minimum quota for Indian recruits in 1919, the figure grew to 37% by 1938. Jeffery attributes this rise more to a shortage of British applicants, given improved employment prospects for doctors in Britain, and to a perceived threat to senior positions inherent in the 1919 reforms, than to a willingness to cede more control to Indian medical officers.

17. R. Jeffery, *The Politics of Health in India*, 64.

18. Ibid., 217–21.

19. *Representation of the Bombay Medical Union*, 1.

20. "Memorandum on the Present Position and Future Prospects of the Indian Medical Service, 1913/14, Medical Appeal Board: Constitution of, Appointment, etc.," British Medical Association, India Office Records, Africa and Pacific Collections, British Library, London, IOR/L/S&G/8/305, 1. Subramanian describes a similar discourse about Indian engineers during the same period. A. Subramanian, *The Caste of Merit*, 37–38.

21. *Royal Commission on the Public Services in India*, 19–30.

22. Ibid., 1–23.

23. P. Chakrabarti, "Signs of the Times: Medicine and Nationhood in British India," *Osiris* 24, no. 1 (2009): 188–21.

24. Mehta's efforts remained anomalous in the wider landscape of medical education in India in the interwar period. Even as the administration of local health policy and bureaucracy was increasingly devolved to the provinces, the colonial government retained central supervision of the IMS rather than allowing nationalist politicians further autonomy. This arrangement entrenched the deep suspicion of the IMS among the nationalists and likely informed the decision to abolish it in 1947 and distribute power over medical civil servants to local governments. P. Chakrabarti, *Bacteriology in British India: Laboratory Medicine and the Tropics* (Rochester: University of Rochester Press, 2012), 84.

25. This was exemplified in Britain by the Beveridge Report of 1942, which presaged the creation of the National Health Service.

26. Government of India, *Health Survey and Development Committee*, 1:1.

27. R. Jeffery, *The Politics of Health in India*, 243.

28. Government of India, *Health Survey and Development Committee*, 4:60.

29. T. N. Madan, *Doctors and Society*, 30. Key figures of the deputation included Henry Sigerist, the communist historian of medicine at Johns Hopkins University; Janet Vaughan, principal of Somerville College, Oxford, who ran the first blood bank in London during the Blitz and was one of the first people to explore the association between illness and poverty; and John Ryle, the Oxford pioneer of social medicine. P. Murthy, A. Sarin, and S. Jain, "International Advisers to the Bhore Committee: Perceptions and Visions for Healthcare," *Economic and Political Weekly* 48, no. 10 (2013): 71–77.

30. A. V. Hill, *A Report to the Government of India*, 17.

31. C. G. Pandit, *My World of Preventive Medicine*, 147.

32. Ibid. In the case of the Indian Institutes of Technology, Subramanian describes a similar impetus to learn from institutions outside India, with the Massachusetts Institute of Technology (MIT) being the particular model of choice. A. Subramanian, *The Caste of Merit*, 69.

33. Ibid., 157, emphasis added.

34. "The Training of Doctors: Report by the Goodenough Committee."

35. C. G. Pandit, *My World of Preventive Medicine*, 158.

36. These were particularly promoted by Professor J. A. Ryle, head of the Department of Preventive and Social Medicine and a pioneer in the field. He described to the committee his method of teaching beyond lectures, including interactive seminars at which

patients were present. "The idea that the disease is a social and economic problem is inculcated," he told the visitors. C. G. Pandit, *My World of Preventive Medicine*, 161.

37. Ibid., original emphasis.

38. Government of India, *Health Survey and Development Committee*, 4:70.

39. Ibid., 165. In the same period, the Sarkar Committee recommended the establishment of the Indian Institutes of Technology. Unlike with AIIMS, however, the IITs were always envisaged as a group of institutions, with four established in different regions between 1951 and 1960. A. Subramanian, *The Caste of Merit*, 71–72.

40. International assistance also came from the US Technical Collaboration Mission in 1960 for construction of the main hospital, and from the Rockefeller Foundation for the purchase of medical equipment and library resources. T. N. Madan, *Doctors and Society*, 36. Nehru acknowledged this assistance in his convocation address in 1964.

41. The politics of knowledge in colonial India as expressed through science and technology has been well documented by historians. D. Raina and S. I. Habib, *Domesticating Modern Science: A Social History of Science and Culture in Colonial India* (Chennai: Tulika, 2004). The postcolonial context has also been analyzed by social scientists, including those who have critiqued the limitations of science as part of the Indian development project, arguing that the epistemic violence of its imperial heritage makes it inherently oppressive. G. Prakash, *Another Reason*; S. Ravi Rajan, "Science, State, and Violence: An Indian Critique Reconsidered," *Science as Culture* 14, no. 3 (2005): 1–17. J. Phalkey, "Introduction: Science, History, and Modern India," *Isis* 104, no. 2 (2013): 330–36. And see A. Subramanian, *The Caste of Merit*, on the specific discourse around engineering as the primary tool of national development in independent India.

42. D. Arnold, "Nehruvian Science and Postcolonial India," *Isis* 104, no. 2 (2013): 360–70. 364; W. Anderson, "Postcolonial Technoscience," *Social Studies of Science* 32, nos. 5–6 (2002): 643–58.

43. See W. Anderson and H. Pols, "Scientific Patriotism: Medical Science and National Self-Fashioning in Southeast Asia," *Comparative Studies in Society and History* 54, no. 1 (2012): 93–113. for examples of scientific patriotism wherein the nationalist movements in several Southeast Asian colonies were dominated by men trained in science and medicine. India's independence movement, by contrast, was dominated by lawyers.

44. J. Phalkey, "Introduction," 331.

45. D. Arnold, "Nehruvian Science," 364.

46. G. Prakash, *Another Reason*, 201–26.

47. Cited in R. Jeffery, *Politics of Health*, 244–45.

48. Government of India, "All India Institute of Medical Sciences Bill," 263.

49. Ibid., 264.

50. The AIIMS Act retains a provision in its Article 14 to "provide for the teaching of humanities in the undergraduate courses." This inclusion might have been encouraged by the advocates of comprehensive social medicine teaching, but there is no evidence to suggest such courses ever took place at AIIMS. Also see T. N. Madan, *Doctors and Society*, 82–83.

51. H. Miller, *Medicine and Society*, vol. 352 (London: Oxford University Press, 1973), 81.

52. D. Arnold, "Nehruvian Science," 366.

53. A. Subramanian, *The Caste of Merit*, 73.

54. D. Arnold, "Nehruvian Science," 366.

55. A. Subramanian, *The Caste of Merit*, 194.

56. Ibid., 72–73.

57. Ibid., 265.

58. Ibid.

59. Ibid.

60. Ibid.

61. V. Ramalingaswami, *Medicine, Health and Development: Ninth Jawaharlal Nehru Memorial Lecture*, 13, 8–9, cited in T. N. Madan, *Doctors and Society*, 103.

62. T. N. Madan, *Doctors and Society*, 105.

63. In his memoir, Pandit laments the failure of AIIMS to become "a teacher training institute for the country as a whole." He lays the blame for this partly on the rapid abolition of the IMS post-independence, which he argues undermined the center-state cooperation necessary to the original plan for the institute. The Mudaliar Committee, tasked in 1962 with reporting on the performance of the health sector since the Bhore Report, noted that the abolition of the IMS "had a certain centrifugal tendency in the sphere of health administration" and recommended that an All India Health Service be established along the lines of the Indian Administrative Service. The proposal was not adopted. C. G. Pandit, *My World of Preventive* Medicine, 166. In a more recent intervention, former health secretary Sujatha Rao has advocated for the creation of a national public health cadre. S. K. Rao, *Do We Care?*

64. C. G. Pandit, *My World of Preventive* Medicine, 162.

CHAPTER 3

1. M. Pentecost and T. Cousins, "The Good Doctor," 7; L. Eisenberg and A. Kleinman, *The Relevance of Social Science to Medicine* (Dordrecht: Reidel, 1981), 12.

2. The contemporary Indian elite, not unlike their predecessors, send their children to the country's most exclusive schools. Afterward, they go abroad for undergraduate study, from where they may or may not return to India as members of a hypermobile global elite. L. Fernandes, *India's New Middle Class*; C. Fuller and H. Narasimhan, "Information Technology Professionals and the New-Rich Middle Class in Chennai (Madras)," *Modern Asian Studies* 41, no. 1 (2007): 121–50.

3. Bourdieu presents "three fundamental guises" of capital. The first is economic: "immediately and directly convertible into money and may be institutionalised in the form of property rights." The second is cultural: "convertible, on certain conditions, into economic capital and may be institutionalised in the form of educational qualifications." And the third is social: "made up of social obligations ('connections'), which is convertible, in certain conditions, into economic capital and may be institutionalised in the form of a title of nobility." P. Bourdieu, "The Forms of Capital," 84. Crucial to this theory is the convertible nature of the different forms of capital and the labor inherent in this process. Bourdieu was particularly concerned with how educational systems act to reproduce social struc-

tures. P. Bourdieu and J. Passeron, *Reproduction in Education, Society and Culture* (London: Sage, 2015).

4. C. Wilson, "The Social Transformation of the Medical Profession in Urban Kerala: Doctors, Social Mobility and the Middle Classes," in *Being Middle Class in India: A Way of Life*, ed. H. Donner (Abingdon, UK: Routledge, 2011), 139–61.

5. C. Fuller and H. Narasimhan, "Information Technology Professionals"; A. Subramanian, "Making Merit: The Indian Institutes of Technology and the Social Life of Caste," *Comparative Studies in Society and History* 57, no. 2 (2015): 291–322; A. Subramanian, *The Caste of Merit*.

6. Although most people who mentioned engineering to me associated it with IT and software engineering, Priya seemed to refer to the more traditional perception of civil engineering, in which an employee might be posted at various sites around the country for certain periods of time. Subramanian notes this new hierarchy within engineering: "the difference between conceptual and practical training has become a crucial part of institutional stratification, with the IITs seen as the most conceptual of engineering colleges." "Making Merit," 316.

7. In Priya's 2011 batch at AIIMS, 20 of the 72 students were female, a slightly higher proportion than subsequent batches, in which the number of female students ranged from 15 to 18.

8. P. Froerer, "Education, Inequality, and Social Mobility in Central India," *European Journal of Development Research* 23 (2011): 695–711; C. Jeffrey, *Timepass*, 64–66. These accounts tend to focus, necessarily, on the transition from primary to secondary education among lower socioeconomic groups, but there is a rich seam of research potential in gender and decision making among middle-class students in higher education. See H. Donner, *Domestic Goddesses: Maternity, Globalisation and Middle-Class Identity in Contemporary India* (Aldershot, UK: Ashgate, 2008) for an example of where this journey begins, as middle-class mothers in Calcutta seek to place their children in "appropriate" preschools. Also C. Jeffrey, *Timepass*, 178, on the need for more research into how women navigate, shape and contend gendered practices.

9. C. Wilson, "The Social Transformation of the Medical Profession in Urban Kerala: Doctors, Social Mobility and the Middle Classes," in *Being Middle Class in India: A Way of Life*, ed. H. Donner (Abingdon, UK: Routledge, 2011), 139–61.

10. In Dandekar's study of medical students in Maharashtra, she found that among general category students the top three motivators were "personal determination," parents, then teachers. Whereas for students in reserved categories the order was teachers, determination, and then parents. V. Dandekar, "Reservations in Medical Education in Maharashtra: An Empirical Study," in *Beyond Inclusion: The Practice of Equal Access in Indian Higher Education*, ed. S. Deshpande and U. Zacharias (New Delhi: Routledge, 2013), 120.

11. In T. N. Madan's survey of AIIMS doctors in the late 1970s, over one-third responded that their parents or other family members had been directly involved in the decision to pursue medicine. *Doctors and Society*, 55.

12. C. Wilson, "The Social Transformation of the Medical Profession," 149.

13. C.L. Wendland, *A Heart for the Work*, 80, 74, 81.

14. M. Pentecost and T. Cousins, "The Good Doctor," 5–6.

15. J. Kasper et al., "All Health Is Global Health, All Medicine Is Social Medicine: Integrating the Social Sciences into the Preclinical Curriculum," *Academic Medicine* 91, no. 5 (2016): 628–35.

16. M. Pentecost and T. Cousins, "The Good Doctor," 6.

17. Ibid., 73.

18. Subramanian reports parallel narratives with regard to engineering in her study of IIT Madras. *The Caste of Merit*, 149.

19. P. Bourdieu, *Distinction: A Social Critique of the Judgement of Taste* (Abingdon, UK: Routledge, 2010).

20. The section title is inspired by Ray Bradbury's Fahrenheit 451: "Peace, Montag. Give the people contests they win by remembering the words to more popular songs or the names of state capitals or how much corn Iowa grew last year. Cram them full of noncombustible data, chock them so damned full of 'facts' they feel stuffed, but absolutely 'brilliant' with information. Then they'll feel they're thinking, they'll get a *sense* of motion without moving. And they'll be happy, because facts of that sort don't change." Ray Bradbury, *Fahrenheit 451* (1953; London: Harper Collins, 1998), 61.

21. P. Jeffery, "Hearts, Minds and Pockets," in *Educational Regimes in Contemporary India*, ed. R. Chopra and P. Jeffery (New Delhi: Sage, 2005), 13–38; K. Kumar, *Political Agenda of Education*; K. N. Panikkar, T. Joseph, Geetha G., and M. A. Lal, *Quality, Access and Social Justice in Higher Education* (New Delhi: Pearson, 2011); M. Priyam, *Contested Politics of Educational Reform in India : Aligning Opportunities with Interests* (New Delhi: Oxford University Press, 2015).

22. P. Bourdieu, "The Forms of Capital"; P. Bourdieu and J. Passaron, *Reproduction in Education*; S. Deshpande, "Exclusive Inequalities: Merit, Caste and Discrimination in Indian Higher Education Today," *Economic and Political Weekly* 41, no. 24 (2006): 2438–44; P. Jeffery, "Hearts, Minds and Pockets."

23. C. Bayly, *Empire and Information: Intelligence Gathering and Social Communication in India, 1780–1870* (Cambridge: Cambridge University Press, 1996); N. Crook, ed., *The Transmission of Knowledge in South Asia: Essays on Education, Religion, History, and Politics* (New Delhi: Oxford University Press, 1996); K. Kumar, *Political Agenda of Education*.

24. Crook suggests a conceptual division of knowledge into raw data and the competence to act on it as a means of understanding histories of education and knowledge transmission (*The Transmission of Knowledge*, 4, 11). In Punjab in the late 1850s, William Arnold, director of public instruction, was preoccupied by a perceived division between practical and theoretical knowledge, suggesting that knowledge in precolonial North India tended to be "specialized and involuted, rather than interactive and generalized." His reports of his tour of the province in 1857–1858 reflect a serious interest in educational methods and ideals, and a general perplexity in the face of existing Indian practices, including the emphasis on memorization, which had often been a means of sharing texts and transmitting knowledge before the printing press reached Punjab in the early nineteenth-century. K. Kumar, *Political Agenda of Education*, 52–56.

25. Bayly questions too rigid a hypothesis about hierarchical and segmented knowledge and "knowing persons," and suggests that by the time the British imposed their own administrative systems, there was already a degree of knowledge sharing and outward orientation among epistemological communities, suggesting that the "revolution" in education associated with colonial power had its seeds in the precolonial Indian landscape of knowledge transmission and transfer. *Empire and Information*, 290–91, 309. For administrators such as Arnold, committed to an educational ideal that promoted the application of critical competence to factual knowledge, the effect of the new curriculum might have been disappointing. In his reports, Arnold had recognized that "consigning to memory large texts and bits of information was the prime skill used in traditional, indigenous pedagogy." Yet his enthusiasm for the "transformation" that had taken place in education in Punjab, that saw boys able to narrate "the early Muhammadan invasions of India," adhere to "the first four rules of arithmetic," and "pass a good exam" in geography, seemed to overlook the explanation that these results were largely obtained using the same rote learning and memorization techniques of which he had so disapproved. K. Kumar, *Political Agenda of Education*, 60.

26. Ibid., 66.

27. The problematic contemporary consequences of the devaluation of the teacher's role include absenteeism and the arbitrary mistreatment of students. See R. Chopra, "Sisters and Brothers: Schooling, Family and Migration," in *Educational Regimes in Contemporary India*, ed. R. Chopra and P. Jeffery (New Delhi: Sage, 2005), 299–315; M. Priyam, *Contested Politics*, 210–17.

28. K. Kumar, *Political Agenda of Education*, 68. For an analysis of the historical trajectory from the colonial Indian Civil Services exam to contemporary mass college entrance exams, see Deshpande, "Pass, Fail, Distinction"; Subramanian, *The Caste of Merit*, 157–63.

29. M. Premchand, "Bade Bhai Sahab" (1910), https://www.scribd.com/doc/6691922/Bade-Bhai-Sahab. My translation.

30. Bayly notes, however, that elite institutions such as Delhi College, the Hindu College, and Jay Narayan Ghosal's college in Banaras did produce "a new type of educated man" who engaged in religious, literary, and historical debate. S. Bayly, *Empire and Information*, 306–7.

31. K. Kumar, *Political Agenda of Education*, 68.

32. P. Bourdieu, "The Forms of Capital," 248.

33. K. Kumar, *Political Agenda of Education*, 39.

34. S. Bayly, "For Family, State and Nation: Achieving Cosmopolitan Modernity in Late-Socialist Vietnam," in *The Social Life of Achievement*, ed. N. J. Long and H. L. Moore (Oxford: Berghahn, 2013), 158–81. See also P. Froerer, "Education, Inequality and Social Mobility," 704; P. Bourdieu, "The Forms of Capital," 95.

35. Oxfam India, "Education to Turn Mirrors into Windows," 2015, https://www.oxfamindia.org/subpage/220.

36. In its figures for 2014, the Ministry of Human Resource Development reports a gross enrollment ratio of 99.3% in primary education (class 1–5), 87.4% in upper primary (class 6–8), declining to 73.6% in secondary (class 9–10) and 49.1% in senior secondary

(class 11–12). Higher education had an enrollment ratio of 21.1% in 2014. "Educational Statistics at a Glance," Government of India, Ministry of Human Resource Development, Bureau of Planning, Monitoring and Statistics, New Delhi, 2014, http://www.education-forallinindia.com/educational_statistics_at_glance-MHRD_2014.pdf.

37. P. Jeffery, "Hearts, Minds and Pockets," 13, original emphasis.

38. B. A. Levinson, D. E. Foley, and D. C. Holland, eds., *The Cultural Production of the Educated Person: An Introduction* (Albany: State University of New York Press, 1996); P. Froerer, "Education, Inequality and Social Mobility," 696.

39. R. Jeffery, C. Jeffrey, and P. Jeffery, "Social Inequalities and the Privatisation of Secondary Schooling in North India," in *Educational Regimes in Contemporary India*, 41–61. In their study of the educational aspirations and outcomes among young men in rural Uttar Pradesh, Jeffrey and colleagues found locally dominant castes consolidating their social position through a change from direct inheritance to a form of "mediated reproduction" that uses existing forms of capital—wealth, status, and social connections—to secure privileged access to superior schooling and government employment. Conversely, the lack of economic, cultural, and social capital among lower castes acts as a formidable barrier to the quality of education they can access, and, by extension, to salaried employment. See M. Ciotti, "In the Past We Were a Bit 'Chamar': Education as a Self- and Community Engineering Process in Northern India," *Journal of the Royal Anthropological Institute* 12, no. 4 (2006): 899–916.

40. P. Bourdieu, "The Forms of Capital," 248. We see another example of this ambiguity in Peggy Froerer's work in "Education, Inequality and Social Mobility" on education and social mobility among Adivasis in rural Chhattisgarh.

41. K. Kumar, *Political Agenda of Education*, 37; O. Mendelsohn and M. Vicziany, *The Untouchables: Subordination, Poverty and the State in Modern India* (Cambridge: Cambridge University Press, 1998), 80–81.

42. V. Benei, *Schooling Passions: Nation, History, and Language in Contemporary Western India* (Stanford, CA: Stanford University Press, 2008); L. Fernandes, *India's New Middle Class*; C. Jeffrey, *Timepass*.

43. See R. Chopra, "Sisters and Brothers" on parental decision making about the different educational trajectories of daughters and sons. On how disadvantages combine to preclude social mobility through education, see A. Krishna, "Examining the Structure of Opportunity and Social Mobility in India: Who Becomes an Engineer?" *Development and Change* 45 (2014): 1–28.

44. P. Froerer, "Education, Inequality and Social Mobility," 710.

45. S. Deshpande, "Pass, Fail, Distinction," 14.

46. Bourdieu and Passaron, *Reproduction in Education*, 153.

47. C. L. Wendland, *A Heart for the Work*, 73.

48. For greatly enriching my analysis of the AIIMS entrance exam in the sections that follow, I am indebted to the work of Satish Deshpande on the exam as a social institution, ("Exclusive Inequalities," "Pass, Fail, Distinction," 2006, 2010) and Ajantha Subramanian on the JEE, the entrance exam for the IITs (The Caste of Merit, 163–213). Amanda Gilbertson's analysis of schooling in middle-class Hyderabad suggests that perceptions

of value in education systems both enable and change with class mobility. Gilbertson found that "international" schools are valued by upper-middle-class parents in communities that recently migrated from rural to urban settings for their emphasis on "exposure," which they anticipate will give their children an advantage in a globalized marketplace over those whose education is based on rote learning. See A. Gilbertson, "'Mugging Up' versus 'exposure': International Schools and Social Mobility in Hyderabad, India," *Ethnography and Education* 9, no. (2014): 210–23; A. Gilbertson, "Cosmopolitan Learning, Making Merit, and Reproducing Privilege in Indian Schools," *Anthropology and Education Quarterly* 47 (2016): 297–313. A concern about the limitations of rote learning was also voiced by wealthier parents in Uttar Pradesh, who sent their children to urban centers for secondary schooling that would instill the critical mindset deemed important for securing upwardly mobile employment. Jeffrey et al., "Social Inequalities," 2092; V. Benei, *Schooling Passions*.

49. Deshpande, "Pass, Fail, Distinction," 33.

50. Subramanian, *The Caste of Merit*, 178–81.

51. U. Rawal and D. Quazi, "Kota Suicides: In This Coaching Hotspot, Stress Snuffs out Lives," *Hindustan Times*, September 19, 2015.

52. S. Malhotra, "The Dream Factories," *Business Today*, May 12, 2013.

53. In 2016, one particular coaching institute produced several top ten AIIMS candidates, and the top three in the JEE. In 2017, suspicions were raised when a single institute claimed all top 10 AIIMS MBBS entrants. Institutes have been accused of "buying" or offering free tuition to promising students in order to maintain their reputation in an increasingly crowded market. See D. H. Quazi, "AIIMS in Bag, Test Toppers Set New Goals: Neurosurgery, Research." *Hindustan Times*, June 15, 2016; *Hindustan Times*, "AIIMS MBBS Result 2017: Top 10 from One Kota Coaching School. Isn't It Odd?" June 15, 2017.

54. S. Bayly, "For Family, State and Nation," 161.

55. C. Bhagat, *Revolution Twenty20* (Delhi: Rupa Publications, 2011).

56. See Subramanian, *The Caste of Merit*, 198–202, on the striking recollection by an IIT Madras alumnus of the punishing routine at a coaching center in south India that he describes as "a prison" and that had a damaging impact on his mental health.

57. T. Ghosh, "Making of an Engineer: My Journey through School, Kota, and Depression," Youth Ki Awaaz, June 30, 2016, http://www.youthkiawaaz.com/2016/06/kota-engineering-led-to-depression/.

58. S. Datta, "Kota Rocked by 5 Student Suicides in 1 Month," *Indian Express*, June 30, 2015; U. Rawal and D. Quazi, "Kota Suicides"; A. H. Quazi, "Student Suicides in Rajasthan's Kota Drop by 70%," *Hindustan Times*, November 8, 2017.

59. Dandekar describes the pressure of coaching loans taken out by poorer students at the college she studied in Maharashtra. "Reservations in Medical Education," 127.

60. S. Deshpande, "Pass, Fail, Distinction," 8; P. Bourdieu and J. Passaron, *Reproduction in Education*, 153–54.

61. S. Deshpande, "Pass, Fail, Distinction," 17.

62. Those who do get in without the English-medium education Sushil deemed necessary

often encounter difficulties managing expectations and the lack of institutional support, as I discuss in chapter 4.

63. In 2014, a group of AIIMS students established an online exam preparation and mentoring service for prospective candidates. A member of their team told me that they focus particularly on training students to answer the reason assertion questions. The company's profile was raised in 2016 after one of their students topped the entrance exam.

64. A. Subramanian, *The Caste of Merit*, 179, original emphasis.

65. S. Deshpande, "Pass, Fail, Distinction," 18. Deshpande suggests that if changes occur in an effort to make mass examinations more effective in identifying potential aptitude for particular careers, they might incorporate multistage and mixed-method testing.

66. S. Deshpande, "Pass, Fail, Distinction," 7.

67. A. Subramanian, *The Caste of Merit*, 171.

68. N. J. Long and H. L. Moore, eds., *The Social Life of Achievement*, 11, 13.

69. C. Stafford, "Numbers and the natural history of imagining the self in Taiwan and China," *Ethnos* 74, no. 1 (2009): 110–26. For a discussion of the slow evolution of the anthropology of numbers—as distinct from the small subfield of ethno-mathematics—beginning with its instigation by Thomas Crump and his interest in "the lore of numbers," see J. I. Guyer, N. Khan, and J. Obarrio, "Number as Inventive Frontier," *Anthropological Theory* 10, nos. 1–2 (2010): 36–61. They remark in detail on the various disciplinary approaches to numbers—from the obvious mathematics, to semiotics and its ideas about mathematical grammars of meaning, philosophy, and cognitive psychology—that might inform an anthropological approach to human relationships with numbers in the ethnographic present. See also T. Crump, *The Anthropology of Numbers* (Cambridge: Cambridge University Press, 1990), 146.

70. A. Appadurai, "Number in the Colonial Imagination," in *Orientalism and the Postcolonial Predicament: Perspectives on South Asia*, ed. C. A. Breckenridge and P. van der Veer (Philadelphia: University of Pennsylvania Press, 1993), 314–39.

71. S. Deshpande, "Pass, Fail, Distinction," 16.

72. S. Deshpande, "Exclusive Inequalities," 2442.

73. S. Deshpande, "Pass, Fail, Distinction," 19.

74. B. Cohn, *The Census, Social Structure and Objectification in South Asia*, in *An Anthropologist among the Historians and Other Essays* (Oxford: Oxford University Press, 1987).

75. N. Peabody, "Cents, Sense, Census: Human Inventories in Late Precolonial and Early Colonial India," *Comparative Studies in Society and History* 43, no. 4 (2001): 821.

76. I. Hacking, "Making Up People," in *Reconstructing Individualism*, ed. T. L. Heller, M. Sosna, and D. E. Wellbery (Stanford, CA: Stanford University Press, 1985) 161–71.

77. A. Appadurai, "Number in the Colonial Imagination," 317.

78. Ibid., 320.

79. C. Stafford, "Numbers," 7.

80. Ibid., 1.

81. A. Appadurai, "Number in the Colonial Imagination," 334.

82. In this spirit, the World Health Organization named its strategy for reviewing maternal deaths "Beyond the Numbers," Geneva, 2004, http://www.who.int/maternal_

child_adolescent/documents/9241591838/en/. For an example of how ethnography can contribute to this effort in an Indian context, see K. Gutschow, "Going 'Beyond the Numbers': Maternal Death Reviews in India," *Medical Anthropology* 35, no. 4 (2016): 322–70.

83. J. I. Guyer et al., "Number as Inventive Frontier," 37, original emphasis.

84. C. Stafford, "Numbers," 7, original emphasis.

85. P. Jeffery, "Hearts, Minds and Pockets," 20; Deshpande, "Pass, Fail, Distinction," 7.

86. S. Bregnbaek, *Fragile Elite: The Dilemmas of China's Top University Students* (Stanford, CA: Stanford University Press, 2016); P. Bourdieu, "The Forms of Capital," 88.

87. S. Deshpande, "Caste and Castelessness."

88. A. Subramanian, "Making Merit."

89. U. Rao, "Biometric Marginality: UID and the Shaping of Homeless Identities in the City," *Economic and Political Weekly* 48, no. 13 (2013): 71–77.

90. Rank is not entirely abstracted from biology, however, in the views of those who still consider intellectual "merit" innate to upper castes and rare among Dalit and Adivasi communities.

91. Subramanian, *The Caste of Merit*, 191.

CHAPTER 4

1. S. Tharu, M. M. Prasad, R. Pappu, and K. Satyanarayana, "Reservations and the Return to Politics," *Economic and Political Weekly* 42, no. 49 (2007): 39–45.

2. In the 1970s, T. N. Madan found that compulsory attendance had been suspended in response to student demands, and subsequently reinstated (*Doctors and Society*, 82). At some point it was suspended once again.

3. The film *Placebo* (2015, dir. Kumar) gives an insight into hostel living at AIIMS, where peeling paint is visible in the same room as a Mac desktop computer. For comparison, see Dandekar's study of students at a government medical college in Maharashtra who spoke of gratitude for their own iron cot (without a mattress) and reliable water and electricity supply. One student reported cycling 20 kilometers to college each day because his family could not afford the subsidized hostel fee ("Reservations in Medical Education," 126). Also see Jeffrey (*Timepass*, 75–78) for an account of poor infrastructure at a college in Meerut.

4. C. Jeffrey, *Timepass*, 81.

5. Pulse, the annual student-organized festival on campus, is considered an important means of "enrichment," as Neha and Priya put it. Organized by third-years, Pulse is a serious business, attracting corporate sponsorship and allegedly offering a more literal means of enrichment to students in key positions. Pulse offers opportunities to be involved in the creative and performance side of P-Wave, the much anticipated opening show, as well as in management and administration tasks. However, the 2007 Thorat Report into caste discrimination at AIIMS cited exclusion from participation in Pulse as one way this manifested. Although students did not raise this as an issue with me, this is not to say that incidents of exclusion do not still occur.

6. While Victor Turner's original description of liminality in *The Forest of Symbols* pertained to coming-of-age initiation rites among the Ndembu in Zambia, scholars have

demonstrated the relevance of the concept in a variety of contemporary contexts. See A. Horvath, B. Thomassen, and H. Wydra, eds., *Breaking Boundaries: Varieties of Liminality* (New York: Berghahn, 2015). For a historical overview of the use of liminality in anthropology, beginning with van Gennep's 1909 Rites of Passage, see B. Thomassen, "Thinking with Liminality: To the Boundaries of an Anthropological Concept," in *Breaking Boundaries*, 39–58.

7. V. Turner, *The Forest of Symbols*, 95–97.

8. Ibid., 105.

9. Any discussion of sex was indirect. It was alluded to when students pointed out that women had unrestricted access to the male hostels, with some taking up semipermanent residence. Or when Ashish told me that he had to buy condoms for a senior student during the month of "ragging" that greets new MBBS arrivals. While ragging has been officially banned on Indian university campuses since 2009, it continues at AIIMS, albeit in a milder form than previously (see *Placebo* 2015, dir. Kumar).

10. L. Abraham, "Bhai-Behen, True Love, Time Pass: Friendships and Sexual Partnerships among Youth in an Indian Metropolis," *Culture, Health and Sexuality* 4, no. 3 (2002): 337–53.

11. V. Turner, *The Forest of Symbols*, 95, 100.

12. For a thorough history of affirmative action in India, see Marc Galanter, *Competing Equalities: Law and the Backward Classes in India* (New Delhi: Oxford University Press, 1984); O. Mendelsohn and M. Vicziany, *The Untouchables*; Z. Hasan, *Politics of Inclusion: Castes, Minorities, and Affirmative Action* (New Delhi: Oxford University Press, 2009). For recent work on the anthropology of affirmative action across South Asia, see A. Shah and S. Shneiderman, "Toward an Anthropology of Affirmative Action," *Focaal* 65 (2013): 3–16.

13. Z. Hasan, *Politics of Inclusion*, 87.

14. C. Jaffrelot, *India's Silent Revolution : The Rise of the Lower Castes* (London: Hurst, 2002).

15. The petition challenged the policy on three grounds. First, that the OBC quota violated the constitutional guarantee of equality of opportunity. Second, that caste was not a reliable indicator of "backwardness." Third, that the proposed quota threatened the efficiency of public services. V. Venkatesan, "The Dynamics of Medicos' Anti-Reservation Protests," 145.

16. Not all agree with the exclusion of affluent OBCs from reservation policies. Deshpande, for example, argues that such a decision empties "the social" of meaning, if discrimination is presumed to dissipate with the accumulation of wealth ("Caste and Castelessness," 37). Tharu and colleagues also discuss the problems of conflating social discrimination with economic deprivation ("Reservations and the Return to Politics"). Hasan writes about historical and contemporary debates over the use of caste rather than economic class to determine eligibility for reservations, and in particular the detrimental consequences this has for Muslims, who continue to be disproportionately deprived and discriminated against as a group (*The Politics of Inclusion*).

17. Z. Hasan, *Politics of Inclusion*, 103; V. Venkatesan, "The Dynamics of Medicos' Anti-Reservation Protests."

18. Z. Hasan, *Politics of Inclusion*, 103.

19. A. Subramanian, "Making Merit."

20. See Subramanian, *The Caste of Merit*, for an in-depth account of how merit became synonymous with upper casteness at IIT Madras.

21. Cited in S. Deshpande, "Caste and Castelessness," 37.

22. A. Subramanian, *The Caste of Merit*. Radhika Chopra has studied teachers' attitudes toward lower-caste children in primary school classrooms, noting an improvement in recent years alongside a persistent belief by some in the inherent "educability" of pupils depending on their caste. R. Chopra, "Sisters and Brothers."

23. Cited in V. Venkatesan, "The Dynamics of Medicos' Anti-Reservation Protests," 148. The eponymous petitioner in the main case, *Ashoka Kumar Thakur v. Union of India*, was an advocate in the Supreme Court. Venkatesan argues on pages 150–51 that by ignoring standard protocol that would demand the writ be rephrased without the use of offensive language, and by including the original phrasing in the 2007 Interim Order that imposed a stay on the implementation of the act, the judiciary betrayed caste prejudice and an alliance with the striking members of the medical community.

24. Z. Hasan, *Politics of Inclusion*, 102–4.

25. Government of India, "Report of the Committee to Enquire into the Allegation of Differential Treatment of SC/ST Students in All India Institute of Medical Science [*sic*]," 2007, http://www.nlhmb.in/reports%20aiims.pdf.

26. Ibid., 60.

27. *Placebo* (2015, dir. Kumar) shows students protesting outside the director's bungalow during Deka's tenure, in the wake of the suicide of an ST student.

28. Government of India, "Report of the Committee," 61–62.

29. A. Dhar, "AIIMS Rejects Thorat Report," *The Hindu*, September 20, 2007.

30. V. Adams, *Doctors for Democracy* (Cambridge: Cambridge University Press, 1998).

31. A. Subramanian, *The Caste of Merit*, 238.

32. V. Venkatesan, "The Dynamics of Medicos' Anti-Reservation Protests."

33. S. Deshpande, "Caste and Castelessness," original emphasis.

34. S. S. Jodhka and K. Newman, "In the Name of Globalisation: Meritocracy, Productivity and the Hidden Language of Caste," *Economic and Political Weekly* 42, no. 41 (2007): 4125–32.

35. "Discrimination" is a freighted term; when associated with caste in an environment with relevant history, like AIIMS, it has dramatic and often violent connotations. In January 2016, Rohith Vemula, a Dalit PhD student at the University of Hyderabad committed suicide following institutional discrimination against him and fellow members of a Dalit political group on campus. The case dominated the headlines and provoked a bout of national outrage before fading from view. P. Donthi, "From Shadows to the Stars: The Defiant Politics of Rohith Vemula and the Ambedkar Students Association," *The Caravan*, May 2016. For a first-person reflection on life as a Dalit student at the same university,

see N. Sukumar, "Quota's Children: The Perils of Getting Educated," in *Beyond Inclusion*, 205–21.

36. While friendship groups were not strictly delineated along lines of category affiliation, such conversations, it seemed, largely were. In Dandekar's study of medical students at GMCM Maharashtra, respondents from the general category reported that 78% of their friends were from the general category and 22% from reserved groups, while those from reserved groups reported 48% of friendships with other students with a reservation and 52% with people in the general category. V. Dandekar, "Reservations in Medical Education," 124.

37. The students from beyond India's Hindi heartland have the additional challenge of improving their Hindi in order to communicate effectively with patients. Some teachers were more understanding than others about this task.

38. A. James, "Keralites Shine in Delhi AIIMS Union Elections, Win All Posts Except One," *International Business Times*, July 23, 2015.

39. Government of India, "Report of the Committee," 53–58.

40. *The Hindu*, "Protest against Denial of Reservation at AIIMS," October 3, 2010; *The Statesman*, "AIIMS Faculty Demands Drive to Fill SC, ST Posts," September 15, 2015.

41. Forum for Rights and Equality, AIIMS, New Delhi, "Forum for Rights and Equality to The Secretary, Ministry of Health and Family Welfare," January 19, 2015.

42. Nikhil's comment about "eating from the same plate" is a reference to the history of discriminatory practices by upper castes who refuse to share utensils with lower castes because they believe they will be "polluted" in the process.

43. Government of India, "Report of the Committee," 32–36. The most explicit bullying, including locking students in their rooms and writing abusive messages on their doors until they agreed to move to a different floor of the hostel, took place in the men's hostels. Fewer female students reported direct bullying, but those in reserved categories tended to form their own social clusters. I obviously cannot be certain that students were not intentionally protecting the image of AIIMS in their discussions with me. The willingness of many of them to critique the institution along various lines, however, including in terms of caste discrimination among faculty, suggests that their reflections were candid. Furthermore, my intention here is not to provide empirical proof one way or the other but to reflect on what students *did* say and what that might tell us about the contemporary life of the institution. For more on methodology, see the appendix.

44. In January 2019, the 124th Amendment to the Indian Constitution established a 10% quota of places for economically weaker sections of the general category in higher education institutions and government employment. At the time of writing, the consequences of this policy have yet to emerge. A recent analysis of 445 higher education institutions shows that this section of students already represents 28% of total places, raising questions about the evidence base for the policy. B. Reddy et al., "New Reservation Policy: Is It Empirically Justifiable?" *Economic and Political Weekly* 54, no. 23 (June 8, 2019): 12–14.

45. A. Subramanian, *The Caste of Merit*, 238.

46. S. Deshpande, "Caste and Castelessness," 38.

47. A. Subramanian, "Making Merit," 293.

48. S. Deshpande, "Caste and Castelessness," 33; A. Subramanian, "Making Merit," 293, *The Caste of Merit*, 141.

49. A. Subramanian, "Making Merit."

50. S. Tharu et al., "Reservations and the Return to Politics."

51. S. Deshpande, "Caste and Castelessness."

52. S. Tharu et al., "Reservations and the Return to Politics," 39.

53. A. Subramanian, *The Caste of Merit*, 174.

54. S. Deshpande, "Caste and Castelessness," 38.

55. Ibid.; A. Beteille, "The Reproduction of Inequality: Occupation, Caste and Family," *Contributions to Indian Sociology* 25, no. 1 (1991): 3–28; L. Fernandes, *India's New Middle Class*.

56. Currently, only the OBC creamy layer is excluded from the quota by court order. However, the fact that Priya appears to consider herself part of the ST creamy layer shows how unstable these categories are and that it is not only upper-caste voices arguing for affirmative action to be adjudged on economic rather than caste criteria. Questions about the creamy layer within SC and ST groups may soon be on the political agenda. Deshpande, "Caste and Castelessness," 37.

57. S. S. Jodhka and K. Newman, "In the Name of Globalisation"; A. M. Shah, "Job Reservations and Efficiency," *Economic and Political Weekly* 26, no. 29 (1991): 1732–24. These objections contain echoes of the modern history of Western political thought, wherein efforts to create more equitable societies were underpinned by an understanding that hierarchies would persist on the basis of people's different innate capabilities. Legitimizing natural intellectual variation allowed for the establishment of societies that could appeal to nature and rationality while promoting "virtues and talents." J. Carson, *The Measure of Merit: Talents, Intelligence, and Inequality in the French and American Republics, 1750–1940* (Princeton, NJ: Princeton University Press, 2006); A. Subramanian, *The Caste of Merit*, 17–18. This discourse has not disappeared in the West. In 2015, the late US Supreme Court justice Antonin Scalia suggested during the hearing of a case about an affirmative action admissions policy at the University of Texas that black students might be better off attending "a slower-track school where they do well" rather than a highly selective college that has taken race into account when admitting them. A. Hartocollis, "With Remarks in Affirmative Action Case, Scalia Steps into 'Mismatch' Debate," New York Times, December 10, 2015, https://www.nytimes.com/2015/12/11/us/with-remarks-in-affirmative-action-case-scalia-steps-into-mismatch-debate.html.

58. A. Deshpande and T. E. Weisskopf, "Does Affirmative Action Affect Productivity in the Indian Railways?" (Working Paper No. 185, Centre for Development Economics, Delhi School of Economics, 2011), http://www.cdedse.org/pdf/work185.pdf; J. Parry, "Two Cheers for Reservation: The Satnamis and the Steel Plant," in *Institutions and Inequalities: Essays in Honour of Andre Beteille*, ed. J. Parry and R. Guha (New Delhi: Oxford University Press, 2009), 128–69.

59. S. Deshpande, "Pass, Fail, Distinction," 7.

60. V. Venkatesan, "The Dynamics of Medicos' Anti-Reservation Protests"; A. Subramanian, "Making Merit."

61. S. Deshpande, "Caste Quotas and Formal Inclusion in Indian Higher Education," in *Beyond Inclusion*, 41.

62. S. Pinto, "Development without Institutions," 358.

63. Ibid.

64. U. Zacharias, "To Race with the Able? Soft Skills and the Psychologisation of Marginality," in *Beyond Inclusion*, 291–92.

65. Snigdha Poonam, in *Dreamers*, describes how personality development is considered important for success among young aspirational Indians beyond the major cities. An increasing number of business ventures cater to this anxiety.

66. U. Zacharias, "To Race with the Able?"; L. Fernandes, *India's New Middle Class*, 68–69; S. Poonam, *Dreamers*.

67. P. Bourdieu, *Language and Symbolic Power*, ed. J. B. Thompson, trans. G. Raymond and M. Adamson (Cambridge, MA: Harvard University Press, 1991), 86.

68. U. Zacharias, "To Race with the Able?," 300. The complex institutional politics of language were thrown into relief during my observation of the opening ceremony of Pulse, when the director of AIIMS addressed students visiting from all over India in *shudh*, or "pure," Hindi. This occurred a few months after the election of a BJP majority government, which made the elevation of Hindi in the bureaucracy a priority.

69. In her study of GMCM Maharashtra, Dandekar found that 80% of SC and ST students reported having difficulties with English as the medium of instruction, compared with (a not insignificant) 15% from the general category. Only 8% of SC and ST students reported facing no difficulties with any aspect of the MBBS course, versus 44% of general category students. V. Dandekar, "Reservations in Medical Education," 122.

70. N. Pandhi, "Clinical Trials," *The Caravan*, October 2015.

71. T. N. Madan, *Doctors and* Society, 79.

72. S. Deshpande "Caste Quotas and Formal Inclusion in Indian Higher Education," 38.

73. Ibid., 15.

74. V. Turner, *The Forest of Symbols*, 101, 108, original emphasis.

75. B. Thomassen, "Thinking with Liminality," 46.

76. B. R. Ambedkar, *The Annihilation of Caste* (London: Verso, 2014).

77. V. Turner, *The Forest of Symbols*, 106.

CHAPTER 5

1. L. Cohen, "Operability: Surgery at the Margin of the State," in *Anthropology in the Margins of the State*, ed. V. Das and D. Poole (Santa Fe, NM: School of American Research Press, 2004), 165–90.

2. A. Pilnick and R. Dingwall, "On the Remarkable Persistence of Asymmetry in Doctor/Patient Interaction: A Critical Review," *Social Science & Medicine* 72, no. 8 (April 1, 2011): 1374–82.

3. M. T. Taussig, "Reification and the Consciousness of the Patient," *Social Science & Medicine. Part B: Medical Anthropology* 14, no. 1 (February 1, 1980): 8.

4. See former health secretary Sujatha Rao's argument in *Do We Care?* for "professionalizing" hospital management (400).

5. T. N. Madan reports being told in the 1970s that a "smugness" had overtaken the teaching program. "The Institute has a split personality," he was told, with some faculty members in favor of scrapping the MBBS altogether. T. N. Madan, *Doctors and Society*, 82.

6. B. Adkoli amd R. Sood, "Faculty Development and Medical Education Units in India: A Survey," *National Medical Journal of India* 22, no. 1 (2009): 28–32; N. Ananthakrishnan and R. Sood, "Curricula Battles: Is It Possible to Win the War Even If a Few Battles Are Lost?" *International Journal of User-Driven Healthcare* 2, no. 1 (2012): 82–85; R. Sood and T. Singh, "Assessment in Medical Education: Evolving Perspectives and Contemporary Trends," *National Medical Journal of India* 25, no. 6 (2012): 357–64.

7. Madan was told during his study in the 1970s that younger faculty members feared expressing disagreement and that open discussion was impeded by hierarchies and rigid institutional structures. T. N. Madan, *Doctors and Society*, 91. This challenge is not unique to AIIMS or to India. On the bureaucratic evolution of British hospitals, see B. S. Turner, *Medical Power and Social Knowledge* (London: Sage, 1987). Serious attention to this question demands a foray into literature on organizational change. On the contribution of anthropology to this field, see S. Wright, ed., *Anthropology of Organizations* (London: Routledge, 1994).

8. R. Baru, "Public Sector Doctors," 89–90.

9. M. Foucault, *The Birth of the Clinic: An Archaeology of Medical Perception* (New York: Vintage, 1994): 107.

10. F. W. Hafferty and R. Franks, "The Hidden Curriculum," 865.

11. B. S. Turner, *Medical Power and Social Knowledge*, 130.

12. A. Petryna, *Life Exposed: Biological Citizens after Chernobyl* (Princeton, NJ: Princeton University Press, 2002). Alice Street pursues this thread, arguing that Madang Hospital in Papua New Guinea is a site in which patients attempt to make themselves seen by the state, being more accustomed to falling through the gaps in its gaze. A. Petryna, *Biomedicine in an Unstable Place*, 13–14. See also J. Copeman, *Veins of Devotion: Blood Donation and Religious Experience in North India* (New Brunswick, NJ: Rutgers University Press, 2009); L. Cohen, "Operability."

13. The vignette in this section is from an outpatient clinic: field notes, April 2014. Following Hafferty and Franks ("The Hidden Curriculum"), O'Donnell notes how the hidden curriculum functions through space as well as speech. O'Donnell, "Introduction: The Hidden Curriculum—a Focus on Learning and Closing the Gap," in *The Hidden Curriculum in Health Professional Education*: 14. Observing the AIIMS environment and the implications of how space is differently organized and maintained might also be considered part of a student's education.

14. P. Bourdieu, *Distinction*. M. Mauss, "Techniques of the Body," in *Sociologie et Anthropologie*, 4th ed. (1935; Paris: Presses Universitaires de France, 1968), 364–86; R. Prentice, *Bodies in Formation*.

15. M. Pentecost and T. Cousins, "'The Good Doctor'" 4; A. Kleinman, *The Illness Narratives: Suffering, Healing, and the Human Condition* (New York: Basic Books, 1988).

16. R. N. Cowell, *The Hidden Curriculum: A Theoretical Framework and a Pilot Study* (EdD diss., Harvard Graduate School of Education, 1972).

17. F. W. Hafferty and R. Franks, "The Hidden Curriculum," 865.

18. K. M. Ludmerer, *Time to Heal: American Medical Education from the Turn of the Century to the Era of Managed Care* (Oxford: Oxford University Press, 2005).

19. D. J. Flinders, N. Noddings, and S. J. Thornton, "The Null Curriculum: Its Theoretical Basis and Practical Implications," *Curriculum Enquiry* 16, no. 1 (2006): 33–42; J. F. O'Donnell, "The Hidden Curriculum," 14.

20. J. S. Taylor and C. L. Wendland, "The Hidden Curriculum," 52.

21. By way of example, on how the hidden curriculum works to reinforce heteronormativity at a medical college in the United States, see M. Murphy, "Hiding in Plain Sight: The Production of Heteronormativity in Medical Education," *Journal of Contemporary Ethnography* 45, no. 3 (2014): 256–89.

22. The vignette in this section is from an outpatient clinic: field notes, May 2015. On the way in which *takleef* can capture the overlaps between "the notion of the symptom, the medical complaint, and the idea of discomfort," see V. Das, *Affliction*, 33.

23. S. Pinto, "'The Tools of Your Chants and Spells': Stories of Madwomen and Indian Practical Healing," *Medical Anthropology* 35, no. 3 (2015): 263–77; K. Ram, "Class and the Clinic"; C. Van Hollen, *Birth on the Threshold: Childbirth and Modernity in South India* (Berkeley: University of California Press, 2003). This is not to suggest that communication in the private sector is unproblematic. V. Datye, K. Kielmann, K. Sheikh, D. Deshmukh, S. Deshpande, J. Porter, and S. Rangan, "Private Practitioners' Communications with Patients around HIV Testing in Pune, India," *Health Policy and Planning* 21, no. 5 (2006): 343–52.

24. V. Das, *Affliction*, 221–22; E. S. Lazarus, "Theoretical Considerations for the Study of the Doctor-Patient Relationship: Implications of a Perinatal Study," *Medical Anthropology Quarterly* 2, no. 1 (1986): 34–58.

25. As I note in chapter 7, a 2017 survey showed 22% of AIIMS patients reporting dissatisfaction with their doctor's behavior. My research assistant Preeti and I regularly assured patients that I was not a representative of AIIMS and that I would not tell anyone at the institution what they said. Nevertheless, I am aware that people may still have been uncertain about why I was asking questions, and may have framed their responses according to what they thought I wanted to hear.

26. On hearing such comments, it is worth recalling the large and diverse nature of private practitioners in India. Given the severity of Sharmila's condition, it is likely that she was talking about doctors in high-profile private hospitals rather than local clinics. As Das notes in *Affliction*, little anthropological work exists comparing quality of care and patient experience between the public and private sectors in India. More research is called for on this front to problematize simplistic public-private dichotomies.

27. J. S. Taylor and C. Wendland, "The Hidden Curriculum."

28. P. Bourdieu, *Distinction*. K. Ram, "Class and the Clinic."

29. R. Prentice, *Bodies in Formation*.

30. V. Das, *Affliction*, 217.

31. M. Foucault, *The Birth of the Clinic*.

32. S. Pinto, "The Tools of Your Chants and Spells," 7, original emphasis. For their early argument that professions have to guard against a "routinization" of knowledge by protecting the hermeneutic dimension of expertise that ensures a power differential between client and professional (even with all other factors being equal), see H. Jamous and B. Peloille, "Professions or Self-Perpetuating Systems? Changes in the French University-Hospital System," in *Professions and Professionalization*, ed. J. A. Jackson (Cambridge: Cambridge University Press, 1970), 109–52.

33. L. Fernandes, *India's New Middle Class*; S. K. Rao, *Do We Care?*

34. Brian Turner describes the divergence of hospital organization from that of traditional Weberian bureaucracy: "The hospital authority structure is fractured around the difference between the rational bureaucratic system and the professional autonomy of the doctor through a system of medical domination." B. Turner, *Medical Power and Social Knowledge*, 160. This point holds at AIIMS, evident in the enduring power of personal networks in accessing services.

35. K. Ram, "Class and the Clinic."

36. Ibid., 204, 207–8.

37. P. Bourdieu, *Language and Symbolic Power*, 37; M. Taussig, "Reification and the Consciousness of the Patient."

38. B. Gerber, "Should We Use Philosophy to Teach Clinical Communication Skills?" *African Journal of Primary Health Care & Family Medicine* 8, no. 1 (November 16, 2016), 2.

39. The vignette in this section is from an outpatient clinic: field notes, February 2015.

40. Reports of "weakness" (*kamzori*) and "body ache" (*badan dard*) are common in Indian clinics and are often cited by doctors to illustrate hypochondria, somatization disorders, or the simplicity of illness among the rural poor in particular. For understandings of *kamzori* in old age, see B. Brijnath, *Unforgotten: Love and the Culture of Dementia Care in India* (New York: Berghahn, 2014); L. Cohen, *No Aging in India: Alzheimer's, The Bad Family, and Other Modern Things* (Berkeley: University of California Press, 1998). For an approach to *kamzori* as a somatized feature of depression among low-income women, see B. Pereira, G. Andrew, S. Pednekar, R. Pai, P. Pelto, and V. Patel, "The Explanatory Models of Depression in Low Income Countries: Listening to Women," *Journal of Affective Disorders* 102 (2007): 209–18. In 1960s Punjab, Kirkpatrick encountered *kamzori* among women on a gynecological ward who associated it with menstruation and multiple childbirths. See J. Kirkpatrick, *The Sociology of an Indian Hospital Ward* (Calcutta: KLM, 1979).

41. This vignette is from an outpatient clinic: field notes, February 2015.

42. M. Foucault, *The Birth of the Clinic*, 114–15; F. Hafferty, "Beyond Curriculum Reform: Confronting Medicine's Hidden Curriculum," *Academic Medicine* 73, no. 4 (1998): 403–7. For a survey of how linguistic anthropology began to tackle medical discourse, see J. C. Kuipers, "'Medical Discourse' in Anthropological Context: Views of Language and Power," *Medical Anthropology Quarterly* 3, no. 2 (1989). 99–123. See J. M. Wilce, "Medical Discourse," *Annual Review of Anthropology* 38 (2009): 199–215, for a rich contemporary account.

43. M. Foucault, *The Birth of the Clinic*, 114. Reflecting on her research on a ward in 1960s Punjab, Kirkpatrick writes that "code switching" between languages was used as a deliberate device to control the information shared with patients; in the paternalistic practice of the time, it was also considered to be a protective mechanism. J. Kirkpatrick, *The Sociology of an Indian Hospital Ward*, 88, 97–98.

44. The vignette in this section is from an outpatient clinic: field notes, February 2015.

45. The tradition of gendered authority was also regularly voiced by patients who addressed female doctors as "sir" or "Doctor Sahab."

46. F. W. Hafferty and R. Franks, "The Hidden Curriculum," 865.

47. The vignette in this section is from an outpatient clinic: field notes, March 2015.

48. See the appendix for a note on methods and the ethics of observation in the clinic.

49. Das has written about the treatment of symptoms rather than the pursuit of diagnosis by many practitioners in low-income neighborhoods, which results in an often chronic condition being understood as an intermittent series of acute episodes. She illustrates this with the example of a young woman who was told that she had "low BP" without the practitioner taking her blood pressure. In this way, she argues, such categories are "neither 'folk' nor 'expert'"—they express linkages to the tensions of difficult living conditions and also carry "the trace of the clinical encounters typical of low-income neighborhoods and their particular ecology of care." V. Das, *Affliction*, 20, 44.

50. The practice of ordering excessive tests for financial gain through a nexus of doctors and private laboratories has become a key trope in the discourse of corruption in Indian healthcare—a discourse from which AIIMS is not exempt. In the case of the patient in this example, and many others at AIIMS, however, the provision of free tests can arguably be understood as an act of health justice.

51. I hesitate to refer to this as an act of eliciting an explanatory model because its intention was not to understand a patient's subjective illness experience, or to acknowledge the power differential between patient and doctor, but to grasp the patient's material context in order to establish a more informed path to an accurate diagnosis. A. Kleinman, *The Illness Narratives: Suffering, Healing, and the Human Condition* (New York: Basic Books, 1988). For a summary of the theoretical responses to the rise of explanatory models in the 1980s, see V. Das, *Affliction*, 27–29; E. S. Lazarus, "Theoretical Considerations."

52. K. Ram, "Class and the Clinic," 206.

53. The vignette in this section is from an outpatient clinic: field notes, February 2015.

54. M. DelVecchio Good, "The Medical Imaginary and the Biotechnical Embrace," in *Subjectivity: Ethnographic Investigations*, ed. J. Biehl, B. Good, and A. Kleinman (Berkeley: University of California Press, 2007), 362–80; S. S. Amrith, *Decolonizing International Health*.

55. In the 1909 preface to his play The Doctor's Dilemma (at pp. 65–67), George Bernard Shaw laments the socioeconomic disconnect between British general practitioners and their patients:

> Suppose it were ascertained that every child in the world could be rendered absolutely immune from all disease during its entire life by taking half an ounce of

radium to every pint of its milk. The world would be none the healthier, because not even a Crown Prince—no, not even the son of a Chicago Meat King, could afford the treatment. Yet it is doubtful whether doctors would refrain from prescribing it on that ground. The recklessness with which they now recommend wintering in Egypt or at Davos to people who cannot afford to go to Cornwall, and the orders given for champagne jelly and old port in households where such luxuries must obviously be acquired at the cost of stinting necessaries, often make one wonder whether it is possible for a man to go through a medical training and retain a spark of common sense. This sort of inconsiderateness gets cured only in the classes where poverty, pretentious as it is even at its worst, cannot pitch its pretenses high enough to make it possible for the doctor (himself often no better off than the patient) to assume that the average income of an English family is about 2,000 pounds a year, and that it is quite easy to break up a home, sell an old family seat at a sacrifice, and retire into a foreign sanatorium devoted to some "treatment" that did not exist two years ago and probably will not exist (except as a pretext for keeping an ordinary hotel) two years hence.

56. S. Pinto, *Where There Is No Midwife*, 139; C. Van Hollen, *Birth on the Threshold*.

57. J. S. Taylor and C. Wendland, "The Hidden Curriculum," 52.

58. For a study of this phenomenon in the Global North, see N. Rose, *The Politics of Life Itself: Biomedicine, Power, and Subjectivity in the Twenty-First Century* (Princeton, NJ: Princeton University Press, 2006).

59. S. Pinto, "Development without Institutions"; S. Pinto, *Where There Is No Midwife*.

60. K. Ram, "Class and the Clinic," 206; S. Pinto, "Development without Institutions."

61. Arthur Kleinman, "The Divided Self, Hidden Values, and Moral Sensibility in Medicine," *The Lancet* 377, no. 9768 (March 5, 2011): 804–5. Also see V. Das, *Affliction*.

62. The vignette in this section is from an outpatient clinic: field notes, March 2015.

63. R. E. Davis-Floyd and C. F. Sargent, eds., *Childbirth and Authoritative Knowledge: Cross-Cultural Perspectives* (Berkeley: University of California Press), 1997; S. Pinto, *Where There Is No Midwife*.

64. In another moment of irony, on our way to the villages to discuss sanitation, someone threw a plastic bag of rubbish from a window at the front of the bus. I watched it arc through the air as we crossed a bridge, falling toward the lackluster river below.

65. See S. Mukherjee, "The Perfect Last Day of Mr Sengupta," *Granta* 124 (2013): 35–42, a US-trained Indian physician, for an account of his shock at the lack of patient privacy at AIIMS.

66. J. S. Taylor and C. Wendland, "The Hidden Curriculum"; M. Lock and D. Gordon, eds., *Biomedicine Examined* (Dordrecht: Kluwer Academic Publishers, 1988).

67. B. Gerber, "Should We Use Philosophy to Teach Clinical Communication Skills?," 1.

68. L. M. Ahearn, *Living Language: An Introduction to Linguistic Anthropology* (Malden, MA: Wiley-Blackwell, 2012), 291; P. Bourdieu, *Language and Symbolic Power*; M. Foucault, "The Subject and Power," in *The Essential Foucault: Selections from the Essential Works of Foucault, 1954–1984*, ed. N. Rose and P. Rabinow (New York: New Press, 1994), 126–44.

69. B. Gerber, "Should We Use Philosophy to Teach Clinical Communication Skills?," 2.

70. A. Kleinman, "The Divided Self," 805.

71. B. Gerber, "Should We Use Philosophy to Teach Clinical Communication Skills?"; D. S. Jones, J. A. Greene, J. Duffin, and J. H. Warner, "Making the Case for History in Medical Education," *Journal of the History of Medicine and Allied Sciences* 70, no. 4 (2015): 623–52.

72. AIIMS Act, Rules and Regulations, All India Institute of Medical Sciences, New Delhi, June 2, 1956, https://www.aiims.edu/images/pdf/aiimsact.pdf.

73. T. N. Madan, *Doctors and Society*, 82–83.

74. V. Das, *Affliction*, 52.

75. A. Pratap and S. Pandit, "Maharashtra Goes on Strike as More Doctors Are Attacked," *Hindustan Times*, March 23, 2017; D. C. Sharma, "Rising Violence against Health Workers in India," *The Lancet* 389 (10080) (2017): 1685.

76. A. Ruddock, "Behind the Self-Defence Lessons for AIIMS Doctors Lies the Failure of Indian Medical Education," *Scroll.in*, May 27, 2017. https://scroll.in/pulse/838661/behind-the-self-defence-lessons-for-aiims-doctors-lies-the-failure-of-indian-medical-education.

77. F. W. Hafferty and R. Franks, "The Hidden Curriculum," 866.

CHAPTER 6

1. M. Pentecost and T. Cousins, "The Good Doctor," 5.

2. As I noted in chapter 1, although medical professionals prefer the more accurate term "subspecialization," I use "superspecialization" to echo the language used by students.

3. J. Chua, *In Pursuit of the Good Life*, 191.

4. N. J. Long and H. L. Moore, *The Social Life of Achievement*.

5. J. Das and J. Hammer, "Strained Mercy: The Quality of Medical Care in Delhi" (Policy Research Working Paper No. 3228, World Bank, September 2004).

6. This shift is illustrated by Madan, who shows that in the 1970s it was not assumed that all MBBS graduates would proceed directly for postgraduate training. T. N. Madan, *Doctors and Society*, 63.

7. B. Lefebvre, "The Indian Corporate Hospitals: Touching Middle Class Lives."

8. There is also an important legal impediment here, which bars non-specialists from undertaking specific medical procedures. In heart surgeon Devi Shetty's example in "Fixing Healthcare," if he were to perform a caesarean section, he could lose his license.

9. At the time of my research, the internship was designed to provide twelve months of clinical experience according to the following rotation: medicine (6 weeks), surgery (6 weeks), rural posting to Ballabhgarh (12 weeks), pediatrics (4 weeks), obstetrics and gynecology (4 weeks), casualty/emergency (4 weeks), anesthesiology (2 weeks), ophthalmology (2 weeks), and elective (8 weeks).

10. On this topic, Madan wrote in 1980: "Some interviewees questioned the wisdom of dispensing with examinations after internship. They maintained that Indian students are examination oriented and the majority of them do not take internship seriously." T. N. Madan, *Doctors and* Society, 81. The National Medical Commission bill proposes a na-

tional MBBS exit exam (NEXT) to address the uneven quality of medical education in the country. Commentators have argued that such an exam should emphasize skills testing along the lines of the US Medical Licensing Examination. S. D. Bhaduri, "The NEXT Promise," *Indian Express*, 8 May, 2018; S. Rao and S. Naik, "Supreme Court Directive on Making NEET Compulsory Is Move in the Right Direction," *Indian Express*, May 10, 2016.

11. "AIIMS PG Topper Interview: Dr. Shuvadeep Ganguly, 10th Rank, November 2015," https://pgblazer.com/aiims-pg-topper-interview-dr-shuvadeep-ganguly-10th-rank-november-2015/.

12. As I write, AIIMS is undergoing a systems upgrade that will include the digitization of medical records. It will be interesting to observe in coming years how this may alter the patient experience of the hospital and the consequences for patient surveillance.

13. The vignette in this section is from an outpatient clinic: field notes, March 2015.

14. V. Das, *Affliction*, 217–18.

15. L. Fernandes, *India's New Middle* Class, xv; R. Lukose, *Liberalization's Children: Gender, Youth, and Consumer Citizenship in Globalizing India* (Durham, NC: Duke University Press, 2009).

16. J. Baudrillard, *The Consumer Society*, 218.

17. This development is in keeping with the historical trend in the United States, another country with little historical state involvement in healthcare provision. G. Weisz, *Divide and Conquer: A Comparative History of Medical Specialization* (Oxford: Oxford University Press, 2008).

18. D. Graeber, *Toward an Anthropological Theory of Value: The False Coin of Our Own Dreams* (New York: Palgrave, 2001), 76; T. Otto and R. Willerslev, "'Value as Theory': Comparison, Cultural Critique, and Guerilla Ethnographic Theory," *HAU: Journal of Ethnographic Theory* 3, no. 1 (2013): 1–20.

19. D. Graeber, *Toward an Anthropological Theory of Value*, 76–77.

20. Ibid., 3.

21. M. Weber, *Economy and Society: An Outline of Interpretive Sociology* (Berkeley: University of California Press, 1978), 205–307.

22. S. Pinto, "The Tools of Your Chants and Spells," 6.

23. J. Chua, *In Pursuit of the Good Life*, 191.

24. N. J. Long and H. Moore, *The Social Life of Achievement*, 13.

25. H. Moore, *Still Life: Hopes, Desires and Satisfactions* (Cambridge, UK: Polity Press, 2011), 76.

26. A. Szakolczai, "Liminality and Experience: Structuring Transitory Situations and Transformative Events," in *Breaking Boundaries*, 11–38.

27. In *Divide and Conquer*, George Weisz offers an elegant comparative overview of the history of specialization in Britain, France, Germany, and the United States, in which concerns about the potential domination of specialization over general practice are common. Work on specialization in low- and middle-income countries remains sparse, with exceptions such as the work of Ecks with Indian gastroenterologists: S. Ecks, "Spectacles of Reason: An Ethnography of Calcutta Gastroenterologists," in *New Politics of Vision*, ed.

J. Edwards, P. Harvey, and P. Wade (Oxford, UK: Berghahn, 2010), 117–35. While interest is growing, the focus so far is on the development of particular specialties, rather than on the nature of specialization itself and its influence over the landscape of illness and medical care. For a valuable recent example regarding the development and regulation of emergency medicine in India: V. Sriram, R. Baru and S. Bennett, "Regulating Recognition and Training for New Medical Specialties in India: The Case of Emergency Medicine," *Health Policy and Planning* (July 2018): 1–13.

Although it was not my focus at AIIMS, the interrogation of the characteristics of particular specialties and the determinants of student choices is an important area of research that, while relatively well established in the Global North, has yet to fully materialize in other contexts. See D. Album and S. Westin 2008, "Do Diseases Have a Prestige Hierarchy? A Survey among Physicians and Medical Students," *Social Science & Medicine* 66 (2008): 182–88; W. Leeming, "Professionalization Theory, Medical Specialists and the Concept of 'National Patterns of Specialization,'" *Social Science Information* 40, no. 3 (2001): 455–85. By way of example from AIIMS about the persistent gender associations of particular fields, Anjali was told by an uncle and former surgeon, that there are certain "things that girls can never do [including surgery] because they have to raise kids."

28. N. J. Long and H. Moore, *The Social Life of Achievement*, 22.

29. The vignette in this section is from an outpatient clinic: field notes, March 2015.

30. S. Bayly, "For Family, State and Nation," 158.

31. Ibid.

32. The film *Ek doctor ki maut* (The death of a doctor; 1990, dir. Sinha) depicts the symbolic death of a promising young research doctor when he is banished to a village having upset the political hierarchy by receiving personal acclaim for his discovery of a leprosy vaccine. Certain individuals who buck the trend are occasionally heroized by the metropolitan elite, such as the AIIMS alumni who run the community health project Jan Swasthya Sahyog in Chhattisgarh (A. Ruddock, "Incorrect Dosage"), but the vast majority of rural doctors are acknowledged only by their patients. Nor is this recognition guaranteed to be positive. In September 2016, a photograph circulated on Twitter of two men leading a funeral procession through a village, carrying a banner with a picture of a doctor's face and text that blamed her for the death of her patient. For examples of doctors being threatened by the dissatisfied families of patients in rural Rajasthan, see J. Killmer, "Village Doctors and Vulnerable Bodies: Gender, Medicine, and Risk in North India" (PhD diss., Syracuse University, 2018).

33. L. Cohen, *No Aging in India*.

34. M. Porecha, "Do You Still Have a Family Physician?" *dna*, February 23, 2014, https://www.dnaindia.com/health/report-do-you-still-have-a-family-physician-1964306.

35. L. Fernandes, *India's New Middle Class*, 134.

36. During my research, the Department of Community Medicine at the six newly created AIIMS had "and Family Medicine" appended to its title, but at the time of writing no family physicians had been recruited to the faculty, not least because AIIMS does not recruit graduates of diploma programs administered by the National Board.

37. K. S. Jacob, "Politics of Medical Education in India," *Economic and Political Weekly*

51, no. 12 (2006): 12–15; R. Jeffery, *Politics of Health in India.* The MCI was under parliamentary review during the writing of this book and is due to be replaced by a National Medical Commission.

38. The fact that by 1974–1975, AIIMS was already seeing over 450,000 outpatients a year testifies to this rapid growth. T. N. Madan, *Doctors and Society*, 45. In a recent television interview, the current director of AIIMS, Dr. Randeep Guleria, stated that "AIIMS is a tertiary hospital but it is also a general hospital."

39. See V. Sriram et al., "Regulating Recognition and Training," on the recent emergence of emergency medicine as a specialty in India.

40. T. N. Madan, *Doctors and Society*, 84, original emphasis.

41. This vignette is from an outpatient clinic: field notes, March 2015.

42. A. Subramanian, "Making Merit," 300.

43. Ibid., 292.

44. C. L. Wendland, *A Heart for the Work*, 157–59; M. Pentecost and T. Cousins, "The Good Doctor," 5.

45. For a quantitative study of emigration among AIIMS alumni, see M. Kaushik, A. Jaiswal, N. Shah, and A. Mahal, "High-End Physician Migration from India," *Bulletin of the World Health Organization* 86, no. 1 (2008): 40–45.

46. T. N. Madan, *Doctors and Society*, 82.

47. R. Baru, "Public Sector Doctors in an Era of Commercialisation"; V. Das, *Affliction*.

48. See P. Varma, *The Great Indian Middle Class* (New Delhi: Penguin, 2007) for a classic version of this narrative. See L. Cohen, *No Aging in India* for examples of how it is employed with regard to the perceived disintegration of traditional family structures.

49. R. Baru, "Public Sector Doctors in an Era of Commercialisation."

50. P. Bala, *Medicine and Medical Policies in India*; S. K. Rao, *Do We Care?*

51. AIIMS faculty are prohibited from doing supplementary work in the private sector, but it is not uncommon for physicians to relocate to corporate hospitals following compulsory retirement from AIIMS. Reflecting the unique status of AIIMS New Delhi, the new All India Institutes have struggled to recruit sufficient faculty. G. S. Mudur, "Mirror AIIMS Hobbled by Faculty Shortage," *The Telegraph*, February 1, 2019.

52. S. Nundy, K. Desiraju, and S. Nagral, *Healers or Predators?*

53. S. Bayly, "For Family, State and Nation," 177.

54. J. Killmer, "Village Doctors and Vulnerable Bodies." There is a long established trope of the Indian village as viewed from the city. For more on the association of the rural with absence, see S. Pinto, *Where There Is No Midwife*. For an account of how perceptions of the village differed in the political thought of Gandhi, Nehru, and Ambedkar, see S. S. Jodhka, "Nation and Village: Images of Rural India in Gandhi, Nehru and Ambedkar," *Economic and Political Weekly* 37, no. 32 (2002): 3343–53. The film *Swades* (2004, dir. Gowariker) depicts the response of a nonresident Indian returning from the United States to rural India; the novel *English, August,* by U. Chatterjee (London: Penguin, 1988), tells the story of an urban civil servant being posted to a village.

55. For an overview of the multiple failings of primary health centers in particular, see Patel et al., "Assuring Health Coverage for All in India," 2426–27. For a comprehensive

overview of efforts to revitalize rural primary healthcare under the National Rural Health Mission in the early 2000s, see S. K. Rao, *Do We Care?*, 298–387.

56. K. D. Rao, S. Ramani, S. Murthy, I. Hazarika, N. Khandpur, M. Choksi, S. Khanna, M. Vujicic, P. Berman, and M. Ryan, "Health Worker Attitudes toward Rural Service in India: Results from Qualitative Research," Health, Nutrition, and Population Unit, Human Development Network, World Bank, 2010, http://siteresources.worldbank.org/HEALTHNUTRITIONANDPOPULATION/Resources/281627-1095698140167/HealthWorkerAttitudesTowardRuralServiceinIndia.pdf. Contrary to urban perceptions, not all doctors reject rural practice. In their study of doctors in rural Chhattisgarh, Sheikh and colleagues found that personal ties to the region, colocation with spouses, an ethic of public service, positive relationships with colleagues, and (small) financial incentives were important factors influencing a commitment to rural practice: K. Sheikh, B. Rajkumari, K. Jain, K. Rao, P. Patanwar, G. Gupta, K. R. Antony, and T. Sundararaman, "Location and Vocation: Why Some Government Doctors Stay on in Rural Chhattisgarh," *International Health* 4 (2012): 192–99. A more recent article drawing on interviews with this same cohort, however, stresses ongoing needs including facility improvements, increased security, improved housing, access to better schools, ongoing training, and recognition of their work by the relevant administrations: K. Sheikh, S. Mondal, P. Patanwar, B. Rajkumari, and T. Sundararaman, "What Rural Doctors Want: A Qualitative Study in Chhattisgarh State." *Indian Journal of Medical Ethics* 1, no. 3 (2016): 138–44.

57. M. Pentecost and T. Cousins, "The Good Doctor," 5.

58. C. Wendland, *A Heart for the Work*, 197–98; J. Livingstone, *Improvising Medicine*.

59. M. DelVecchio Good, "The Medical Imaginary," 324.

60. A. Gupta, *Red Tape: Bureaucracy, Structural Violence, and Poverty in India* (Durham, NC: Duke University Press, 2012); S. Pinto, *Where There Is No Midwife*; B. Singh, *Poverty and the Quest for Life: Spiritual and Material Striving in Rural India* (Chicago: University of Chicago Press, 2015).

61. See J. Killmer, "Village Doctors and Vulnerable Bodies" for the frustrations of doctors working without necessary equipment in rural Rajasthan who feel their position has been reduced to one of triage.

62. Again, this is not new. Discussing the same topic, one of Madan's interlocutors responded: "It is a painful waste of talent and resources . . . you do not need specialists like us to cater to the routine medical care needs of the population." T. N. Madan, *Doctors and Society*, 93–94.

63. A. Subramanian, *The Caste of Merit*, 154.

64. C. L. Wendland, *A Heart for the Work*, 172–92.

65. V. Das, *Affliction*, 25.

66. Samuel Shem depicts this culture in his famous novel about medical training, *House of God* (London: Black Swan, 1978). Also see H. S. Becker, B. Geer, E. C. Hughes, and A. L. Strauss, *Boys in White: Student Culture in Medical School* (Chicago: University of Chicago Press, 1961); D. Pollock, "Training Tales: U. S. Medical Autobiography," *Cultural Anthropology* 11, no. 3 (1996): 339–61; S. Sinclair, *Making Doctors: An Institutional Apprenticeship* (Oxford, UK: Berg, 1997).

67. C. L. Wendland, *A Heart for the Work*, 203.

68. Ibid., 108.

69. M. Pentecost and T. Cousins, "The Good Doctor," 3.

70. In chapter 4 I discussed the experiences of Purush and Sushil as students in the SC and ST reserved categories at AIIMS. Without further research, I cannot suggest ideas about the relationship between these affiliations, their relative politicization, and their career aspirations. In her PhD dissertation on students at Jawaharlal Nehru University in Delhi, Garalytė challenges a narrative that interprets Dalit social mobility as necessarily entailing an impulse to "pay back to society" as discussed by Naudet. K. Garalytė, "Dalit Student Movement in India: From Identity Politics to Counter Culture Movement" (Kaunas, Lithuania: Vytautas Magnus University, 2016); J. Naudet, "'Paying Back to Society': Upward Social Mobility among Dalits," *Contributions to Indian Sociology* 42, no. 3 (October 1, 2008): 413–41. While other AIIMS students in reserved categories spoke of wanting to reform health and governance systems (Santosh and Tashi, for example), so did some of their upper-caste batchmates (including Anjali and Neha). The extent to which they will fulfill these aspirations is yet to be seen, but it remains the case that of these four it was Anjali and Neha who planned, for their own reasons, to apply for postgraduate study in the United States. Meanwhile, Priya, also an ST student, was abstractly inclined to contribute to her ancestral village but had more immediate ambitions to open a private dermatology clinic and spa in South Delhi.

71. During a similar discussion in the 1970s, Madan was asked by one of his interlocutors, "Why am I expected to be like Jesus Christ?" T. N. Madan, *Doctors and Society*, 71.

72. K. Sheikh and J. Porter, "Disempowered Doctors? A Relational View of Public Health Policy Implementation in Urban India," *Health Policy and Planning* 26 (2011): 83–92. Also see K. Kielmann, D. Deshmukh, S. Deshpande, and S. Rangan, "Managing Uncertainty around HIV/AIDS in an Urban Setting: Private Medical Providers and Their Patients in Pune, India," *Social Science & Medicine* 61, no. 7 (2005): 1540–50.

73. Trehan founded the multiple-specialty hospital Medanta in Gurgaon, outside Delhi, in 2009, following a career as a cardiac surgeon in New York. He is considered to wield significant influence over the direction of government health policy, allegedly in the direction of private interests: V. Krishnan, "Private Practice: How Naresh Trehan Became One of India's Most Influential Doctor-Businessmen," *The Caravan*, February 2015. Trehan and Prathap Reddy, another cardiologist, and the founder of India's first corporate hospital chain, Apollo, are arguably India's most famous doctor-businessmen. Their impact on the landscape of private medicine is an indicator that the transformation by clinicians of "health, power, and other aspects of social life" can be understood from a variety of perspectives. S. M. Holmes, A. C. Jenks, and S. Stonington, "Clinical Subjectification: Anthropologies of Contemporary Biomedical Training," *Culture, Medicine, and Psychiatry* 35, no. 2 (2011): 105.

74. D. Graeber, "It Is Value That Brings Universes into Being," *HAU: Journal of Ethnographic Theory* 3, no. 2 (2013): 231.

75. P. Chatterjee, "You Must Repay Society's Debt, Modi Tells Young AIIMS Doctors," *Indian Express*, October 21, 2014.

76. A. Kalra, "India Slashes Health Budget, Already One of the World's Lowest," *Reuters*, December 23, 2014.

77. M. Foucault, "Technologies of the Self," in *Technologies of the Self: A Seminar with Michel Foucault*, ed. L. H. Martin, H. Gutman, and P. H. Hutton (Amherst: University of Massachusetts Press, 1988); A. Pandian, "Devoted to Development: Moral Progress, Ethical Work, and Divine Favor in South India," *Anthropological Theory* 8, no. 2 (2008): 159–79; L. Cohen, "Operability"; M. Pentecost and T. Cousins, "The Good Doctor."

CHAPTER 7

1. The head of PHFI, Dr. Srinath Reddy, is a former head of the AIIMS cardiology department.

2. S. Pinto, "Development without Institutions," 355.

3. T. N. Madan, *Doctors and Society*, 79.

4. A. Ruddock, "AIIMS Teaches Its Doctors What to Ask a Patient: It Must Also Teach Them How," Scroll.In, February 22, 2017, https://scroll.in/pulse/829959/aiims-teaches-its-doctors-what-to-ask-a-patient-it-must-also-teach-them-how-to.

5. M. M. A. Bhat, "Hate Crimes in India," Jindal Global Law Review, August 4, 2020, https://doi.org/10.1007/s41020-020-00119-0.

6. P. B. Mehta, *The Burden of Democracy*, 120.

7. C. Bambra et al., "The COVID-19 Pandemic and Health Inequalities," *Journal of Epidemiology and Community Health*, June 13, 2020, 1–5.

8. S. Sengupta and M. K. Jha, "Social Policy, COVID-19 and Impoverished Migrants: Challenges and Prospects in Locked Down India," *International Journal of Community and Social Development* 2, no. 2 (2020): 152–72.

9. L. Lingam and R. S. Sapkal, "COVID-19, Physical Distancing and Social Inequalities: Are We All Really in This Together?," *International Journal of Community and Social Development* 2, no. 2 (2020): 173–90; A. Konikkara, "How a Healthcare System Partial to Privatization Fails the Poor," *The Caravan*, July 29, 2020, https://caravanmagazine.in/health/how-healthcare-partial-to-privatisation-fails-the-poor.

10. R. Wilkinson and K. Pickett, *The Spirit Level: Why Equality Is Better for Everyone*, Penguin Sociology (London: Penguin Books, 2010).

11. M. M. A. Bhat, "Hate Crimes in India."

12. The Wire, "After 3-Year Delay, Government Releases Farmer Suicide Data," November 8, 2019, https://thewire.in/agriculture/farmer-suicides-data.

13. D. Narayan, "India's Abuse of Women Is the Biggest Human Rights Violation on Earth," *The Guardian*, April 27, 2018, https://www.theguardian.com/commentisfree/2018/apr/27/india-abuse-women-human-rights-rape-girls.

14. S. Deshpande, "Pass, Fail, Distinction," 5.

15. Ibid.

16. V. Ramalingaswami, *Medicine, Health and Development*, 8–9.

17. J. S. Taylor and C. Wendland, "The Hidden Curriculum," 51, original emphasis.

18. Government of India, "All India Institute of Medical Sciences Act, 1956," 6.

19. B. Gerber, "Should We Use Philosophy to Teach Clinical Communication Skills?"; D. S. Jones, J. A. Greene, J. Duffin, and J. H. Warner, "Making the Case for History in Medical Education"; A. Kleinman, "The Divided Self"; M. Pentecost and T. Cousins, "The Good Doctor."

20. A. Kleinman, "The Divided Self," 805.

21. According to Virchow, "The politician, the practical anthropologist, must find the means for their actual solution." J. P. Mackenbach, "Politics Is Nothing but Medicine at a Larger Scale: Reflections on Public Health's Biggest Idea," *Journal of Epidemiology and Community Health* 63, no. 3 (March 1, 2009): 181–84; H. Jack Geiger, "The Political Future of Social Medicine: Reflections on Physicians as Activists," *Academic Medicine* 92, no. 3 (2017): 282–84.

22. M. Pentecost and T. Cousins, "The Good Doctor," 7.

23. V. Adams and S. R. Kaufmann, "Ethnography and the Making of Modern Health Professionals," *Culture, Medicine, and Psychiatry* 35, no. 2 (2011): 318.

1. A. Gupta, *Red Tape*; M. S. Hull, *Government of Paper: The Materiality of Bureaucracy in Urban Pakistan* (Berkeley: University of California Press, 2012).

2. For a longer version of this tale, see A. Ruddock, "Notes from the Waiting Room: Seeking Research Access to the All India Institute of Medical Sciences (AIIMS)," LSE Field Research Method Lab, June 16, 2017, https://blogs.lse.ac.uk/fieldresearch/2017/06/16/notes-from-the-waiting-room-aiims/.

3. P. Abrams, "Notes on the Difficulty of Studying the State," *Journal of Historical Sociology* 1 (1988): 58–89.

4. M. Inhorn, "Privacy, Privatization, and the Politics of Patronage: Ethnographic Challenges to Penetrating the Secret World of Middle Eastern, Hospital-Based In Vitro Fertilization," *Social Science & Medicine* 59, no. 10 (2004): 2095–2108.

5. A. Street, *Biomedicine in an Unstable Place*, 31.

6. C. Geertz, *The Interpretation of Cultures: Selected Essays* (New York: Basic Books, 2000).

7. On archetypal powerful individuals, see M. Inhorn, "Privacy, Privatization," 2097.

8. D. Fassin, "Why Ethnography Matters," 630; M. Inhorn, "Privacy, Privatization," 2096.

9. See M. Inhorn, "Privacy, Privatization," 2100, for her reflections on a similar experience at a university hospital in Cairo.

10. I had a single meeting with the director of AIIMS, which resulted in one of the more disorientating moments of my long effort to gain access as he sent me back down the chain of command to the dean I had begun with a year earlier but whose post had since—fortuitously, it turned out—been occupied by a different person. I attempted to arrange an interview with the director before I left Delhi, but I received no response to my requests.

11. G. Wind, "Negotiated Interactive Observation," 83–85.

12. S. Zaman, "Poverty and Violence, Frustration and Inventiveness: Hospital Ward Life in Bangladesh," *Social Science & Medicine* 59, no. 10 (2004): 2025–36; M. Nichter,

Global Health: Why Cultural Perceptions, Social Representations, and Biopolitics Matter (Tucson: University of Arizona Press, 2008).

13. Kirsten Bell's thoughtful article "Resisting Commensurability," about what she considers the incommensurability of informed consent and research ethics, with particular reference to ethnographic practice, explores these themes in depth. "Resisting Commensurability: Against Informed Consent as an Anthropological Virtue." *American Anthropologist* 112, no. 3 (2015): 1–12. Also see Charles Bosk, "Irony, Ethnography, and Informed Consent," in *Bioethics in Social Context*, ed. C. Barry Hoffmaster (Philadelphia: Temple University Press, 2001); S. van der Geest, "Confidentiality and Pseudonyms: A Fieldwork Dilemma from Ghana," *Anthropology Today* (2003): 14–18.

14. S. van der Geest, "Confidentiality and Pseudonyms."

15. S. Turner, "The Silenced Assistant: Reflections of Invisible Interpreters and Research Assistants," *Asia Pacific Viewpoint* 51 (2010): 206–19.

16. As I discuss in chapter 6, the intern year is used by many as an opportunity to study for the postgraduate entrance exams at the expense of gaining greater clinical experience.

17. J. Clifford, "Introduction: Partial Truths," in *Writing Culture: The Poetics and Politics of Ethnography*, ed. J. Clifford and G. E. Marcus (Berkeley: University of California Press, 1986), 1–26.

18. C. Wendland, *A Heart for the* Work, 235. As Wendland notes, a longitudinal approach is in many ways the ideal method for a study of doctors in formation, but faced with the logistical constraints of limited time and funding this is rarely possible. In her work on reservations in medical education in Maharashtra, Dandekar did seek out graduates of the college she had studied (although no one she had known as a student) to track career trajectories and lifestyles. Dandekar, "Reservations in Medical Education in Maharashtra," 128–29.

19. J. Clifford and G. E. Marcus, eds., *Writing Culture: The Poetics and Politics of Ethnography*; M. Lynch, "Against Reflexivity as an Academic Virtue and Source of Privileged Knowledge," *Theory, Culture and Society* 17, no. 3 (2000): 26–54.

20. D. J. Banks, "Minorities in American Anthropology: A Personal View," *Histories of Anthropology Annual* 3, no. 1 (2007): 222–46; D. A. Davis and C. Craven, *Feminist Ethnography: Thinking through Methodologies, Challenges, and Possibilities* (Lanham, MD: Rowman & Littlefield Publishers, 2016); E. Lewin and W. L. Leap, *Out in Public: Reinventing Lesbian/Gay Anthropology in a Globalizing World* (Hoboken, NJ: Wiley, 2009).

21. Z. Wool, "What I Wish I Knew About Anthropology and Disability: Notes toward a More Enabling Anthropology," *Anthro{dendum}* (blog), January 10, 2018, https://anthrodendum.org/2018/01/10/what-i-wish-i-knew-about-anthropology-and-disability-notes-toward-a-more-enabling-anthropology/.

22. For the experiences in academia of early career academics with chronic illnesses, see A. Ruddock, "Making Visible: Chronic Illness and the Academy," *Sociological Review* (blog), October 17, 2017, https://www.thesociologicalreview.com/making-visible-chronic-illness-and-the-academy/.

23. E. Samuels, "Six Ways of Looking at Crip Time," *Disability Studies Quarterly* 37, no. 3 (2017), https://dsq-sds.org/article/view/5824/4684.

24. In *Where There Is No Midwife*, Sarah Pinto weaves her own pregnancy through the narrative of birth and loss in rural North India and reflects on the influence it has on her interactions with rural women, up to and including the point at which she is compelled to return home to the United States for medical care. Although my illness has no similar presence in this book, it is accurate to say that I experienced moments of empathy with patients that were made poignant by the gulf between the material conditions of our lives. Such moments expressed the reality of the AIIMS experience for patients in a way that made, while not necessarily a more accurate, certainly a more emphatic and affecting impression on me than could be accessed through sympathetic observation and interviews alone. For reflections on this theme, see K. Narayan, *Alive in the Writing: Crafting Ethnography in the Company of Chekhov* (Chicago: University of Chicago Press, 2012).

BIBLIOGRAPHY

Abraham, L. "Bhai-Behen, True Love, Time Pass: Friendships and Sexual Partnerships among Youth in an Indian Metropolis." *Culture, Health and Sexuality* 4, no. 3 (2002): 337–53. https://doi.org/10.1080/13691050110120794.

Abrams, P. "Notes on the Difficulty of Studying the State." *Journal of Historical Sociology* 1 (1988): 58–89.

Acharya, S. S. "Health Equity in India: An Examination through the Lens of Social Exclusion." *Journal of Social Inclusion Studies* 4, no. 1 (2018): 104–30. https://doi.org/10.1177/2394481118774489.

Adams, V. *Doctors for Democracy.* Cambridge: Cambridge University Press, 1998.

Adams, V., and S. R. Kaufmann. "Ethnography and the Making of Modern Health Professionals." *Culture, Medicine, and Psychiatry* 35, no. 2 (2011): 313–20. https://doi.org/10.1007/s11013-011-9216-0.

Adkoli, B., and R. Sood. "Faculty Development and Medical Education Units in India: A Survey." *National Medical Journal of India* 22, no. 1 (2009): 28–32.

Ahearn, L. M. *Living Language: An Introduction to Linguistic Anthropology.* Malden, MA: Wiley-Blackwell, 2012.

Album, D., and S. Westin. "Do Diseases Have a Prestige Hierarchy? A Survey among Physicians and Medical Students." *Social Science & Medicine* 66 (2008): 182–88. https://doi.org/10.1016/j.socscimed.2007.07.003.

Ambedkar, B. R. *Annihilation of Caste: The Annotated Critical Edition.* Edited by S. Anand. London: Verso, 2014.

Amrith, S. S. *Decolonizing International Health: India and Southeast Asia, 1930–65.* Basingstoke, UK: Palgrave Macmillan, 2006.

Ananthakrishnan, N., and R. Sood. "Curricula Battles: Is It Possible to Win the War Even If a Few Battles Are Lost?" *International Journal of User-Driven Healthcare* 2, no. 1 (2012): 82–85.

Anderson, W. "Postcolonial Technoscience." *Social Studies of Science* 32, no. 5–6 (2002): 643–58.

Anderson, W., and H. Pols. "Scientific Patriotism: Medical Science and National Self-Fashioning in Southeast Asia." *Comparative Studies in Society and History* 54, no. 1 (2012): 93–113. https://doi.org/10.1017/S0010417511000600.

Appadurai, A. "Number in the Colonial Imagination." In *Orientalism and the Postcolonial Predicament: Perspectives on South Asia*, edited by C. A. Breckenridge and P. van der Veer, 314–39. Philadelphia: University of Pennsylvania Press, 1993.

Arnold, D. *Colonizing the Body: State Medicine and Epidemic Disease in Nineteenth-Century India*. Berkeley: University of California Press, 1993.

———. "Nehruvian Science and Postcolonial India." *Isis* 104, no. 2 (2013): 360–70.

Arnoldy, B. "In India, the Challenge of Building 50,000 Colleges." *Christian Science Monitor*, January 16, 2012. https://www.csmonitor.com/World/Asia-South-Central/2012/0116/In-India-the-challenge-of-building-50-000-colleges.

Baer, H., M. Singer, and I. Susser, eds. *Medical Anthropology and the World System: Critical Perspectives*. Santa Barbara, CA: Praeger, 2013.

Bajpai, V., and A. Saraya. "For a Realistic Assessment: A Social, Political and Public Health Analysis of Bhore Committee." *Social Change* 41, no. 2 (2011): 215–31.

Bala, P. *Medicine and Medical Policies in India: Social and Historical Perspectives*. Lanham, MD: Lexington Books, 2007.

Bambra, C., R. Riordan, J. Ford, and F. Matthews. "The COVID-19 Pandemic and Health Inequalities." *Journal of Epidemiology and Community Health* 74, no. 11 (2020): 964–68. https://doi.org/10.1136/jech-2020-214401.

Banerjee, M. *Why India Votes?* Abingdon, UK: Routledge, 2014.

Banks, D. J. "Minorities in American Anthropology: A Personal View." *Histories of Anthropology Annual* 3, no. 1 (2007): 222–46. https://doi.org/doi: 10.1353/haa.0.0028.

Baru, R. "Public Sector Doctors in an Era of Commercialisation." In *Health Providers in India: On the Frontlines of Change*, edited by K. Sheikh and A. George, 81–96. Routledge: New Delhi, 2010.

Baru, R., A. Acharya, S. Acharya, K. Nagarak, and A. K. Shiva Kumar. "Inequities in Access to Health Services in India: Caste, Class and Region." *Economic and Political Weekly* 55, no. 38 (2010): 49–58.

Baudrillard, J. *The Consumer Society: Myths and Structures*. London: Sage, 1998.

Bayly, C. *Empire and Information: Intelligence Gathering and Social Communication in India, 1780–1870*. Cambridge: Cambridge University Press, 1996.

Bayly, S. "For Family, State and Nation: Achieving Cosmopolitan Modernity in Late-Socialist Vietnam." In *The Social Life of Achievement.*, edited by N. J. Long and H. L. Moore, 158–81. Oxford, UK: Berghahn, 2013.

Baziak, A. T., and R. K. Denton. "The Language of the Hospital and Its Effects on the Patient." In *Social Interaction and Patient Care*, edited by J. K. Skipper and R. C. Leonard, 272–77. Philadelphia: J. B. Lippincott, 1965.

Becker, H. S., B. Geer, E. C. Hughes, and A. L. Strauss. *Boys in White: Student Culture in Medical School*. Chicago: University of Chicago Press, 1961.

Bell, K. "Resisting Commensurability: Against Informed Consent as an Anthropological Virtue." *American Anthropologist* 112, no. 3 (2015): 1–12. https://doi.org/10.14288/1.0223104.

Benei, V. *Schooling Passions: Nation, History, and Language in Contemporary Western India*. Stanford, CA: Stanford University Press, 2008.

Beteille, A. "The Reproduction of Inequality: Occupation, Caste and Family." *Contributions to Indian Sociology* 25, no. 1 (1991): 3–28.

Bhaduri, S. D. "The NEXT Promise." *Indian Express*, May 8, 2018. http://indianexpress. com/article/opinion/columns/mci-next-medical-education-mbbs-exam-5167293/.

Bhat, M. Mohsin Alam. "Hate Crimes in India." *Jindal Global Law Review*, August 4, 2020. https://doi.org/10.1007/s41020-020-00119-0.

Bhatia, P. "Government Directs AIIMS to Go Bilingual." *Medical Dialogues*, January 26, 2015.

Bosk, C. "Irony, Ethnography, and Informed Consent." In *Bioethics in Social Context*, edited by C. Barry Hoffmaster, 199–220. Philadelphia: Temple University Press, 2001.

Bourdieu, P. *Distinction: A Social Critique of the Judgement of Taste.* Abingdon, UK: Routledge, 2010.

———. "The Forms of Capital." In *Handbook of Theory and Research for the Sociology of Education*, edited by J. Richardson, 241–58. New York: Greenwood Books, 1986.

———. *Language and Symbolic Power.* Edited by J. B. Thompson. Translated by G. Raymond and M. Adamson. Cambridge, MA: Harvard University Press, 1991.

Bourdieu, P., and J. Passeron. *Reproduction in Education, Society and Culture.* London: Sage, 2015.

Bradbury, R. *Fahrenheit 451.* London: HarperCollins, 1998.

Bregnbæk, S. *Fragile Elite: The Dilemmas of China's Top University Students.* Stanford, CA: Stanford University Press, 2016.

Brijnath, B. *Unforgotten: Love and the Culture of Dementia Care in India.* New York: Berghahn, 2014.

Business Standard. "AIIMS at 60: Tree Planted by Queen Elizabeth Lost to Termites," October 2, 2016. http://www.business-standard.com/article/pti-stories/aiims-at-60-tree-planted-by-queen-elizabeth-lost-to-termites-116100200124_1.html.

———. "Harsh Vardhan Upholds Power to Remove Chaturvedi from AIIMS," September 28, 2014. http://www.business-standard.com/article/economy-policy/harsh-vardhan-upholds-power-to-remove-chaturvedi-from-aiims-114092500037_1.html.

———. "Nadda Urged to Increase Accommodation for AIIMS Doctors," July 28, 2016. http://www.business-standard.com/article/news-ians/nadda-urged-to-increase-accommodation-for-aiims-doctors-116072801224_1.html.

———. "Sanjiv Chaturvedi: The Man Who Uncovered AIIMS Corruption," July 29, 2015. https://www.business-standard.com/article/current-affairs/aiims-whistle-blower-sanjiv-chaturvedi-wins-ramon-magsaysay-award-115072900348_1.html

Carson, J. *The Measure of Merit: Talents, Intelligence, and Inequality in the French and American Republics, 1750–1940.* Princeton, NJ: Princeton University Press, 2006.

Chakrabarti, P. *Bacteriology in British India: Laboratory Medicine and the Tropics.* Rochester, NY: University of Rochester Press, 2012.

———. *Medicine and Empire: 1600–1960.* Basingstoke, UK: Palgrave Macmillan, 2013.

———. "'Signs of the Times': Medicine and Nationhood in British India." *Osiris* 24, no. 1 (January 1, 2009): 188–211. https://doi.org/10.1086/605975.

Chandra, N. "Eight Hours, 30 Doctors and a New Lease of Life. Conjoined Twins with Fused Chest, Abdomen Separated Successfully at AIIMS." *India Today* 22 (July 2013): 10.

Chatterjee, P. "You Must Repay Society's Debt, Modi Tells Young AIIMS Doctors." *Indian Express* (October 21, 2014). http://indianexpress.com/article/delhi/you-must-repay-societys-debt-modi-tells-young-aiims-doctors/.

Chatterjee, U. *English, August*. London: Penguin, 1988.

Chopra, R. "Sisters and Brothers: Schooling, Family and Migration." In *Educational Regimes in Contemporary India*, edited by R. Chopra and P. Jeffery, 299–315. New Delhi: Sage, 2005.

Chua, J L. *In Pursuit of the Good Life: Aspiration and Suicide in Globalizing South India*. Berkeley: University of California Press, 2014.

Ciotti, M. "In the Past We Were a Bit 'Chamar': Education as a Self- and Community Engineering Process in Northern India." *Journal of the Royal Anthropological Institute* 12, no. 4 (2006): 899–916. https://doi.org/10.1111/j.1467-9655.2006.00369.x.

Clifford, J. "Introduction: Partial Truths." In *Writing Culture: The Poetics and Politics of Ethnography*, edited by G. E. Marcus and J. Clifford, 1–26. Berkeley: University of California Press, 2009.

Clifford, J., and G. E. Marcus, eds. *Writing Culture: The Poetics and Politics of Ethnography*. Berkeley: University of California Press, 2009.

Cohen, L. *No Aging in India: Alzheimer's, The Bad Family, and Other Modern Things*. Berkeley: University of California Press, 1998.

———. "Operability: Surgery at the Margin of the State." In *Anthropology in the Margins of the State*, edited by V. Das and D. Poole, 165–90. Santa Fe, NM: School of American Research Press, 2004.

Cohn, B. "The Census, Social Structure and Objectification in South Asia." In *An Anthropologist among the Historians and Other Essays*, 224–54. Oxford: Oxford University Press, 1987.

Coser, R. L. *Life in the Ward*. East Lansing: Michigan State University Press, 1962.

Crawford, D. G. *A History of the Indian Medical Service 1600–1913*. 2 vols. London: W. Thacker, 1914.

Crook, N., ed. *The Transmission of Knowledge in South Asia: Essays on Education, Religion, History, and Politics*. New Delhi: Oxford University Press, 1996.

Crump, T. *The Anthropology of Numbers*. Cambridge: Cambridge University Press, 1990.

Dandekar, V. "Reservations in Medical Education in Maharashtra: An Empirical Study." In *Beyond Inclusion: The Practice of Equal Access in Indian Higher Education*, edited by S. Deshpande and U. Zacharias, 95–144. New Delhi: Routledge, 2013.

Das, J. "India's Informal Doctors Are Assets Not Crooks." SciDevNet, April 24, 2016. http://www.scidev.net/global/health/opinion/india-informal-doctors-assets-crooks.html.

Das, J., and J. Hammer. "Strained Mercy: The Quality of Medical Care in Delhi." World Bank Policy Research Working Paper 3228 (September 2004). https://openknowledge.worldbank.org/handle/10986/14725.

Das, V. *Affliction: Health, Disease, Poverty*. New Delhi: Orient Blackswan, 2015.

Datye, V., K. Kielmann, K. Sheikh, D. Deshmukh, S. Deshpande, J. Porter, and S. Rangan, Private practitioners' communications with patients around HIV testing in Pune, India,

Health Policy and Planning 21, no. 5 (2006): 343–52. https://doi.org/10.1093/heapol/czlo21.

Davis, D. A., and C. Craven. *Feminist Ethnography: Thinking through Methodologies, Challenges, and Possibilities.* Lanham, MD: Rowman & Littlefield Publishers, 2016.

Davis-Floyd, R. E., and C. F. Sargent, eds. *Childbirth and Authoritative Knowledge: Cross-Cultural Perspectives.* Berkeley: University of California Press, 1997.

DelVecchio Good, M. "The Medical Imaginary and the Biotechnical Embrace." In *Subjectivity: Ethnographic Investigations,* edited by J. Biehl, B. Good, and A. Kleinman, 362–80. Berkeley: University of California Press, 2007.

Deo, M. G. "Doctor Population Ratio for India—The Reality." *Indian Journal of Medical Research* 137, no. 4 (2014): 632–35.

Deshpande, A., and T. E. Weisskopf. "Does Affirmative Action Affect Productivity in the Indian Railways?" Working Paper No. 185, Centre for Development Economics, Delhi School of Economics, 2011. http://www.cdedse.org/pdf/work185.pdf.

Deshpande, S. "Caste and Castelessness: Towards a Biography of the 'General Category.'" *Economic and Political Weekly* 47, no. 15 (2013): 32–39.

———. "Exclusive Inequalities: Merit, Caste and Discrimination in Indian Higher Education Today." *Economic and Political Weekly* 41, no. 24 (2006): 2438–44.

Deshpande, S., and U. Zacharias, eds. "Caste Quotas and Formal Inclusion in Indian Higher Education." In *Beyond Inclusion: The Practice of Equal Access in Indian Higher Education,* 13–47. New Delhi: Routledge, 2013.

Deshpande, S. "Pass, Fail, Distinction: The Examination as Social Institution." Third Marjorie Sykes Memorial Lecture presented at the National Council of Educational Research and Training, Regional Institute of Education, Ajmer, March 3, 2010. https://www.academia.edu/36917384/Pass_Fail_Distinction_The_Examination_as_a_Social_Institution.

Dhar, A. "AIIMS Rejects Thorat Report." *The Hindu,* September 20, 2007. https://www.thehindu.com/todays-paper/tp-national/tp-newdelhi/AIIMS-rejects-Thorat-report/article14838292.ece.

Donner, H. *Domestic Goddesses: Maternity, Globalisation and Middle-Class Identity in Contemporary India.* Aldershot, UK: Ashgate, 2008.

Donthi, P. "From Shadows to the Stars: The Defiant Politics of Rohith Vemula and the Ambedkar Students Association." *The Caravan,* May 2016.

Drèze, J., and A. Sen. *An Uncertain Glory: India and its Contradictions.* London: Allen Lane, 2013.

D'Silva, J. "India's Private Medical Colleges and Capitation Fees." *BMJ,* no. 350 (2015). http://dx.doi.org/10.1136/bmj.h106.

Duranti, A. *Linguistic Anthropology.* Cambridge: Cambridge University Press, 1997.

Dutta, S. "Kota Rocked by 5 Student Suicides in 1 Month." *Indian Express,* June 30, 2015. https://indianexpress.com/article/india/india-others/love-affair-home-sickness-academic-pressure-behind-rising-suicide-cases-in-kota-police/.

Ecks, S. "Bodily Sovereignty as Political Sovereignty: "'Self-Care' in Kolkata (India)." *An-*

thropology & Medicine 11, no. 1 (2004): 75–89. https://doi.org/10.1080/13648470420 00204906.

———. "Spectacles of Reason: An Ethnography of Calcutta Gastroenterologists." In *New Politics of Vision*, edited by J. Edwards, P. Harvey, and P. Wade, 117–35. Oxford: Berghahn, 2010.

Economic Times. "Govt Plans Exit Exam for All MBBS Students." *Economic Times*, July 27, 2016. http://health.economictimes.indiatimes.com/news/industry/govt-plans-exit-exam-for-all-mbbs-students/53409969.

Eisenberg, L., and A. Kleinman. *The Relevance of Social Science to Medicine*. Dordrecht: Reidel, 1981.

Farmer, P. *Infections and Inequalities: The Modern Plagues*. Berkeley: University of California Press, 1999.

Fassin, D. "Why Ethnography Matters: On Anthropology and Its Publics." *Cultural Anthropology* 28, no. 4 (2013): 621–46. https://doi.org/10.1111/cuan.12030.

Fernandes, L. *India's New Middle Class: Democratic Politics in an Era of Economic Reform*. Minneapolis: University of Minnesota Press, 2006.

Finkler, K. "Biomedicine Globalized and Localized: Western Medical Practices in an Outpatient Clinic of a Mexican Hospital." *Social Science & Medicine* 59, no. 10 (2004): 2037–51. https://doi.org/doi: 10.1016/j.socscimed.2004.03.008.

Flinders, D. J., N. Noddings, and S. J. Thornton. "The Null Curriculum: Its Theoretical Basis and Practical Implications." *Curriculum Enquiry* 16, no. 1 (1986): 33–42.

Forum for Rights and Equality, AIIMS, New Delhi. "Forum for Rights and Equality to the Secretary, Ministry of Health and Family Welfare," January 19, 2015.

Foucault, M. *The Birth of the Clinic: An Archaeology of Medical Perception*. New York: Vintage, 1994.

———. "The Subject and Power." In *The Essential Foucault: Selections from the Essential Works of Foucault, 1954–1984*, edited by N. Rose and P. Rabinow, 126–44. New York: New Press, 1994.

Fox, R. "Medical Uncertainty Revisited." In *Handbook of Social Studies*, edited by G. L. Albrecht, R. Fitzpatrick, and S. Scrimshaw, 409–25. London: Sage, 2000.

———. "The Evolution of Medical Uncertainty." *Health and Society* 58, no. 1 (1980): 1–49.

Froerer, P. "Education, Inequality, and Social Mobility in Central India." *European Journal of Development Research* 23 (2011): 695–711. https://doi.org/10.1057/ejdr.2011.43.

Fuller, C. J., and H. Narasimhan. "Information Technology Professionals and the New-Rich Middle Class in Chennai (Madras)." *Modern Asian Studies* 41, no. 1 (2007): 121–50. https://doi.org/10.1017/S0026749X05002325.

Galanter, Marc. *Competing Inequalities: Law and the Backward Classes in India*. New Delhi: Oxford University Press, n.d.

Galbraith, J. K. *The Affluent Society*. New York: Houghton Mifflin, 1998.

Garalytė, K. "Dalit Student Movement in India: From Identity Politics to Counter Culture Movement." Kaunas: Vytautas Magnus University, n.d.

Geest, S. van der, and K. Finkler. "Hospital Ethnography: Introduction." *Social Sci-*

ence & Medicine 59, no. 10 (2004): 1995–2001. https://doi.org/10.1016/j.socscimed
.2004.03.004.

Geiger, H. J. "The Political Future of Social Medicine: Reflections on Physicians as Activists." *Academic Medicine* 92, no. 3 (2017): 282–84.

Gerber, B. "Should We Use Philosophy to Teach Clinical Communication Skills?" *African Journal of Primary Health Care & Family Medicine* 8, no. 1 (November 16, 2016): e1–e4. https://doi.org/10.4102/phcfm.v8i1.1292.

Gesler, W. M. "Therapeutic Landscapes: Medical Issues in Light of the New Cultural Geography." *Social Science & Medicine* 34, no. 7 (1992): 735–46.

Ghosh, T. "Making of an Engineer: My Journey through School, Kota, and Depression," June 30, 2016. http://www.youthkiawaaz.com/2016/06/kota-engineering-led-to
-depression/.

Gilbertson, A. "Cosmopolitan Learning, Making Merit, and Reproducing Privilege in Indian Schools." *Anthropology and Education Quarterly* 47 (2016): 297–313. https://
doi.org/10.1111/aeq.12157.

———. "'Mugging up' versus 'Exposure': International Schools and Social Mobility in Hyderabad, India." *Ethnography and Education* 9, no. 2 (2014): 210–23. https://doi.org
/10.1080/17457823.2013.878512.

Government of India. The All India Institute of Medical Sciences Act, 1956. https://www.
aiims.edu/images/pdf/aiimsact.pdf.

———. "Health Survey and Development Committee, Vols I–III." Calcutta, 1946. https://
www.nhp.gov.in/sites/default/files/pdf/Bhore_Committee_Report_VOL-1.pdf.

———. *Lok Sabha Debates*. Vol. 1, no. 2. New Delhi: Lok Sabha Secretariat, 1956.

———. "National Health Policy 2002." https://nhm.gov.in/images/pdf/guidelines/nrhm-
guidelines/national_nealth_policy_2002.pdf.

———. "National Health Policy 2015 Draft." https://www.nhp.gov.in/sites/default/files/
pdf/draft_national_health_policy_2015.pdf.

———. "Report of the Committee to Enquire into the Allegation of Differential Treatment of SC/ST Students in All India Institute of Medical Science [*sic*]," 2007. https://
atrocitynews.files.wordpress.com/2008/05/reports-aiims.pdf.

Gowariker, A. *Swades*. DVD. Moserbaer, 2006.

Graeber, D. "It Is Value That Brings Universes into Being." *HAU: Journal of Ethnographic Theory* 3, no. 2 (2013): 219–43. https://doi.org/10.14318/hau3.2.012.

———. *Toward an Anthropological Theory of Value: The False Coin of Our Own Dreams*. New York: Palgrave, 2001.

Guha, R., and J. Parry, eds. "Two Cheers for Reservation: The Satnamis and the Steel Plant." In *Institutions and Inequalities: Essays in Honour of Andre Beteille*, 128–69. New Delhi: Oxford University Press, 1999.

Gupta, A. "Blurred Boundaries: The Discourse of Corruption, the Culture of Politics, and the Imagined State." *American Ethnologist* 22, no. 2 (1995): 375–402.

———. *Red Tape: Bureaucracy, Structural Violence, and Poverty in India*. A John Hope Franklin Center Book. Durham, NC: Duke University Press, 2012.

Gupta, D. "Tidy Up Delhi's AIIMS before Building Many More across India." *Times of India*, July 21, 2014. http://blogs.timesofindia.indiatimes.com/toi-editorials/tidy-up-delhis-aiims-before-building-many-more-across-india/.

Gutschow, K. "Going 'Beyond the Numbers': Maternal Death Reviews in India." *Medical Anthropology* 35, no. 4 (2016): 322–37. https://doi.org/10.1080/01459740.2015.1101460.

Guyer, J. I., N. Khan, and J. Obarrio. "Introduction: Number as Inventive Frontier." *Anthropological Theory* 10, nos. 1–2 (2010): 36–61. https://doi.org/10.1177/1463499610365388.

Hacking, I. "Making Up People." In *Reconstructing Individualism*, ed. T. L. Heller, M. Sosna, and D. E. Wellbery, 161–71. Stanford, CA: Stanford University Press, 1985.

Hafferty, F. "Beyond Curriculum Reform: Confronting Medicine's Hidden Curriculum." *Academic Medicine* 73, no. 4 (1998): 403–7. https://doi.org/10.1097/00001888-199804000-00013.

Hafferty, F. W., and R. Franks. "The Hidden Curriculum, Ethics Teaching, and the Structure of Medical Education." *Academic Medicine* 69, no. 11 (1994): 861–71. https://doi.org/10.1097/00001888-199411000-00001.

Haller, D., and C. Shore, eds. *Corruption: Anthropological Perspectives*. London: Pluto, 2005.

Hardiman, D., and P. B. Mukharji, eds. *Medical Marginality in South Asia: Situating Subaltern Therapeutics*. London: Routledge, 2012.

Harrison, M. *Public Health in British India: Anglo-Indian Preventive Medicine 1859–1914*. Cambridge: Cambridge University Press, 1994.

Hartocollis, A. "With Remarks in Affirmative Action Case, Scalia Steps into 'Mismatch' Debate." *New York Times*, December 10, 2015. https://www.nytimes.com/2015/12/11/us/with-remarks-in-affirmative-action-case-scalia-steps-into-mismatch-debate.html.

Hasan, Z. *Politics of Inclusion: Castes, Minorities, and Affirmative Action*. New Delhi: Oxford University Press, 2009.

Hill, A. V. "A Report to the Government of India on Scientific Research in India." Royal Society, 1944.

The Hindu. "Protest against Denial of Reservation at AIIMS," October 3, 2010. http://www.thehindu.com/todays-paper/tp-national/tp-newdelhi/protest-against-denial-of-reservation-at-aiims/article810496.ece.

Hindustan Times. "22 New AIIMS Coming up across the Country, Says Health Minister Nadda." August 25, 2018. https://www.hindustantimes.com/india-news/22-new-aiims-coming-up-across-the-country-says-health-minister-nadda/story-tVpsnOCrvUpkbr2U4Xm5sJ.html.

———. "AIIMS MBBS Result 2017: Top 10 from One Kota Coaching School. Isn't It Odd?" June 15, 2017. https://www.hindustantimes.com/editorials/aiims-mbbs-result-2017-top-10-from-one-kota-coaching-school-isn-t-it-odd/story-6mm65fff3DhyMBu5gIYvVK.html.

———. "AIIMS MBBS 2017 Results: Men Outperform Women, Only 4,905 out of 2.8 Lakh Candidates Clear Exam." June 15, 2017. http://www.hindustantimes.com/education/aiims-mbbs-2017-results-men-outperform-women-only4905-of-2-84-lakh-candidates-clear-exam/story-05fBvANVRBLaMbHpqCyodP.html.

————. "Meet AIIMS MBBS Entrance Topper: Haryana Boy Navsheen Singhal." June 19, 2015.

Hull, M. S. *Government of Paper: The Materiality of Bureaucracy in Urban Pakistan*. Berkeley: University of California Press, 2012.

Illich, I. *Medical Nemesis: The Expropriation of Health*. New York: Pantheon Books, 1982.

India Today. "17 Kg Tumour Removed from Woman's Abdomen." March 4, 2015. http://indiatoday.intoday.in/story/aiims-doctor-remove-17-kg-tumour-from-bihar-woman-abdomen/1/422254.html.

Inhorn, M. "Privacy, Privatization, and the Politics of Patronage: Ethnographic Challenges to Penetrating the Secret World of Middle Eastern, Hospital-Based In Vitro Fertilization." *Social Science & Medicine* 59, no. 10 (2004): 2095–2108. https://doi.org/10.1016/j.socscimed.2004.03.012.

Iqbal, N. "Kashmir Pellet Gun Victims Pin Their Hopes on Doctors at AIIMS." *Indian Express*, July 27, 2016. https://indianexpress.com/article/india/india-news-india/kashmir-pellet-gun-victims-aiims-2938977/.

Jacob, K. S. "Politics of Medical Education in India." *Economic and Political Weekly* 51, no. 12 (2016): 12–15.

Jaffrelot, C. *India's Silent Revolution : The Rise of the Lower Castes*. London: Hurst, 2002.

James, A. "Keralites Shine in Delhi AIIMS Union Elections, Win All Posts Except One." *International Business Times*, July 23, 2015. http://www.ibtimes.co.in/keralites-shine-delhi-aiims-union-elections-win-all-posts-except-one-640243.

Jamous, H. and B. Peloille. "Professions or Self-Perpetuating Systems? Changes in the French University-Hospital System." In *Professions and Professionalization*, edited by J. A. Jackson, 109–52. Cambridge: Cambridge University Press, 1970.

Jayal, N. G. *Citizenship and Its Discontents: An Indian History*. Cambridge, MA: Harvard University Press, 2013.

Jeffery, P. "Introduction: Hearts, Minds and Pockets." In *Educational Regimes in Contemporary India*, edited by R. Chopra and P. Jeffery, 13–38. New Delhi: Sage, 2005.

Jeffery, R. "Recognizing India's Doctors: The Institutionalization of Medical Dependency, 1918–39." *Modern Asian Studies* 13, no. 2 (1979): 301–26.

————. *The Politics of Health in India*. Berkeley: University of California Press, 1988.

Jeffery, R., C. Jeffrey, and P. Jeffery. "Social Inequalities and the Privatisation of Secondary Schooling in North India." In *Educational Regimes in Contemporary India*, edited by R. Chopra and P. Jeffery, 41–61. New Delhi: Sage, 2005.

Jeffrey, C. *Timepass: Youth, Class, and the Politics of Waiting in India*. Stanford, CA: Stanford University Press, 2010.

Jeffrey, C., P. Jeffery, and R. Jeffery. "Reproducing Difference? Schooling, Jobs, and Empowerment in Uttar Pradesh, India." *World Development* 33, no. 12 (2005): 2085–2101. https://doi.org/10.1016/j.worlddev.2005.07.006.

Jha, D. N. "Humble till the End: A Patient AIIMS Will Remember Forever—Times of India." *Times of India*, August 27, 2018. https://timesofindia.indiatimes.com/city/delhi/humble-till-the-end-a-patient-aiims-will-remember-forever/articleshow/65446154.cms.

———. "No Takers for Seats in AIIMS Patna, Raipur." *Times of India*, October 2014. http://timesofindia.indiatimes.com/home/education/news/No-takers-for-seats-in-AIIMS-Patna-Raipur/articleshow/44646599.cms.

Jodhka, S. S. "Nation and Village: Images of Rural India in Gandhi, Nehru and Ambedkar." *Economic and Political Weekly* 37, no. 32 (2002): 3343–53.

Jodhka, S. S., and K. Newman. "In the Name of Globalisation: Meritocracy, Productivity and the Hidden Language of Caste." *Economic and Political Weekly* 42, no. 41 (2007): 4125–32.

Jones, D. S., J. A. Greene, J. Duffin, and J. H. Warner. "Making the Case for History in Medical Education." *Journal of the History of Medicine and Allied Sciences* 70, no. 4 (2015): 623–52.

Kafka, F. *The Castle*. London: Vintage, 2005.

Kalra, A. "India Slashes Health Budget, Already One of the World's Lowest." *Reuters*, December 23, 2014. https://www.reuters.com/article/idUSKBN0K10XZ20141223.

Kasper, J., J. A. Greene, P. E. Farmer, and D. S. Jones. "All Health Is Global Health, All Medicine Is Social Medicine: Integrating the Social Sciences Into the Preclinical Curriculum." *Academic Medicine* 91, no. 5 (2016). https://journals.lww.com/academicmedicine/Fulltext/2016/05000/All_Health_Is_Global_Health,_All_Medicine_Is.15.aspx.

Kaur, R. A. "Speech to Parliament," 1956.

Kaushik, M., A. Jaiswal, N. Shah, and A. Mahal. "High-End Physician Migration from India." *Bulletin of the World Health Organization* 86, no. 1 (2008): 40–45.

Kielmann, K., D. Deshmukh, S. Deshpande, and S. Rangan. "Managing Uncertainty around HIV/AIDS in an Urban Setting: Private Medical Providers and Their Patients in Pune, India." *Social Science & Medicine* 61, no. 7 (2005): 1540–50. https://doi.org/o.1016/j.socscimed.2005.02.008.

Killmer, J. "Village Doctors and Vulnerable Bodies: Gender, Medicine, and Risk in North India." PhD, Syracuse University, 2018.

Kirkpatrick, J. *The Sociology of an Indian Hospital Ward*. Calcutta: KLM, 1979.

Kleinman, A. *The Illness Narratives: Suffering, Healing, and the Human Condition*. New York: Basic Books, 1988.

Kleinman, A. "The Divided Self, Hidden Values, and Moral Sensibility in Medicine." *The Lancet* 377, no. 9768 (March 5, 2011): 804–5. https://doi.org/10.1016/S0140-6736(11)60295-X.

Kluckhohn, C. "Values and Value-Orientations in the Theory of Action: An Exploration in Definition and Classification." In *Toward a General Theory of Action*, edited by T. Parsons and E. Shils. Cambridge, MA: Harvard University Press, 1951.

Kohli, A. *Poverty amid Plenty in the New India*. Cambridge: Cambridge University Press, 2006.

Konikkara, A. "How a Healthcare System Partial to Privatization Fails the Poor." *The Caravan*, July 29, 2020. https://caravanmagazine.in/health/how-healthcare-partial-to-privatisation-fails-the-poor.

Krishna, A. "Examining the Structure of Opportunity and Social Mobility in India:

Who Becomes an Engineer?" *Development and Change* 45 (2014): 1–28. https://doi. org/10.1111/dech.12072.

Krishnan, V. "Most Medical Colleges Show Little Interest in Research: Study." *The Hindu*, 2016. http://www.thehindu.com/todays-paper/tp-national/most-medical-colleges-show-little-interest-in-research-study/article8501007.ece.

———. "Private Practice: How Naresh Trehan Became One of India's Most Influential Doctor-Businessmen." *The Caravan*, February 2015. https://caravanmagazine.in/ reportage/naresh-trehan-medanta-private-practice.

Kuipers, J. C. "'Medical Discourse' in Anthropological Context: Views of Language and Power." *Medical Anthropology Quarterly* 3, no. 2 (1989): 99–123.

Kumar, A. *Placebo*. Storyteller Ink. Netflix, 2014.

Kumar, K. *Political Agenda of Education: A Study of Colonialist and Nationalist Ideas*. New Delhi: Sage, 2005.

Kumar, R. "Why Family Medicine Is a Good Career Choice for Indian Medical Graduates?" *Journal of Family Medicine and Primary Care* 3, no. 1 (2014): 1–2.

Lahariya, C. "Mohalla Clinics of Delhi, India: Could These Become Platform to Strengthen Primary Healthcare?" *Journal of Family Medicine and Primary Care* 6, no. 1 (2017): 1–10. https://doi.org/10.4103/jfmpc.jfmpc_29_17.

Lambert, H. "Medical Pluralism and Medical Marginality: Bone Doctors and the Selective Legitimation of Therapeutic Expertise in India." *Social Science & Medicine* 74, no. 7 (April 1, 2012): 1029–36. https://doi.org/10.1016/j.socscimed.2011.12.024.

Leeming, W. "Professionalization Theory, Medical Specialists and the Concept of 'National Patterns of Specialization.'" *Social Science Information* 40, no. 3 (2001): 455–85. https://doi.org/10.1177/ 053901801040003005.

Lefebvre, B. "The Indian Corporate Hospitals: Touching Middle Class Lives." In *Patterns of Middle Class Consumption in India and China*, edited by C. Jaffrelot and P. van der Veer, 88–109. New Delhi: Sage, 2008.

Levinson, B. A., D. E. Foley, and D. C. Holland, eds. *The Cultural Production of the Educated Person: An Introduction*. Albany: State University of New York Press, 1996.

Lewin, E., and W. L. Leap. *Out in Public: Reinventing Lesbian / Gay Anthropology in a Globalizing World*. Readings in Engaged Anthropology. Wiley, 2009.

Lingam, L., and R. S. Sapkal. "COVID-19, Physical Distancing and Social Inequalities: Are We All Really in This Together?" *International Journal of Community and Social Development* 2, no. 2 (2020): 173–90. https://doi.org/10.1177/2516602620937932.

Livingston, J. *Improvising Medicine: An African Oncology Ward in an Emerging Cancer Epidemic*. Durham, NC: Duke University Press, 2012.

Lock, M., and D. Gordon, eds. *Biomedicine Examined*. Dordrecht, The Netherlands: Kluwer Academic Publishers, 1988.

Long, N. J., and H. L. Moore, eds. *The Social Life of Achievement*. Oxford, UK: Berghahn, 2013.

Ludmerer, K. M. *Time to Heal: American Medical Education from the Turn of the Century to the Era of Managed Care*. Oxford: Oxford University Press, 2005.

Lukose, R. *Liberalization's Children: Gender, Youth, and Consumer Citizenship in Globalizing India*. Durham, NC: Duke University Press, 2009.

Lynch, M. "Against Reflexivity as an Academic Virtue and Source of Privileged Knowledge." *Theory, Culture and Society* 17, no. 3 (2000): 26–54. https://doi.org/10.1177/026327 60022051202.

Mackenbach, J P. "Politics Is Nothing but Medicine at a Larger Scale: Reflections on Public Health's Biggest Idea." *Journal of Epidemiology and Community Health* 63, no. 3 (March 1, 2009): 181–84. https://doi.org/10.1136/jech.2008.077032.

Madan, T. N., ed. *Doctors and Society: Three Asian Case Studies: India, Malaysia, Sri Lanka*. Ghaziabad: Vikas, 1980.

Malhotra, S. "The Dream Factories." *Business Today*, May 12, 2013. http://www.business-today.in/magazine/cover-story/kota-coaching-institutes-brand-iit/story/194170.html.

Manuel, T. "India Produces 50,000 Doctors a Year. If Only Medical Education Were Better Regulated." *The Wire* 28 (August 2015). http://thewire.in/9427/medical-colleges-mci-mbbs/.

Mehta, P. B. *The Burden of Democracy*. New Delhi: Penguin Random House India, 2003.

Mendelsohn, O., and M. Vicziany. *The Untouchables: Subordination, Poverty and the State in Modern India*. Cambridge: Cambridge University Press, 1998.

Miller, H. *Medicine and Society*. Vol. 352. London: Oxford University Press, 1973. http://www.bmj.com/content/352/bmj.i1338.

Moore, H. L. *Still Life: Hopes, Desires and Satisfactions*. Cambridge, UK: Polity Press, 2011.

Mudur, G. S. "Mirror AIIMS Hobbled by Faculty Shortage." *The Telegraph*, January 2, 2019.

Mukherjee, S. "The Perfect Last Day of Mr Sengupta." *Granta* 124 (2013): 35–42.

Murphy, M. "Hiding in Plain Sight: The Production of Heteronormativity in Medical Education." *Journal of Contemporary Ethnography* 45, no. 3 (November 6, 2014): 256–89. https://doi.org/10.1177/0891241614556345.

Murthy, P., A. Sarin, and S. Jain. "International Advisers to the Bhore Committee: Perceptions and Visions for Healthcare." *Economic and Political Weekly* 48, no. 10 (2013): 71–77.

Mutha, S., and J. I. Takayama. "Insights into Medical Students' Career Choices Based on Third- and Fourth-Year Students' Focus-Group Discussions." *Academic Medicine* 72, no. 7 (1997): 635–40.

Nagarajan, R. "State Councils Blame MCI for Mess in Data on Doctors." *Times of India*, August 16, 2018.

Nampoothiri, D. D. "Confronting Social Exclusion: A Critical Overview of the CREST Experience." In *Beyond Inclusion: The Practice of Equal Access in Indian Higher Education*, edited by S. Deshpande and U. Zacharias, 252–88. New Delhi: Routledge, 2013.

Narain, J. P. "Is Ayushman Bharat a Game Changer?" *Indian Express*, February 7, 2018. http://indianexpress.com/article/opinion/is-ayushman-bharat-a-game-changer-national-health-insurance-scheme-5054394/.

Narayan, D. "India's Abuse of Women Is the Biggest Human Rights Violation on Earth."

The Guardian, April 27, 2018. https://www.theguardian.com/commentisfree/2018/apr/27/india-abuse-women-human-rights-rape-girls.

Narayan, K. *Alive in the Writing: Crafting Ethnography in the Company of Chekhov.* Chicago: University of Chicago Press, 2012.

Naudet, J. "'Paying Back to Society': Upward Social Mobility among Dalits." *Contributions to Indian Sociology* 42, no. 3 (October 1, 2008): 413–41. https://doi.org/10.1177/006996670804200304.

Nehru, J. *Jawaharlal Nehru's Speeches.* Vol. 2, *1949–1953.* Delhi: The Publications Division, 1958.

Nichter, M. *Global Health: Why Cultural Perceptions, Social Representations, and Biopolitics Matter.* Tucson: University of Arizona Press, 2008.

Nundy, S., K. Desiraju, and S. Nagral, eds. *Healers Or Predators? Healthcare Corruption in India.* Oxford University Press, 2018.

O'Donnell, J. F. "Introduction: The Hidden Curriculum—A Focus on Learning and Closing the Gap." In *The Hidden Curriculum in Health Professional Education*, edited by J. F. O'Donnell and F. W. Hafferty, 1–20. Lebanon, NH: Dartmouth College Press, 2014.

Otto, T., and R. Willerslev. "'Value as Theory': Comparison, Cultural Critique, and Guerrilla Ethnographic Theory." *HAU: Journal of Ethnographic Theory* 3, no. 1 (2013): 1–20.

Oxfam India. "Education to Turn Mirrors into Windows," 2015. https://www.oxfamindia.org/subpage/220.

Pandey, D. "Child Rape Victim Shifted to AIIMS as Outrage Spreads." *The Hindu*, April 20, 2013. http://www.thehindu.com/todays-paper/child-rape-victim-shifted-to-aiims-as-outrage-spreads/article4635436.ece.

Pandhi, N. "Clinical Trials." *The Caravan*, October 2015.

Pandian, A. "Devoted to Development: Moral Progress, Ethical Work, and Divine Favor in South India." *Anthropological Theory* 8, no. 2 (June 1, 2008): 159–79. https://doi.org/10.1177/1463499608090789.

Pandit, C. G. *My World of Preventive Medicine.* New Delhi: Leipzig Press, 1982.

Panikkar, K. N., T. Joseph, Geetha G., and M. A. Lal. *Quality, Access and Social Justice in Higher Education.* New Delhi: Pearson, 2011.

Patel, V., R. Parikh, S. Nandraj, P. Balasubramaniam, K. Narayan, V. K. Paul, A. K. S. Kumar, M. Chatterjee, and K. S. Reddy. "Assuring Health Coverage for All in India." *Lancet* 386 (2015): 2422–35.

Pentecost, M., and T. Cousins. "'The Good Doctor': The Making and Unmaking of the Physician Self in Contemporary South Africa." *Journal of Medical Humanities*, August 23, 2019. https://doi.org/10.1007/s10912-019-09572-y.

Pereira, B., G. Andrew, S. Pednekar, R. Pai, P. Pelto, and V. Patel. "The Explanatory Models of Depression in Low Income Countries: Listening to Women." *Journal of Affective Disorders* 102 (2007): 209–18.

Petryna, A. *Life Exposed: Biological Citizens after Chernobyl.* Princeton, NJ: Princeton University Press, 2002.

Phadke, A. "Regulation of Doctors and Private Hospitals in India." *Economic and Political Weekly* 41, no. 6 (2016): 46–55.

Phalkey, J. "Introduction: Science, History, and Modern India." *Isis* 104, no. 2 (2013): 330–36.

Pilnick, A., and R. Dingwall. "On the Remarkable Persistence of Asymmetry in Doctor/Patient Interaction: A Critical Review." *Social Science & Medicine* 72, no. 8 (April 1, 2011): 1374–82. https://doi.org/10.1016/j.socscimed.2011.02.033.

Pinto, S. "Development without Institutions: Ersatz Medicine and the Politics of Everyday Life in North India." *Cultural Anthropology* 19, no. 3 (2004): 337–64. https://doi.org/10.1525/can.2004.19.3.337.

———. "'The Tools of Your Chants and Spells': Stories of Madwomen and Indian Practical Healing." *Medical Anthropology* 35, no. 3 (2015): 263–77.

———. *Where There Is No Midwife: Birth and Loss in Rural India*. Oxford, UK: Berghahn, 2008.

Pollock, D. "Training Tales: U.S. Medical Autobiography." *Cultural Anthropology* 11, no. 3 (1996): 339–61.

Poonam, S. *Dreamers: How Young Indians Are Changing Their World*. Delhi: Penguin Random House India, 2018.

Porecha, M. "Do You Still Have a Family Physician?" *dna*, February 2014. http://www.dnaindia.com/health/report-do-you-still-have-a-family-physician-1964306.

Potnuru, B. "Aggregate Availability of Doctors in India: 2014–2030." *Indian Journal of Public Health* 61, no. 3 (January 7, 2017): 182. https://doi.org/10.4103/ijph.IJPH_143_16.

Powell-Jackson, T., A. Acharya, and A. Mills. "An Assessment of the Quality of Primary Health Care in India." *Economic and Political Weekly* 48, no. 19 (2013): 53–61.

Prakash, G. *Another Reason: Science and the Imagination of Modern India*. Princeton, NJ: Princeton University Press, 1999.

Pratap, A., and S. Pandit. "Maharashtra Goes on Strike as More Doctors Are Attacked." *Hindustan Times*, March 23, 2017. https://www.hindustantimes.com/mumbai-news/maharashtra-strike-goes-on-as-another-doctor-is-hit/story-kwBngewRpYk5XzqH9KXafP.html.

Premchand, M. *Bade Bhai Sahab*. https://www.scribd.com/doc/6691922/Bade-Bhai-Sahab, 1910.

Prentice, R. *Bodies in Formation: An Ethnography of Anatomy and Surgery Education*. Durham, NC: Duke University Press, 2013.

Priyam, M. *Contested Politics of Educational Reform in India: Aligning Opportunities with Interests*. New Delhi: Oxford University Press, 2015.

Qadeer, I., K. Sen, and R. Nayar. *Public Health and the Poverty of Reforms: The South Asian Predicament*. New Delhi: Sage, 2001.

Quazi, A. H. "AIIMS in Bag, Test Toppers Set New Goals: Neurosurgery, Research." *Hindustan Times*, June 15, 2016. http://www.hindustantimes.com/education/aiims-in-bag-test-toppers-set-new-goals-neurosurgery-research/story-moYwSyIjiuMvTDfQjJsJNL.html.

————. "Student Suicides in Rajasthan's Kota Drop by 70%." *Hindustan Times*, November 8, 2017. https://www.hindustantimes.com/india-news/student-suicides-in-rajasthan-s-kota-drops-by-70/story-2Msn5Kwn8EFHqzZ8zIDS8L.html.

Raina, D., and S. I. Habib. *Domesticating Modern Science: A Social History of Science and Culture in Colonial India*. Chennai: Tulika, 2004.

Rajshekhar, M. "High Patient Inflow, Corruption, Nepotism and Talent Exodus: The Problems That Have Plagued AIIMS." *The Economic Times*, March 2015. http://articles .economictimes.indiatimes.com/2015-03-12/news/60048160_1_new-aiims-delhi-aiims-aiims-metro-station.

Ram, K. "Class and the Clinic: The Subject of Medical Pluralism and the Transmission of Inequality." *South Asian History and Culture* 1, no. 2 (2010): 199–212. https://doi.org/10.1080/19472491003590676.

Ramalingaswami, V. *Medicine, Health and Development. Ninth Jawaharlal Nehru Memorial Lecture, 13*. New Delhi, 1975.

Ramanna, M. *Western Medicine and Public Health in Colonial Bombay: 1845–1895*. New Perspectives in South Asian History Series. Sangam Books, 2002.

Rao, K. D., A. Bhatnagar, and P. Berman. "So Many, yet Few: Human Resources for Health in India." *Human Resources for Health* 10, no. 1 (August 13, 2012): 19. https://doi.org/10.1186/1478-4491-10-19.

Rao, K. D., S. Ramani, S. Murthy, I. Hazarika, N. Khandpur, M. Choksi, S. Khanna, M. Vujicic, P. Berman, and M. Ryan. "Health Worker Attitudes toward Rural Service in India: Results from Qualitative Research." Health, Nutrition, and Population Unit, Human Development Network, World Bank, 2010. http://siteresources.worldbank.org/ HEALTHNUTRITIONANDPOPULATION/Resources/281627-1095698140167/ HealthWorkerAttitudesTowardRuralServiceinIndia.pdf.

Rao, K. D., and A. Sheffel. "Quality of Clinical Care and Bypassing of Primary Health Centers in India." *Social Science & Medicine* 207 (2018): 80–88. https://doi.org/10.1016/j.socscimed.2018.04.040.

Rao, S., and S. Naik. "Supreme Court Directive on Making NEET Compulsory Is Move in the Right Direction." *Indian Express*, May 10, 2016.

Rao, S. K. *Do We Care? India's Health System*. New Delhi: Oxford University Press, 2017.

Rao, U. "Biometric Marginality: UID and the Shaping of Homeless Identities in the City." *Economic and Political Weekly* 48, no. 13 (2013): 71–77.

Rashid, T. "Dr. Ramadoss Plays the Boss, Pushes AIIMS Chief to Brink." *Indian Express*, June 15, 2006. http://archive.indianexpress.com/news/dr-ramadoss-plays-the-boss-pushes-aiims-chief-to-brink————/6562/0.

Ravi Rajan, S. "Science, State, and Violence: An Indian Critique Reconsidered." *Science as Culture* 14, no. 3 (2005): 1–17.

Rawal, U., and D. Quazi. "Kota Suicides: In This Coaching Hotspot, Stress Snuffs Out Lives." *Hindustan Times*, September 19, 2015.

Reddy, A., B. S. Jose, P. Ambedkar, V. S. Reddy, and V. S. Nishikanth. "New Reservation Policy: Is It Empirically Justifiable?" *Economic and Political Weekly* 54, no. 23 (June 8, 2019): 12–14.

Rose, N. *The Politics of Life Itself: Biomedicine, Power, and Subjectivity in the Twenty-First Century.* Princeton, NJ: Princeton University Press, 2006.

Rosenberg, C. E. *Our Present Complaint: American Medicine, Then and Now.* Baltimore: Johns Hopkins University Press, 2007.

Ruddock, A. "AIIMS Teaches Its Doctors What to Ask a Patient. It Must Also Teach Them How." *Scroll.In*, February 22, 2017. https://scroll.in/pulse/829959/aiims-teaches-its-doctors-what-to-ask-a-patient-it-must-also-teach-them-how-to.

———. "Behind the Self-Defence Lessons for AIIMS Doctors Lies the Failure of Indian Medical Education." *Scroll.In*. https://scroll.in/pulse/838661/behind-the-self-defence-lessons-for-aiims-doctors-lies-the-failure-of-indian-medical-education.

———. "Incorrect Dosage." *The Caravan*, October 27, 2015. http://www.caravanmagazine.in/perspectives/incorrect-dosage-india-blinkered-preference-specialist-doctors.

———. "Making Visible: Chronic Illness and the Academy." *Sociological Review* (blog), October 17, 2017. https://www.thesociologicalreview.com/making-visible-chronic-illness-and-the-academy/.

———. "Notes from the Waiting Room: Seeking Research Access to the All India Institute of Medical Sciences (AIIMS)." LSE Field Research Method Lab, June 16, 2017. https://blogs.lse.ac.uk/fieldresearch/2017/06/16/notes-from-the-waiting-room-aiims/.

Ruddock, A., and P. Chakrabarti. "The 'Indian Predicament': Medical Education and the Nation in India, 1880–1956." In *Medical Education: Historical Case Studies of Teaching, Learning, and Belonging in Honour of Jacalyn Duffin*, edited by D. Gavrus and S. Lamb. Montreal: McGill-Queens University Press, forthcoming.

Saez, L., and A. Sinha. "Political Cycles, Political Institutions and Public Expenditure in India, 1980–2000." *British Journal of Political Science* 40, no. 1 (2010): 91–113. https://doi.org/10.1017/S0007123409990226.

Samuels, E. "Six Ways of Looking at Crip Time." *Disability Studies Quarterly* 37, no. 3 (2017). https://dsq-sds.org/article/view/5824/4684.

Sarangapani, P. M. *Knowledge, Curricula, and Teaching Methods: The Case of India. Revue Internationale d'éducation de Sèvres*, 2014. http://ries.revues.org/3851.

Sengupta, S., and M. K. Jha. "Social Policy, COVID-19 and Impoverished Migrants: Challenges and Prospects in Locked Down India." *International Journal of Community and Social Development* 2, no. 2 (2020): 152–72. https://doi.org/10.1177/2516602620933715.

Sethi, A. "The Mystery of India's Deadly Exam Scam." *The Guardian*, December 17, 2015. http://www.theguardian.com/world/2015/dec/17/the-mystery-of-indias-deadly-exam-scam.

Sethi, N. "Parliamentary Standing Committee Report on Corruption in the Hospital Has No Foundation: AIIMS." *Business Standard*, June 3, 2016. http://www.business-standard.com/article/current-affairs/parliamentary-panel-report-on-corruption-baseless-aiims-116060300042_1.html.

Shah, A., and S. Shneiderman. "Toward an Anthropology of Affirmative Action." *Focaal* 65 (2013): 3–162.

Shah, A. M. "Job Reservations and Efficiency." *Economic and Political Weekly* 26, no. 29 (1991): 1732–24.

Sharma, D. C. "Rising Violence against Health Workers in India." *The Lancet* 389, no. 10080 (May 5, 2017): 1685. https://doi.org/10.1016/S0140-6736(17)31142-X.

Sharma, D. C. "India Still Struggles with Rural Doctor Shortages." *The Lancet* 386, no. 10011 (2015): 2381–82. https://doi.org/doi: 10.1016/S0140–6736(15)01231-3.

Shaw, G. B. *The Doctor's Dilemma: A Preface on Doctors*. Project Gutenberg, 2009.

Sheikh, K., and A. George, eds. *Health Providers in India: On the Frontlines of Change*. New Delhi: Routledge, 2010.

Sheikh, K., S. Mondal, P. Patanwar, B. Rajkumari, and T. Sundararaman. "What Rural Doctors Want: A Qualitative Study in Chhattisgarh State." *Indian Journal of Medical Ethics* 1, no. 3 (2016): 138–44. https://doi.org/10.20529/IJME.2016.040.

Sheikh, K., and J. Porter. "Disempowered Doctors? A Relational View of Public Health Policy Implementation in Urban India." *Health Policy and Planning* 26 (2011): 83–92. https://doi.org/10.1093/heapol/czq023.

Sheikh, K., B. Rajkumari, K. Jain, K. Rao, P. Patanwar, G. Gupta, K. R. Antony, and T. Sundararaman. "Location and Vocation: Why Some Government Doctors Stay on in Rural Chhattisgarh." *International Health* 4 (2012): 192–99. https://doi.org/10.1016/j.inhe.2012.03.004.

Shem, S. *House of God*. London: Black Swan, 1978.

Shetty, D. "Fixing Healthcare." *Seminar*, September 2015. https://www.india-seminar.com/2015/675/675_devi_shetty.htm

Singh, B. [Baldev], ed. *Jawaharlal Nehru on Science and Society: A Collection of His Writings and Speeches*. New Delhi: Nehru Memorial Museum and Library, 1988.

Singh, B. [Brighupati]. *Poverty and the Quest for Life: Spiritual and Material Striving in Rural India*. Chicago: University of Chicago Press, 2015.

Singh, J. "Budget Allocation for Health Less than Half of 12th Plan Promises." *Live Mint*, April 28, 2016. http://www.livemint.com/Politics/BtgaCDbm8HWoAaRojrGfMN/Budget-allocation-for-health-less-than-half-of-12th-Plan-pro.html.

Sinha, T. *Ek doctor ki maut*. Shemaroo, 1990.

Sood, R., and B. V. Adkoli. "Medical Education in India—Problems and Prospects." *Journal of the Indian Academy of Clinical Medicine* 1, no. 3 (2000): 210–12.

Sood, R., and T. Singh. "Assessment in Medical Education: Evolving Perspectives and Contemporary Trends." *National Medical Journal of India* 25, no. 6 (2012): 357–64.

Sriram, V., R. Baru, and S. Bennett. "Regulating Recognition and Training for New Medical Specialties in India: The Case of Emergency Medicine." *Health Policy and Planning*, July 23, 2018, 1–13. https://doi.org/10.1093/heapol/czy055.

Sriram, V., A. Hyder, and S. Bennett. "The Making of a New Medical Specialty: A Policy Analysis of the Development of Emergency Medicine in India." *International Journal of Health Policy and Management*, July 16, 2018. https://doi.org/10.15171/ijhpm.2018.55.

Sruthijith, K. K. "Delhi's Upscale Hospitals Are Turning Away the Poor in Whose Name They Got Land, Subsidies." *Huffington Post* (blog), September 20, 2015.

Stafford, C. "Numbers and the Natural History of Imagining the Self in Taiwan and China." *Ethnos* 74, no. 1 (2009): 110–26. https://doi.org/10.1080/00141840902751238.

The Statesman. "AIIMS faculty demands drive to fill SC, ST posts," September 15, 2015. http://www.thestatesman.com/news/delhi/aiims-faculty-demands-drive-to-fill-sc-st-posts/96957.html.

Still, C. "'They Have It in Their Stomachs but They Can't Vomit It Up'": Dalits, Reservations, and 'Caste Feeling' in Rural Andhra Pradesh." *Focaal* 65 (2013): 68–79. https://doi.org/10.3167/fcl.2013.650107.

Street, A. "Affective Infrastructure: Hospital Landscapes of Hope and Failure." *Space and Culture* 15, no. 1 (2012): 44–56. https://doi.org/10.1177/1206331211426061.

———. *Biomedicine in an Unstable Place: Infrastructure and Personhood in a Papua New Guinean Hospital.* Durham, NC: Duke University Press, 2014.

Street, A., and S. Coleman. "Introduction: Real and Imagined Spaces." *Space and Culture* 15, no. 1 (2012): 4–17. https://doi.org/10.1177/1206331211421852.

Subramanian, A. "Making Merit: The Indian Institutes of Technology and the Social Life of Caste." *Comparative Studies in Society and History* 57, no. 2 (2015): 291–322. https://doi.org/10.1017/S0010417515000043.

———. *The Caste of Merit: Engineering Education in India.* Cambridge, MA: Harvard University Press, 2019.

Sukumar, N. "Quota's Children: The Perils of Getting Educated." In *Beyond Inclusion: The Practice of Equal Access in Indian Higher Education*, edited by S. Deshpande and U. Zacharias, 205–21. New Delhi: Routledge, 2013.

Sundar, N. "India's Higher Education Troubles." *New York Times*, August 5, 2018, sec. Opinion. https://www.nytimes.com/2018/08/03/opinion/india-higher-education-modi-ambani-rss-trouble.html.

Sundararaman, T., I. Mukhopadhyay, and V. R. Muraleedharan. "No Respite for Public Health." *Economic and Political Weekly* 51, no. 16 (2016).

Szakolczai, A. "Liminality and Experience: Structuring Transitory Situations and Transformative Events." In *Breaking Boundaries: Varieties of Liminality*, edited by A. Horvath, B. Thomassen, and H. Wydra, 11–38. New York: Berghahn, 2015.

Taussig, M. T. "Reification and the Consciousness of the Patient." *Social Science & Medicine. Part B: Medical Anthropology* 14, no. 1 (February 1, 1980): 3–13. https://doi.org/10.1016/0160-7987(80)90035-6.

Taylor, J. S., and C. Wendland. "The Hidden Curriculum in Medicine's 'Culture of No Culture.'" In *The Hidden Curriculum in Health Professional Education*, edited by F. W. Hafferty and J. F. O'Donnell, 53–62. Lebanon, NH: Dartmouth College Press, 2014.

Tharu, S., M. M. Prasad, R. Pappu, and K. Satyanarayana. "Reservations and the Return to Politics." *Economic and Political Weekly* 42, no. 49 (2007): 39–45.

Thomassen, B. "Thinking with Liminality: To the Boundaries of an Anthropological Concept." In *Breaking Boundaries: Varieties of Liminality*, edited by A. Horvath, B. Thomassen, and H. Wydra, 39–58. New York: Berghahn, 2015.

Times of India. "Tribal Student Hangs Self at AIIMS," March 10, 2012. http://timesof

india.indiatimes.com/city/delhi/Tribal-student-at-AIIMS-hangs-self/articleshow /12139294.cms.

Turner, B. S. *Medical Power and Social Knowledge*. London: Sage, 1987.

Turner, S. "The Silenced Assistant: Reflections of Invisible Interpreters and Research Assistants." *Asia Pacific Viewpoint* 51 (2010): 206–19.

Turner, V. *The Forest of Symbols: Aspects of Ndembu Ritual*. Ithaca, NY: Cornell University Press, 1967.

UNFPA. "State of World Population 2017," 2017. https://www.unfpa.org/swop.

Unnikrishnan, M. K., and Sharma, A. "Misplaced Reverence for Super-Specialists Has Led to Lopsided Public Health Priorities in India." *Economic and Political Weekly* 53, no. 44 (November 3, 2018). https://www.epw.in/engage/article/misplaced-reverence-for-super-specialists-has-led-to-lop-sided-public-health-priorities-in-india.

Unnikrishnan, V. "AIIMS Director Mishra in Trouble: RS MPs Seek Privilege Motion." *Catch News*, August 3, 2016. http://www.catchnews.com/health-news/aiims-director-misra-in-trouble-rs-mps-seek-privilege-motion-1470225969.html/fullview.

van Gennep, A. *The Rites of Passage*. Translated by M. B. Vizedom and G. L. Caffee. Chicago: University of Chicago Press, 1961.

Van Hollen, C. *Birth on the Threshold: Childbirth and Modernity in South India*. Berkeley: University of California Press, 2003.

Varma, P. *The Great Indian Middle Class*. New Delhi: Penguin, 2007.

Venkatesan, V. "The Dynamics of Medicos' Anti-Reservation Protests of 2006." In *Health Providers in India: On the Frontlines of Change*, edited by K. Sheikh and A. George, 142–57. New Delhi: Routledge, 2010.

Weber, M. *Economy and Society: An Outline of Interpretive Sociology*. Berkeley: University of California Press, 1978.

Weisz, G. *Divide and Conquer: A Comparative History of Medical Specialization*. Oxford: Oxford University Press, 2005.

Wendland, C. L. *A Heart for the Work: Journeys Through an African Medical School*. Chicago: University of Chicago Press, 2010.

Wilce, J. M. "Medical Discourse." *Annual Review of Anthropology* 38 (2009): 199–215. https://doi.org/10.1146/annurev-anthro-091908-164450.

Wilkinson, R., and K. Pickett. *The Spirit Level: Why Equality Is Better for Everyone*. Penguin Sociology. London: Penguin Books, 2010.

Wilson, C. "The Social Transformation of the Medical Profession in Urban Kerala: Doctors, Social Mobility and the Middle Classes." In *Being Middle Class in India: A Way of Life*, edited by H. Donner, 139–61. Abingdon, UK: Routledge, 2011.

Wind, G. "Negotiated Interactive Observation: Doing Fieldwork in Hospital Settings." *Anthropology and Medicine* 15, no. 2 (2008): 79–89. https://doi.org/10.1080/13648470802127098.

The Wire. "After 3-Year Delay, Government Releases Farmer Suicide Data." *The Wire*, November 8, 2019. https://thewire.in/agriculture/farmer-suicides-data.

Wool, Z. "What I Wish I Knew about Anthropology and Disability: Notes toward a More

Enabling Anthropology." *Anthro{dendum}* (blog), January 10, 2018. https://anthro
dendum.org/2018/01/10/what-i-wish-i-knew-about-anthropology-and-disability-
notes-toward-a-more-enabling-anthropology/.

Wright, S., ed. *Anthropology of Organizations*. London: Routledge, 1994.

Zacharias, U. "To Race with the Able? Soft Skills and the Psychologisation of Marginality." In *Beyond Inclusion: The Practice of Equal Access in Indian Higher Education*, edited
by S. Deshpande and U. Zacharias, 289–327. Routledge: New Delhi, 2013.

Zaman, S. *Broken Limbs, Broken Lives: Ethnography of a Hospital Ward in Bangladesh*. Amsterdam: Het Spinhuis, 2005.

———. "Poverty and Violence, Frustration and Inventiveness: Hospital Ward Life
in Bangladesh." *Social Science & Medicine* 59, no. 10 (2004): 2025–36. https://doi.
org/10.1016/j.socscimed.2004.03.007.

ALSO PUBLISHED IN THE SOUTH ASIA IN MOTION SERIES